Exile, Non-Belonging and Statelessness in Grangaud, Jabès, Lubin and Luca

COMPARATIVE LITERATURE AND CULTURE

Series Editors
TIMOTHY MATHEWS AND FLORIAN MUSSGNUG

Comparative Literature and Culture explores new creative and critical perspectives on literature, art and culture. Contributions offer a comparative, cross-cultural and interdisciplinary focus, showcasing exploratory research in literary and cultural theory and history, material and visual cultures, and reception studies. The series is also interested in language-based research, particularly the changing role of national and minority languages and cultures, and includes within its publications the annual proceedings of the 'Hermes Consortium for Literary and Cultural Studies'.

Timothy Mathews is Emeritus Professor of French and Comparative Criticism, UCL.

Florian Mussgnug is Reader in Italian and Comparative Literature, UCL.

Exile, Non-Belonging and Statelessness in Grangaud, Jabès, Lubin and Luca

No man's language

Greg Kerr

UCLPRESS

First published in 2021 by
UCL Press
University College London
Gower Street
London WC1E 6BT

Available to download free: www.uclpress.co.uk

A CIP catalogue record for this book is available from The British Library.

ISBN: 978-1-78735-675-7 (Hbk)
ISBN: 978-1-78735-674-0 (Pbk)
ISBN: 978-1-78735-673-3 (PDF)
ISBN: 978-1-78735-676-4 (epub)
ISBN: 978-1-78735-677-1 (mobi)
DOI: https://doi.org/10.14324/111.9781787356733

Contents

List of figures

Acknowledgements

This book was in large part made possible by the award of a Marie Skłodowska-Curie Actions Individual Fellowship at the Analyse et traitement informatique de la langue française laboratory in Nancy during the academic year 2016–17. My primary personal debt of gratitude is to Véronique Montémont, without whose great expertise, support and inspiration (and deep knowledge of the work of Armen Lubin) the project would not have been possible in the first place.

I would like to thank Gérard Malkassian for the opportunity to present some of this work at the Conférences du Salon seminar series, held at the Maison des étudiants arméniens at the Cité universitaire, Paris, and Krikor Beledian for a similar opportunity at the Institut national des langues et civilisations orientales. I am grateful to both for their numerous astute suggestions in relation to my research on Armen Lubin, and to Sophie Balastre and Johana Dunlop for their help on other matters Armenian.

I wish to thank Nimet Frascaria Jabès and Viviane Jabès Crasson for permission to reproduce the drawings by Edmond Jabès in the chapter devoted to his writings, and Éditions Gallimard for permission to reproduce images from the *Livre des questions*. Much of the archival work on Armen Lubin and Ghérasim Luca was made possible by the permission of the late Arpik Missakian and of Micheline Catti to consult manuscripts at the Bibliothèque littéraire Jacques Doucet. Philippe Blanc and Dominique Nobécourt Mutarelli of that library were also extremely helpful, as were Anne Mary-Verdure and Guillaume Delaunay of the Bibliothèque nationale de France. Further archival work at the Office français de protection des réfugiés et apatrides was made possible with the assistance of Aline Angoustures and Marie Gonzalez-Perez.

Previous versions of some of the material contained in this book have appeared in the following articles, and I am grateful to the editors of those publications for permission to reproduce the material here: '"Travail d'abolition": Illness and statelessness in Armen Lubin', *Irish Journal of*

French Studies 14 (2014): 39–53, and (co-authored with Véronique Montémont) 'Introduction [to special collection]: Between Borders: French-language poetry and the poetics of statelessness', *Modern Languages Open* 1 (2019), http://doi.org/10.3828/mlo.v0i0.208.

I am grateful for exceptionally generous and insightful suggestions regarding drafts of some of the material from yasser elhariry, Krzysztof Fijalkowski, Barnaby Norman, Éanna O'Ceallacháin and David Scott. A similar debt of gratitude is owed to the peer reviewers of this manuscript for their extensive comments. I also wish to thank Chris Penfold and the editorial team at UCL Press for their assistance in the final stages, and Jill Bowie for her superb copy-editing.

Colleagues and friends at Nancy were a great source of support and encouragement during the academic year 2016–17, especially the following: Thomas Beuchot, Laurent Gobert, Toma Gotkova, Yan Greub, Sarah Kremer and Lou Lee.

The advice and friendship of numerous colleagues at the University of Glasgow have been vital, as has the precious support of those close to me over this time.

This project has received funding from the European Union's Horizon 2020 research and innovation programme under the Marie Skłodowska-Curie grant agreement No. 704528.

Introduction

At least since the age of European romanticism, poetry has often been understood as a powerful vector of collective belonging, particularly at the level of the nation. From Johann Wolfgang von Goethe to Taras Shevchenko to Alexander Pushkin to Dionysios Solomos, those figures consecrated by tradition as 'national poets' often stand in metonymic relation to a territory, a language and a literary system. On the announcement of the death of the poet Seamus Heaney in 2013, the then Taoiseach of the Republic of Ireland, Enda Kenny, declared that Heaney had been the 'keeper of our language, our codes, our essence as a people'. Kenny remarked that the passing of the Nobel laureate had brought a 'great sorrow to Ireland' and that only the poet himself 'could describe the depth of his loss to the nation'.[1] Invoking an idea of shared intimacy and familiarity, this tribute to the poet affirms a conviction in a sense of collective ownership over a language ('our language, our codes, our essence'), in this case, English as it is spoken on the island of Ireland, established through a figure considered to be its privileged guardian or keeper.

The promotion of this emblematic relation of poet and national culture is one of the chief means by which the institution of literature historicises itself, inscribes itself in a shared cultural past and supplies modes of belonging to those who consume it. But what, then, of the exiled, migrant or translingual poet in this connection? How might exophonic writing, that is, the practice of creative writing in a language other than one's mother tongue, stand to complicate this picture of the relation between poet, national or majoritarian language and literary system? What of those for whom the practice of poetry is inseparable from a sense of restlessness or unease, suggesting a condition of not being at home in any one language, even their mother tongue?

These questions are crucial for the four French-language poets whose work is the focus of this book: Armen Lubin (1903–74), Ghérasim Luca (1913–94), Edmond Jabès (1912–91) and Michelle Grangaud

(1941–). Their work displays characteristics that are in keeping with the development of poetry in French over the twentieth century: the diminishing emphasis on poetry as the expression of a personalised lyric subjectivity; the decline of metre and rhyme in favour of modes of organisation which instead exploit visual motifs and the space of the page; the emergence of a kind of metadiscursive commentary as a feature of poetic work alongside its more traditionally aesthetic and figurative modes; distrust of the image; and the pursuit of effects of provisionality, to name but a few. Chronologically, they mark a set of bridging points between movements such as surrealism in the early part of the century and the latter-day activities of the Oulipo group. Taken together, they prepare the ground for the more recent poetic *extrême contemporain* [extreme contemporary], the representatives of which re-perform what Jérôme Game calls that 'historic poetic gesture of *mise en crise* of classical subjectivity … in favour of a dubious subjectivity, precarious and in process'.[2] What Game refers to as the *mise en crise* [placing in crisis] of subjectivity has been integral to the development of modern poetry at least since Arthur Rimbaud or Stéphane Mallarmé, and this book argues that a distinct phase of this crisis is reflected in the selection of work studied here.

In the array of poetic practices under consideration in this book, it is often not simply that the poetic subject is divided or displaced; what they in different ways disclose are the limits of what Jacques Derrida calls the 'métaphysique du propre' ['metaphysics of the proper'][3] or what Roberto Esposito terms a 'semantics of proprium',[4] that is, conceptual frameworks or signifying practices that can be apprehended only via the proprietary attributes of a subject, and the semantics of having or belonging. In diverse ways, Grangaud, Jabès, Lubin and Luca engage formally and thematically with questions of exile, statelessness and non-belonging. The French poetic field in the twentieth century is a valuable one for study in this context, particularly given France's status as a *terre d'asile* [land of asylum] for some of the poets in question and for the populations to which they belonged; this is a book which thus touches on the historical legacies of Ottoman Turkey, Gamal Nasser's Egypt, wartime Romania and French colonial Algeria.[5]

In terms of conceptual treatments of the topic of exile, one of the most influential is that of Maurice Blanchot, who notes in *L'Entretien infini* ['The infinite conversation']: 'L'exode, l'exil indiquent un rapport positif avec l'extériorité dont l'exigence nous invite à ne pas nous contenter de ce qui nous est propre (c'est-à-dire de notre pouvoir de tout assimiler, de tout identifier, de tout rapporter à notre Je)' ['Exodus and exile indicate a positive relation to exteriority, whose exigency invites us not to be content with what is proper to us (that is, with our power to assimilate everything, to identify everything, to bring everything back to our I'].[6] Although an intuitive understanding might view the exile primarily as one who crosses a border or who has left a given place and journeys towards another, Blanchot casts the phenomenon as much in terms of an internal displacement and that displacement's profound, unsettling effects. Exile, here, is not simply spatial or geographical, but places the 'I' at a distance from its accustomed ways of being, knowing and appropriating the world. Exile thus opens onto a radical exteriority, an 'outside' of discursive thought and the intellectual operations laid down by the latter, operations that set out the world within the purview of the 'I', usually shoring up its authority and identity.

Following Blanchot, this book argues that exile, statelessness and non-belonging bring about a crisis in the domain of the proper.[7] This is a crisis of all that can be assimilated to the 'I', its scope of operation and its 'proper' attributes (among them the proper name, the *langue propre* or language one considers one's own, and the semantic currency of having and belonging). In French, the term *propre* encompasses meanings ranging from possession and belonging to literalness, cleanliness, propriety and appropriateness, unity of meaning and self-identity. The writings selected here attest to an unsettling of these effects of the proper; of the particular form of discursive rationality which the proper supports, and the symbolic operations it accomplishes within language. This characteristic of the four *oeuvres* speaks acutely to the circumstances of exile and/or linguistic and cultural non-belonging with which each poet is engaged. Yet, when we look at their work collectively, it also discloses a profound ontological uncertainty of the poetic itself, as a category continually confronted, in the period under consideration, with the question of its specificity and proper definition. The very precariousness of poetry's being, Michael G. Kelly suggests, is 'a central aporetic concept or *case vide* in modern French poetic practice's attempts at self-analysis', and is thus, by extension, a catalyst in the evolution of that practice.[8]

Throughout the book, the four *oeuvres* in question are examined through the lenses of exile, statelessness and non-belonging, a set of frameworks which both bring into focus the dislocation of the proper and help to account for the precarious specificity of poetry. If statelessness is one of these frameworks, it is not least because the term captures the political and ideological conditions which produce the situation of exile for two of the writers under consideration, Armen Lubin and Ghérasim

Luca. While exile is immemorial, the term '*state*lessness' references the political project of the modern state, a structure requiring bureaucratic administration and recognised rules of inclusion and exclusion. Central to the project of the state are institutions such as a national language or languages, and the documenting and control of identity through passports or the civil register, the civil register providing the formal basis on which social belonging is made possible. While it is well established in the social and political sciences,[9] scholarship on such themes in literary studies is a more recent phenomenon. In a study of modernism, in which she explores tensions between authors' cosmopolitan ideals and the state management of international mobility, Bridget Chalk has shown how the modern passport system represents 'an institutionalized form into which the individual must be inserted in order to be socially legible and legally legitimate'. She goes on to examine the effects produced by the passport, demonstrating how modernist writers' 'struggles with identity documentation' lead 'into ... experiments with forms of narrative identity construction'.[10] In a related fashion, part of the aim of the present study is to explore how the condition of statelessness comes to inflect the creative engagements of Lubin and Luca in conditions where the proper and its effects are acutely at stake.

Both within and beyond the realm of political philosophy, the most influential account of statelessness to this day remains that of Hannah Arendt. In *The Origins of Totalitarianism*, Arendt examines the condition of political refugees who become displaced by mass persecution or revolution and who are constrained to exist beyond the legal protection of any polity, all the while becoming the object of practices of identity control.[11] The diminished political existence of stateless individuals renders them effectively speechless, according to Arendt, for it sunders the close articulation of subjectivity, action and language on which, she says, political existence is grounded. Thus, in a more abstract perspective, 'state*lessness*' also suggests a kind of erasure of particularity of that which is proper: it can involve a loss of one's homeland or 'proper' place, or of those attributes or identifying characteristics peculiar to individual subjects regardless of their location (among them nationality and the proper name as guaranteed by identity papers).

While the terms of Arendt's analysis have been subject to critical revision by later authors such as Giorgio Agamben[12] or Jacques Rancière,[13] the notion that statelessness can be understood in terms of a diminished kind of participation in a language and a world held in common is one which is taken up and interrogated in different ways by both Lubin and Luca. The approach adopted here is to address the condition of statelessness partly in its technical sense in relation to these poets, but also in a more extended one. Because it is a term that is more broadly identified by a grammar of negative categories of lack or absence, in addition to connoting a loss of belonging, poetic work completed under the sign of statelessness suggests marked abstractive possibilities that stand to expose the exclusionary effects of the proper and to illuminate something of the precarious being of poetry. Thus, for Lubin, the condition of statelessness is inseparable from his experience of lifelong illness, genocidal trauma and a perception of the 'weakening' of language's affirmative aspect. Meanwhile, for Luca, the poet's engagement with statelessness suggests a posture of nonconformity with the idea that a text is governed by certain criteria, such as internal coherence and non-contradiction, semantic continuity, or a hierarchy of values (for instance, those of the written over the spoken).

Whether or not the poets are stateless, exiled or in other ways engaged with the question of non-belonging, the works discussed here invariably lead the reader to the confines of the proper, a term which is key to Jacques Derrida's analysis in his celebrated essay *Le Monolinguisme de l'autre – ou la prothèse de l'origine*. Throughout this text, Derrida examines the persistence of the category of the 'propre' in mediating a subject's relation to their mother tongue, understood as an object of possession or dispossession. Drawing on his own experience in this work, Derrida addresses the paradoxical situation of a person who is unable to consider as truly their own the language with which they are most intimately familiar and with which they identify. The event which motivated this reflection on Derrida's part was the summary revocation by France's Vichy government of the Crémieux decree which had awarded French citizenship to the Jewish community of French Algeria. Lasting from 1940 to 1943, this judicial measure effectively rendered Derrida and other members of the Jewish community stateless and dramatically altered their relationship to the French language, perhaps the most powerful index of their sense of belonging to the wider national community of French Algeria.

In the essay, Derrida acknowledges the need not to underplay the significance of the relationship of oppressed peoples to the language they use, yet he argues for a 'universalisation prudente et différenciée' ['careful and differentiated universalisation'][14] of the notion that no one stands in a relationship of mastery to their mother tongue. Giving rise to fantasies of appropriation or reappropriation, the subject's 'langue « propre »' ['"own" language'], Derrida argues, can never be fully assimilated to him or her precisely because it is in the nature of all language to interfere with or elude the mechanisms of appropriation, property and the proper.[15] The peculiar situation of the French-speaking Jewish community of North Africa to which he belonged led Derrida to understand that any claim which an individual or group might sustain to a language, or indeed to citizenship on the basis of mastery of and sole attachment to that language, whether it be on the basis of natural, national, birth-related or ontological claims, can be usurped, through the intervention of state power.[16]

This in turn complicates our understanding of language as a property of which one can be dispossessed: 'Si elle paraît être aussi bien, et par-là même, la première et dernière condition de l'appartenance, la langue est aussi l'expérience de l'expropriation, d'une irréductible *exapropriation*. La langue dite « maternelle » est déjà « langue de l'autre »' ['While it seems to be the first and last condition of belonging, language is also the experience of expropriation, of an irreducible "exapropriation". The so-called "mother tongue" is already "the language of the other"'].[17] Thus, by this reading, every language, even the language one acquires as one's first language, exceeds the possibility of identification with the natural or historical properties of a community.[18] Derrida's analysis is important here because it points to a place of 'intimité déconcertante' ['disconcerting intimacy'] *within* the monolingual which corresponds to what he calls the 'nonidentité à soi de toute langue' ['non-identity to itself of every language'].[19] As Marc Crépon writes, commenting on this text, what Derrida ascertains here is effectively a form of 'exil de la langue dans la langue, un exil de celui qui parle, dans « sa langue maternelle », à l'intérieur de sa propre langue, une *autre* langue qui n'est pourtant pas une langue étrangère' ['exile of language within language, an exile of the one who speaks, in "his mother tongue", inside his own language, an *other* language which is nonetheless not a foreign language'].[20]

It follows from Derrida's argument that no one of multilingual, translingual or monolingual forms of expression is more advantageously placed than the others to enact the displacement of the proper in the pursuit of the interiorised 'other language', to borrow Crépon's terms. Via his adoption of the neologism 'exapropriation', Derrida hypothesises a way of inhabiting one's own language that retains a sense of its alterity, thus indicating a movement outside a relation of appropriation or possession. 'Exapropriation' is 'pas simplement une façon d'être chez soi dans sa langue, mais une manière d'expérimenter l'étrangeté ou l'impropriété ou l'altérité de notre langue' ['not simply a way to be at home in one's language, but a way to experience the strangeness or impropriety or alterity of our language'].[21] Derrida's approach thus betokens what

Yasemin Yildiz describes as 'an ethical injunction to transcending proprietary thinking vis-à-vis languages'.[22] It also thwarts what Paul Audi terms 'le démon de l'appartenance' ['the demon of belonging'], that is, the persistence of the category of belonging in attempts to conceptualise identity.[23]

Derrida's concern in *Le Monolinguisme de l'autre* is not with poetry, however, so what might be the specificity of poetry in the context of a critical reflection on the workings of the proper? Giorgio Agamben, writing in an essay on the Italian poet Giorgio Caproni in *The End of the Poem*, is a thinker who sees in poetry a privileged space for a relinquishment of the will to appropriation. In this essay, Agamben firstly considers some comments by Caproni on the *res amissa*, that is, the paradox of a gift that is so well concealed or intimately possessed by its recipient that it becomes inadvertently, irrevocably hidden or lost; he then goes on to discuss poetic language as the site of a tension between two contrasting features of style and manner.

In relation to this latter point of discussion in the essay, we customarily think of style as a particular unmistakable quality of a particular writer or *oeuvre*, and manner as a self-conscious cultivation of the distinguishing features of a style. For Agamben, these distinctions can be elucidated in terms of the maturation of an individual writer: 'If style marks the artist's most characteristic trait, manner registers an inverse process of expropriation and exclusion. It is as if the old poet, who found this style and reached perfection in it, now forgets it in order to advance the singular claim of expressing himself solely through impropriety.'[24] Put otherwise, if style is taken to be the most distinguishing attribute of a particular writer or *oeuvre*, manner, manifesting itself through features such as digression or parataxis, is by contrast marked by what Agamben calls an 'irreducibility to a procedure of stylistic evolution' and a departure from the norms of the literary genre with which it is associated; turning to Friedrich Hölderlin, Agamben argues that the poet's late work was no longer recognisable in terms of those stylistic or generic attributes that had erstwhile come to define it.[25] In this way, poetry becomes a process of navigation between the two poles of what Agamben terms 'expropriating appropriation' (or literary *style*) and 'appropriating expropriation' (or *manner*), one that is commensurate with 'the perpetual oscillation between a homeland and an exile – dwelling'.[26]

Agamben argues that this evolution internal to a given poetic *oeuvre* has the capacity to 'call into question the very borders between languages'[27] for it corresponds to the 'site of a dislocation and experimental change' that 'according to Benjamin stands between languages without coinciding with any of them (and whose proper place he found in translation)'.[28] For Agamben, this pattern can be discerned in the trajectories of individual poets: that of Caproni primarily, but also of Johann Wolfgang von Goethe; Agamben cites claims by the linguist Ernst Lewy that the German of the late Goethe reflects a shift from a morphology characteristic of Indo-European languages to one suggestive of agglutinative languages such as Turkish.[29] In the case of Goethe, it is obviously not the case that the poet is writing *in* Turkish or in another agglutinative language, but that his word- and sentence-formation no longer coincides with a particular dominant idea of the German language and its accumulated stylistic possibilities and 'proper' characteristics: the late Goethe seems to be writing another language *within* German that is nonetheless not a foreign language. If the question of the border is at issue in this latter example, it is as much so in terms of the crossing of an external border (separating one language from another) as that of an internal one (an exile within the poet's mother tongue).

The temporal play, or process of navigation between the two facets Agamben identifies, is important here, because what happens in the poetic text is not simply or exclusively a reappropriation, a 'taking back' or 'reclaiming' of a means of expression; this would be in the sense that one takes back ownership, taking something back into a place of stability and security, in such a way that language could be considered as a criterion of belonging. The play or navigation peculiar to poetry is one also of being taken away from the place of the *langue propre* and taken forward into a space of articulate uncertainty and exposure, a space exempted from the demands and responsibilities associated with recourse to one's mother tongue. 'Lo hanno portato via / dal luogo della sua lingua' ['They took him away / from the place of his language'], as a poem by Giorgio Caproni, 'Lo Spatriato' ['The expatriate'], puts it.[30]

For Agamben, by dint of its oscillation between what he terms language's 'homeland' and its 'exile', poetry is analogous with the *res amissa*, that thing that, while always already lost and inappropriable, is the object of a special form of care or attention. As Paolo Bartoloni argues, Agamben's understanding of poetry as *res amissa* intimates 'not so much … that which is said by language as that which exceeds language's saying'.[31] As this book argues, it is the care or protection of this excess, this excess by dint of loss, that is constitutive of poetry. Thus, for Edmond Jabès, in terms similar to the Capronian *res amissa*, the unsayable 'n'est pas ce qui ne peut être dit mais, au contraire, ce qui a été si intimement, si *totalement* dit qu'il ne dit plus que cette intimité, cette totalité indicible' ['is not what cannot be said, but, rather, what has been said so intimately, what has been so *totally* said that it no longer says anything but this intimacy, this unsayable totality'].[32] A poem may produce and preserve an unsayable excess that is lost to language, and therein lies its singularity and fragility. This excess emerges precisely at the moment of dislocation of the proper, an aspect that as a consequence confers a distinctive meaning on the notion of the poet as a 'keeper' of language. Following Richard Stamelman, loss is 'the *fait accompli* of the modern poem, the experience from which poetry emerges into being'.[33] In the selection of poetry studied in this book, 'keeping' remains an operative term, then, not so much in the sense of a substantial essence preserved, but to designate an attitude of care *in* language for what lies beyond language's reach.

The first chapter of the study takes as its focus Chahnour Kerestedjian, an Istanbul-born writer and member of the Armenian diaspora, who emigrated to France in 1923 following the Armenian genocide, and in whose French-language poet-persona, Armen Lubin, the horizons of writer, invalid and stateless person come to intersect. Consigned by chronic tuberculosis of the bones to a lengthy cycle of sojourns in French hospitals and sanatoria, Lubin's poor health rendered him unfit for military service, thereby obstructing his attempts to secure naturalisation in France. Eliciting an underlying connection between the medical and juridical domains, this poet-patient went on to produce an *oeuvre* which inflects the condition of statelessness in a lingering opacity and ironic deflation, and in a language which figures, and deflects, those disciplinary logics of which the stateless individual finds him- or herself the object.

As Lyndsey Stonebridge writes, in her account of the trajectories of stateless writers at the mid-twentieth century, the 'legal, political, and moral forms of internationalism' sometimes offered displaced people 'exits from danger and new homes, but also, and more often than not, spaces in which to disappear'.[34] For refugees like Lubin, one of the paradoxes of the experience of being without legal or moral recognition is that these spaces of disappearance are paradoxically also spaces of maximal exposure to the sanction of legal and institutional powers. Thus, when Lubin suggests a form of equivalence between the inarticulate cries of the terminally ill and the condition of the undocumented exile in works such as *Transfert nocturne* and *Sainte patience*, what tentatively emerges is a sense of the inadequacy of medicalised or national-juridical frameworks in accounting for a diminished, yet irreducible life of the suffering individual which murmurs its presence in his texts.

In an essay on Paul Celan, Jean-Christophe Bailly writes that a poet 'doit à chaque instant non pas « surveiller son langage » (au contraire !) mais maintenir son état de veille dans le langage, et tenir par-là même que le langage soit une veille' ['must at all times not "watch one's language" (quite the opposite!) but maintain a waking state in language, and thereby maintain that language is wakefulness'].[35] Similarly, a central preoccupation of Lubin's poetics is to 'watch over' a weakening of the structures of affirmation, as if the condition of detachment and watchfulness in which the poet found himself by dint of genocidal trauma, statelessness and a chronic, lifelong medical condition made him especially receptive to language's own malaise.

The second chapter turns on the question of the visuality of language and the problematic status of the image within the writings of Edmond Jabès, a writer of Jewish origin forced by nationalism in his native Egypt to leave that country and go into exile in France in 1957. While a traditional conception of the image is of a feature that centralises and organises literary language, articulating the relationship between literal and figurative levels of discourse and between signifiers and signifieds, Jabès aims to abstract writing from the image's binding efficacy. Although he responds to a long tradition of reflection on the image within modern poetry in French, Jabès's writings offer a unique understanding of the place of the image within the framework of exile. Through a thematic orientation away from personalised experience and all but the most featureless of topographies, the deployment of a lexicon of absence and erasure, and an interruptive spacing of textual matter, Jabès inscribes silence and the unsayable at the heart of his multivolume *Livre des questions*. Amid this cycle of published work and in his manuscripts, Jabès produces diagrams and scribbles. He also meditates on a strand of abstract artworks by artists such as Jean Degottex and Eduardo Chillida, which, removed from figurative intent, underscore the author's desire to situate his writing at a limit-position between the graphic qualities of letters ordained for legibility and the alien opacity of the nonalphabetic, of black marks on a white surface. Bringing to the fore the significance of this disjuncture of the seeable and the sayable, and of vision and knowledge, this chapter argues that Jabès's writings offer a privileged site within which questions of exile, especially as they concern visuality and the image, are engaged.

The third chapter explores the poetry of Ghérasim Luca, a Romanian-born writer of Jewish origin. Through his writings and the incantatory spoken performances of his work, Luca sets out to disturb a kind of monolingual serenity that is associated with the 'naturalised', 'articulate' uses of French. Leaving behind post-war Romania for France, he for most of his life deliberately eluded the possibility of naturalisation as a French citizen: 'Fondamentalement et même légalement je suis nécessairement apatride. Ni ma langue passée ni ma langue présente ne justifient à mes yeux (après Auschwitz) l'appartenance à un patrimoine national' ['Fundamentally and even legally, I am necessarily stateless. Neither my past language nor my present one justify in my eyes (after Auschwitz) belonging to a national heritage'].[36]

Following an assessment of Luca's critique of the axiomatic status accorded to the Oedipal complex in Western civilisation, this chapter reads his poetry as motivated by a rejection of genealogy (and its associated paradigms of filiation, nativity, kinship and so on) as the foundational mechanism of culture. For Luca, the genealogical ordering of culture brings with it a set of causal explanations and explanatory paradigms that induce a kind of linguistic and epistemological strait-jacketing around the real. Proverbial forms of speech, for instance, assert a form of patrimony, subtly affirming a collective inheritance of or ownership over language, one which Luca at every turn seeks to contest in his pursuit of a radical 'no man's langue' ['no man's language']. In his work, the linguistic accident and the cognitive associations determined by homophony and haphazard word play are elevated to a creative and critical principle, signalling that the poet sought to maintain a relationship of exteriority not only with respect to the language of his country of origin, but also to that of his country of adoption. Luca frequently substitutes syntactical progression with a kind of dizzying circularity. Speech decomposes into its constituent phonemic matter and is invested with novel combinatory possibilities, as originary *logos* decomposes into a radical, disseminatory phonesis, and the conventionality of text is jettisoned in pursuit of the contingency of spoken performance and the 'improper' accidents of orality.

The work of Michelle Grangaud is the focus of the final chapter. For her, non-belonging is not linked to a personal experience of migration in the same way as for the other poets considered here. This is despite the fact that her early life was one marked by the traumas of postcolonial transition and that she was more or less compelled by historical circumstance to leave French Algeria, where she was born. She is perhaps most noted for her inventive approach to the anagram in the collections *Mémento-fragments* and *Stations*. However, as a member of the Ouvroir de littérature potentielle [Workshop of Potential Literature], or Oulipo, Grangaud is also the author of a range of works variously organised around other textual constraints such as the inventory, lipograms and anadiplosis. Just as is the case for other members of Oulipo, Grangaud's work eschews emphasis on personal expression and the values of lyric, and instead promotes a conception of the text primarily as an artefact or construct. Despite its elevation of procedure and rule, for Grangaud, constrained writing has a paradoxically liberating quality, because it leads to a creative production unhindered by the conventions of the 'free' expression of the self.

Grangaud's work on the anagram, this chapter argues, thus opens onto a kind of *impropriety*, in that it underscores a general condition of language, which is that of language's inability to contain itself; to contain itself, that is, to the sphere of the proper and the purview of an individual subject. In these conditions, constraints offer a momentary, controlled production of that improprietous excess of language, the poet herself identifying the anagram as a 'mode de multiplication du langage par lui-même' ['a method of multiplication of language by itself'].[37] Grangaud's sense of non-belonging is not intensely bound up with exile in the way it is for Jabès, Lubin and Luca. Yet her text *État civil* ['Civil status'] points to a fascination with what haunts the category of the individuated, sedentary subject designated by name, and shows how Grangaud views a form of linguistic non-belonging as coincident with our contemporary social condition. That sense of non-belonging is integral to her playful critique of a semantics ordered around the cornerstone of the proper noun, with the latter's connotations of univocity, indivisibility and self-identicality. Her publications thus disclose a fascination with the potential of the anagram, anadiplosis and other constraints to subvert those connotations that attach to the proper noun, that is, to names and identities of all kinds.

This book draws to varying degrees on a range of frameworks and methodologies, including trauma and attestation (Lubin), Jewish studies and theories of word and image (Jabès), historical linguistics and the critique of monolingualism (Luca), and aspects of post-foundationalist political philosophy (Grangaud). Amid this diversity of approach, the various individual studies reveal a related set of poetic interrogations of a focal theme. From Lubin's vigilance in language, to Jabès's understanding of writing as a drawing back from speech, to Luca's contrasting elevation of phonesis over *logos*, or Grangaud's work on the anagram which underscores language's 'uncontainability' as its general condition, the poetry explored in this book attests to a crisis of the proper, one that is particularly acute in the context of exile and non-belonging. In doing so, it shows the possibilities of a creative engagement abstracted from the categories of selfhood, citizenship and nation, albeit, as the following chapters show, one that is sometimes shadowed by dramatically new conceptions of individuality, community and being-together.

Notes

1 *TheJournal.ie*, 'Taoiseach: "Seamus Heaney's death brings great sorrow to Ireland"', last modified 30 August 2013, accessed 13 January 2021, https://www.thejournal.ie/enda-kenny-tribute-seamus-heaney-1061640-Aug2013/.
2 Jérôme Game, *Poetic Becomings: Studies in contemporary French literature* (Oxford: Peter Lang, 2011), 4.
3 Jacques Derrida, *L'Écriture et la différence* (Paris: Seuil, 1967), 271.
4 Roberto Esposito, *Communitas: The origin and destiny of community*, trans. by Timothy Campbell (Stanford, CA: Stanford University Press, 2010), 2.
5 Furthermore, while forced migration may equate to dispossession, literary success in France may mark a certain 'consecration' for the writer. See: Pascale Casanova, *La République mondiale des lettres* (Paris: Seuil, 1999).
6 Maurice Blanchot, *L'Entretien infini* (Paris: Gallimard, 1969), 168.
7 Luke Bouvier's *Writing, Voice and the Proper: Jules Vallès and the politics of orality* (Amsterdam: Rodopi, 1998) and Nicholas Royle's *The Uncanny* (Manchester: Manchester University Press, 2003) are two major studies that also adopt the framework of a disturbance in the field of the proper to interrogate literature's engagement with political radicalism and the uncanny, respectively. The term the 'crisis of the proper' appears in the opening pages of Royle's book.
8 Kelly, Michael G., *Strands of Utopia: Spaces of poetic work in twentieth-century France* (Oxford: Legenda, 2008), 101.
9 On the significance of the paradigm of identification for modern practices of governmentality in a French context, see: Gérard Noiriel, *L'Identification. Génèse d'un travail d'État* (Paris: Belin, 2007).
10 Bridget T. Chalk, *Modernism and Mobility: The passport and cosmopolitan experience* (New York: Palgrave Macmillan, 2014), 30–1.
11 Hannah Arendt, *The Origins of Totalitarianism* (New York: Harcourt, Brace and Company, 1951).
12 Giorgio Agamben, *Homo Sacer: Sovereign power and bare life*, trans. by Daniel Heller-Roazen (Stanford, CA: Stanford University Press, 1998).
13 Jacques Rancière, *Aux bords du politique* (Paris: Gallimard, 2004).
14 Jacques Derrida, *Le Monolinguisme de l'autre – ou la prothèse d'origine* (Paris: Galilée, 1996), 45.
15 Derrida, *Le Monolinguisme de l'autre*, 46.
16 Derrida, *Le Monolinguisme de l'autre*, 45.
17 Jacques Derrida and Anne Dufourmantelle, *De l'hospitalité* (Paris: Calmann-Lévy, 1997), 83.
18 See also Étienne Balibar's discussion of this text in: Étienne Balibar, *Citoyen sujet et autres essais d'anthropologie philosophique* (Paris: PUF, 2011), 184–5.
19 Derrida, *Le Monolinguisme de l'autre*, 123.
20 Marc Crépon, *Langues sans demeure* (Paris: Galilée, 2005), 12.
21 Jacques Derrida, *Moscou aller-retour* (La Tour d'Aigues: Aube, 1995), 121.
22 Yasemin Yildiz, *Beyond the Mother Tongue: The postmonolingual condition* (New York: Fordham University Press, 2012), 42.
23 Paul Audi, *Le Démon de l'appartenance* (Paris: Encre Marine, 2014).
24 Giorgio Agamben, *The End of the Poem: Studies in poetics*, trans. by Daniel Heller-Roazen (Stanford, CA: Stanford University Press, 1999), 97.
25 Agamben, *The End of the Poem*, 97.
26 Agamben, *The End of the Poem*, 98.
27 Agamben, *The End of the Poem*, 96.
28 Agamben, *The End of the Poem*, 97.
29 Agamben, *The End of the Poem*, 96.
30 Giorgio Caproni, *L'Opera in versi*, ed. by Luca Zuliani and Pier Vincenzo Mengaldo (Milan: Mondadori, 2009), 461.
31 Paolo Bartoloni, 'Thinking Thingness: Agamben and Perniola', *Annali d'Italianistica*, 29 (2011): 158.

32 Edmond Jabès, *Le Petit Livre de la subversion hors de soupçon* (Paris: Gallimard, 1982), 55.
33 Richard Stamelman, *Lost Beyond Telling: Representations of death and absence in modern French poetry* (London: Cornell University Press, 1990), ix–x.
34 Lyndsey Stonebridge, *Placeless People: Writings, rights, and refugees* (Oxford: Oxford University Press, 2018), 168.
35 Jean-Christophe Bailly, 'L'action solitaire du poème', in « *Toi aussi, tu as des armes* »*: Poésie et politique*, ed. by Jean-Christophe *Bailly* et al. (Paris : La Fabrique, 2011), 22.
36 Quoted in: Dominique Carlat, *Gherasim Luca l'intempestif* (Paris: José Corti Editions, 1998), 251.
37 P.O.L, '*Mémento fragment*', accessed 13 January 2021, http://www.pol-editeur.com/index.php?spec=livre&ISBN=2-86744-090-4.

Bibliography

Agamben, Giorgio. *The End of the Poem: Studies in poetics*, translated by Daniel Heller-Roazen. Stanford, CA: Stanford University Press, 1999.
Agamben, Giorgio. *Homo Sacer: Sovereign power and bare life*, translated by Daniel Heller-Roazen. Stanford, CA: Stanford University Press, 1998.
Arendt, Hannah. *The Origins of Totalitarianism*. New York: Harcourt, Brace and Company, 1951.
Audi, Paul. *Le Démon de l'appartenance*. Paris: Encre Marine, 2014.
Bailly, Jean-Christophe. 'L'action solitaire du poème'. In « *Toi aussi, tu as des armes* »*: Poésie et politique*, edited by Jean-Christophe *Bailly* et al. Paris: La Fabrique, 2011.
Balibar, Étienne. *Citoyen sujet et autres essais d'anthropologie philosophique*. Paris: PUF, 2011.
Bartoloni, Paolo. 'Thinking Thingness: Agamben and Perniola', *Annali d'Italianistica* 29 (2011): 141–62.
Blanchot, Maurice. *L'Entretien infini*. Paris: Gallimard, 1969.
Bouvier, Luke. *Writing, Voice and the Proper: Jules Vallès and the politics of orality*. Amsterdam: Rodopi, 1998.
Caproni, Giorgio. *L'Opera in versi*, edited by Luca Zuliani and Pier Vincenzo Mengaldo. Milan: Mondadori, 2009.
Carlat, Dominique. *Gherasim Luca l'intempestif.* Paris: José Corti Editions, 1998.
Casanova, Pascale. *La République mondiale des lettres*. Paris: Seuil, 1999.
Chalk, Bridget T. *Modernism and Mobility: The passport and cosmopolitan experience*. New York: Palgrave Macmillan, 2014.
Crépon, Marc. *Langues sans demeure*. Paris: Galilée, 2005.
Derrida, Jacques. *L'Écriture et la différence*. Paris: Seuil, 1967.
Derrida, Jacques. *Le Monolinguisme de l'autre – ou la prothèse d'origine*. Paris: Galilée, 1996.
Derrida, Jacques. *Moscou aller-retour*. La Tour d'Aigues: Aube, 1995.
Derrida, Jacques, and Anne Dufourmantelle. *De l'hospitalité*. Paris: Calmann-Lévy, 1997.
Esposito, Roberto. *Communitas: The origin and destiny of community*, translated by Timothy Campbell. Stanford, CA: Stanford University Press, 2010.
Game, Jérôme. *Poetic Becomings: Studies in contemporary French literature*. Oxford: Peter Lang, 2011.
Jabès, Edmond. *Le Petit Livre de la subversion hors de soupçon*. Paris: Gallimard, 1982.
Journal.ie, The. 'Taoiseach: "Seamus Heaney's death brings great sorrow to Ireland"', last modified 30 August 2013. Accessed 13 January 2021. https://www.thejournal.ie/enda-kenny-tribute-seamus-heaney-1061640-Aug2013/.
Kelly, Michael G. *Strands of Utopia: Spaces of poetic work in twentieth-century France*. Oxford: Legenda, 2008.
Noiriel, Gérard. *L'Identification. Genèse d'un travail d'État*. Paris: Belin, 2007.
P.O.L. '*Mémento fragment*'[*sic*]. Accessed 13 January 2021. http://www.pol-editeur.com/index.php?spec=livre&ISBN=2-86744-090-4.
Rancière, Jacques. *Aux bords du politique*. Paris: Gallimard, 2004.
Royle, Nicholas. *The Uncanny*. Manchester: Manchester University Press, 2003.
Stamelman, Richard. *Lost Beyond Telling: Representations of death and absence in modern French poetry*. London: Cornell University Press, 1990.
Stonebridge, Lyndsey. *Placeless People: Writings, rights, and refugees.* Oxford: Oxford University Press, 2018.
Yildiz, Yasemin. *Beyond the Mother Tongue: The postmonolingual condition*. New York: Fordham University Press, 2012.

1
Solemn attestation: illness and statelessness in Armen Lubin

According to Emil Cioran in his essay 'Avantages de l'exil' ['Advantages of exile'], the condition of stateless persons is comparable with that of the modernist writing subject, who attempts to wrest him- or herself away from local or national ties:

> S'arracher au monde, quel travail d'abolition ! L'apatride, lui, y parvient sans se mettre en frais, par le concours – par l'hostilité – de l'histoire. Point de tourments, de veilles, pour qu'il se dépouille de tout ; les événements l'y obligent. En un certain sens, il ressemble au malade, lequel, comme lui, s'installe dans la métaphysique ou la poésie sans mérite personnel, par la force des choses, par les bons offices de la maladie.[1]
>
> [What a labour of abolition it is to tear oneself away from the world! The stateless person manages to do so at no great expense to himself, by the aid – or indeed the antagonism – of history. No torments or sleepless nights are necessary for him to rid himself of everything; events oblige him to do so. In a certain way, he resembles the patient who, like him, sinks into metaphysics or poetry without any personal merit, by force of circumstances, by the good offices of illness.]

In passing, the same essay thus also equates the modernist writer and the stateless individual with the invalid, a figure dispossessed of corporeal agency. The first chapter of this study is concerned with the work of Chahnour Kerestedjian (1903–74), an Istanbul-born writer and member of the Armenian diaspora, who emigrated to France in 1923 following the systematic persecution of Armenians in the Ottoman Empire. In his

French-language poet-persona, Armen Lubin, the horizons of all three figures invoked by Cioran – writer, invalid and stateless person – come to intersect.

If the present chapter retains a focus on the poet's statelessness, it is not least because Lubin shows an acute, and at times strongly historicised, sensitivity to the institutional conditions which produce his situation of non-belonging. Moving from the poet's origins in Ottoman-era Istanbul to his exile in France and literary efforts in French and Armenian, the following analysis endeavours to show a poet marked by the traumas of genocide, statelessness and lifelong illness. Indeed, this is a body of work which remains centrally engaged with the legacy of such traumas to a writing subject struggling to reconcile his presence within a new cultural order with the institutional reality that he does not possess the minimum entitlements to validate meaningful participation within that order.

Lubin's hospital narrative *Transfert nocturne* ['Night transfer'] can be considered a work of central importance for his *oeuvre* at large, for it enables the reader to ascertain the lineaments of the poetics of verse collections such as *Sainte Patience* ['Blessed patience'] and *Les Hautes Terrasses* ['The heavenly platforms']. It is in this work that the effective dehumanisation of the gravely ill in a hospital context is staged as a kind of becoming stateless, through the suspension of any relation of belonging with respect to the social body. Illness and statelessness stood in close relation for the poet: just as Lubin's physical health wavered for the remainder of his life subsequent to his diagnosis with tuberculosis, his civil status following the effective loss of his nationality also remained unresolved long after his arrival in France:

> Avant, il était écrit sur mes papiers : *réfugié d'origine arménienne*, alors que maintenant (il y est inscrit) ex-arménien. Bien, bien ! Dans le passé j'étais arménien ; mais qui suis-je maintenant ? À quelle nation j'appartiens ? Mes inénarrables papiers n'en disent rien.[2]
>
> [Previously, the words written on my papers were *refugee of Armenian origin*, whereas now it's ex-Armenian. So it is! In the past, I was Armenian, but who am I now? To what nation do I belong? My preposterous papers give no clue.]

At stake in this quotation and across much of the poet's *oeuvre* is what could be called an anxiety of explication – that is, the pressure to yield an account of the signature attributes of one's self within the terms defined by governing discursive and institutional structures. As Lubin's exasperated questions suggest, the inability to make oneself answerable to authority in this respect brings about a sense of linguistic and ontological lack. Lubin is in this way always sensitive to the effects of his own exclusion from the normative matrix of physical health and nativity (understood as the fact of birth within a given place and into a given linguistic community) within which social identities are forged.

Nonetheless, if the particulars recorded on the papers alluded to above amount to a forced or misdirected act of identity attribution, the poet saw potential for a more speculative and authorially directed gesture in his own adoption of distinct literary identities in Armenian (Chahan Chahnour) and French (Armen Lubin). While on the one hand, the proper name attested by official certificates offers, according to Pierre Bourdieu, 'l'attestation visible de l'identité de son porteur à travers les temps et les espaces sociaux' ['the visible attestation of the identity of its bearer through time and social spaces'],[3] the pseudonym, on the other hand, might be said to situate its bearer in a more uncertain space, much like that occupied by the immigrant (to cite another essay by Bourdieu), 'à la frontière de l'être et du non-être social' ['at the border of social being and nonbeing'].[4] Arguably, as an invalid, refugee author who held literary identities in two different languages, Lubin sought precisely to exploit the productive uncertainty opened up by his adoption of pseudonyms.

In this vein, in an October 1946 letter, the author responds to the request of publisher Jean Paulhan to elaborate on his choice of the pseudonym corresponding to his French poetic persona:

> Armen est pour Arménien, ce que France est pour François. Je vous avoue que je n'en sais pas davantage. ... Je pense que la forme française d'Armen Lubin, c'est Arsène Lupin. Et pourquoi pas ? Les poètes et les artistes de la rue Ravignan qui enchantèrent ma jeunesse prônaient bien la supériorité de Fantômas sur M. Paul Bourget. Il est impossible de les oublier. Il est plus impossible encore d'aimer la littérature, sans en ressentir en même temps un profond dégoût (une haine plutôt) qui nous pousse à narguer et à défier les déviations de la littérature, en opposant à ces déviations une déviation encore plus grande.[5]
>
> [Armen is for Armenian, what France is for François. I have to say, that's all I know. ... I think that the French version of Armen Lubin

is Arsène Lupin. And why not? The poets and artists of the rue Ravignan who enchanted my youth made sure to advocate the superiority of Fantômas over Monsieur Paul Bourget. It is impossible to forget them. It is even more impossible to love literature, without at the same time feeling a deep disgust (or rather, a hatred) which pushes us to flout and to challenge literature's divergence from the norm, pushing back against it with an even greater divergence of our own.]

Among the more notable features of this commentary are these: the poet's somewhat equivocal response, combined with his sensitivity to the nationality effects engendered by his choice of pseudonym; his vision of the literary idiom as constituted by successive instances of rupture with aesthetic norms; and his lightly worn acquaintance with French literature, both canonical and popular. Yet if his choice of pseudonym suggests an easy identification with the culture of France, the poet's declared affinity with the figure of the fictional gentleman burglar Arsène Lupin also simultaneously articulates something of his abiding sense of his own illicit presence within the country as a 'passager clandestin' ['stowaway'], to recall the title of one of his verse collections.

In addition to such speculative onomastics, for Lubin, it is above all the poem which offers the most privileged arena within which a subject can elaborate on its own diminished answerability when confronted with the question of its origins. From those collected in *Le Passager clandestin* to those of *Sainte Patience*, Lubin's poems frequently work to dramatise situations in which agency is limited or suspended, and where the communicative function of language periodically recedes. The conditions of poetic language are thus themselves analogous with those in which the clandestine subject finds itself. As Lubin declares: 'la poésie, la vraie, ne circule que sous le manteau. On a beau dire et beau faire, elle refuse de marcher en plein jour' ['poetry, the real kind, only goes out in disguise. No matter what you say or do, it refuses to go out and about in broad daylight'].[6] While occasionally thematised directly, at a more tacit level the condition of statelessness is inflected in this *oeuvre* in a lingering opacity and ironic deflation, and in the way poetic language figures, and deflects, those disciplinary logics of which the *apatride* [stateless person] finds himself the object. The poem's privileged mode for Lubin is, as this chapter argues, ultimately that of attestation, as a form of utterance in which a subject is placed in a relation of uncertainty to its own foundation and to the legitimacy of its speech.

Istanbulite beginnings: reading and recording

Chahnour Kerestedjian was born in 1903 in Ottoman-era Istanbul. His paternal grandfather was of Greek origin, and a tailor within the Ottoman Court, while his father was likewise a tailor. The family name itself is of Turkish derivation, and is likely to originate in a nineteenth-century custom of adopting an ancestor's profession as surname.[7] Kerestedjian attended the Armenian school founded by the educationalist Reteos Berberian in the suburb of Üsküdar, where he excelled in Armenian literature and French. Early contacts with literature came also through an uncle on his mother's side of the family, Teotoros Lapçinciyan (1873–1928), alias Teotig, author of a series of popular yearbooks. Entitled *Ամէնուն Տարեցոյցը* ['Everyone's almanac'], the annuals formed a kind of encyclopaedia of Armenian cultural life in Istanbul, comparable to the Hachette series of almanacs common in France. 'Ces almanachs allaient sauver de l'oubli d'innombrables reliques et documents de la culture et de la pensée arméniennes' ['These almanacs would go on to save countless relics and records of Armenian culture and thought from oblivion'], wrote Teotig's nephew years later, with the retrospective awareness that they constituted an archive of a community which was itself to become largely obliterated in the years to come.[8]

Kerestedjian had just entered adolescence in 1915 at the outset of the Armenian genocide, the systematic extermination by the Ottoman Empire of up to 1.5 million of its Armenian subjects in pursuit of an ethnically and religiously homogeneous state. In the wake of the subsequent campaign of imprisonment, forced labour and deportations resulting in the death or massacre of Armenians in the Syrian desert, Kerestedjian's uncle Teotig in 1919 published details of those Armenian intellectuals who had been the focus of the first deportations; these began on 24 April 1915 in Istanbul following an order by the Ottoman Ministry of the Interior. Teotig's publication (which has since appeared in French translation in 2016 with the title *Mémorial du 24 avril* ['Memorial for 24 April']) features hundreds of short entries on members of the Armenian intelligentsia and includes dates of birth, photographs, biographical details and information on the circumstances of death or deportation.

A subsequent publication project by Teotig resulted in *Գողգոթա հայ հոգեւորականութեան*, a work first published in 1921 whose title translates as 'Golgotha of the Armenian clergy'. Drawing on biographical questionnaires which had been issued since 1912 to all Armenian priests and bishops by their church's Patriarch, this latter book served to document the atrocities committed against the Armenian clergy during the massacres and deportations. In pursuit of this work, Teotig made visits to Armenian orphanages and refugee camps in Istanbul and the vicinity, and was assisted in compiling the information from the questionnaires by his nephew. Deeply marked by this experience, which seems to have consisted primarily in lengthy hours spent inventorying the macabre physical and sexual abuse administered to the clergy, Kerestedjian would himself later recall the episode in a 1967 memoir devoted to his uncle, *Զոյգ մը կարմիր տետրակներ* ['A pair of red notebooks'].[9] In a biography of Teotig published in 2010, Rita Soulahian Kuyumjian translates a telling passage from this work:

> We read. We recorded. When we went to eat a bite downstairs, we were wasted, unable to exchange a word. The food had no taste. He was so taken by the task at hand that sometimes on discovering the circumstances of the death of a bishop he rejoiced in an odd way ...[10]

Teotig himself was deported in 1916, but survived. It was in this atmosphere of persecution that his nephew went into exile, emigrating to France in 1923. Documents held at the Office français de protection des réfugiés et apatrides [French Office for the Protection of Refugees and Stateless People] in Paris show that Chahnour Kerestedjian obtained a Nansen passport,[11] and spent the following 15 years in Paris where he worked on behalf of a Parisian photographic agency as a retoucher, making alterations or additions to photographic images. During this period, he wrote under the pseudonym Շահան Շահնուր; romanised in French as Chahan Chahnour, the name was seemingly inspired by the name of the principal of his secondary school, Chahan Berberian, son of the school's founder.[12] While articles appeared in the Paris-based Armenian newspaper *Haratch* ['Forwards'] and the literary review *Menk* ['We'], it was his 1929 novel *Նահանջը առանց երգի* ['Retreat without song'] (first serialised in *Haratch*, beginning in 1928) which most decisively signalled his entry onto the Armenian literary scene.

A past that cannot become past: *La Retraite sans fanfare*

This novel, which has come to feature prominently in the Armenian canon, addresses tensions between assimilation and the preservation of cultural identity among a group of Armenians who lose all ties to their ancestral homeland. However, despite the fact that it was written and published in France, it was not to be translated into French until 2009, under the title *La Retraite sans fanfare* ['Retreat without song'].[13] The novel is largely based on Kerestedjian's own personal experiences as a refugee in this period, and it chronicles the fortunes of a dissolute band of six young Armenians who have evidently been forced by persecution in their homeland to seek refuge in France. The tone of the text is bitter and aggressive, and indeed much of this bitterness is directed at the Armenian nation, the Armenian Apostolic Church and older generations of Armenians. The chief protagonist of the text is an individual alternately referred to as Bédros or by the gallicised version of his name, Pierre. Following his arrival from Istanbul, Bédros/Pierre secures employment as the manager of a Parisian photographic studio, and enters into a turbulent, ill-fated relationship with a French woman, Jeanne, also known as Nénette. In view of its polemical tone and sexual content, the novel generated considerable controversy among the Armenian readership.[14] Although a thorough consideration of Chahnour's Armenian *oeuvre* and its place within the literature of the Armenian genocide is far beyond the scope of this study, some aspects of *La Retraite sans fanfare* are worthy of mention in the context of the poetics elaborated in the author's French-language works.

Among the more striking aspects of the novel is that it does not at any point recount the events of the genocide, and indeed directly alludes to the events which have precipitated the Armenians' exile only once in a fleeting mention of 'les premiers mois de la catastrophe' ['the first months of the catastrophe']: 'Dans les premiers mois de la catastrophe, les jeunes gens encore enfants pour la plupart, jetés sur le pavé parisien, s'étaient blottis les uns contre les autres, liés les uns aux autres par un amour et une affection sans borne' ['In the first months of the catastrophe, the young people, most of whom were still children, were cast out onto the footpaths of Paris where they huddled against each other, each linked by boundless love and affection'].[15] The genocide is thus cast not as an isolated, localised event or set of events; rather, the wording 'les premiers mois de ...' ['the first months of ...'] supposes an ongoing, affect-laden state which persists long after its first manifestation. Of significance here also is the term 'catastrophe', for it is by this word, translated from the Armenian 'Աղետ' ('Aghet'), that the events of the genocide are typically invoked in Armenian culture. As Marc Nichanian has observed eloquently, such is the traumatic nature of genocidal experience that it ultimately eludes figural representation, belonging instead to the order of the unsayable:

> This something beyond the representable, beyond all possible narration … has no name. One cannot fix it, look at it directly, make of it an idea or a concept, nor can one make of it an object of science or knowledge. … It is still the past event that cannot become past, linked to the extreme experience of trauma. … The Catastrophe is the anaphoric object that passes across discourses, that never presents itself as such (as an object) for the gaze.[16]

Such concerns go to the core of the uncertain epistemology of *La Retraite sans fanfare*, a text in which 'ambivalent use of figurative language', as Michael Pifer argues, 'suggests a figural relationship with prior experiences it does not or cannot depict'.[17] Chahnour's narrative repeatedly dramatises the self-estrangement of Bédros/Pierre as an estrangement from language, as is clear from the novel's opening line: 'Il ne parvint pas à donner une définition des mots « prostituée » et « Dieu »' ['He was unable to give a definition of the words "prostitute" and "God"'].[18] From the first, the moral predicament of the central character is confirmed as emblematic of the plight of the Armenian diaspora, whose loss must be seen in linguistic as well as human terms: 'En retraite parents, enfants, oncles, gendres. En retraite mœurs, conceptions, morale, amour. En retraite la langue, en retraite la langue, en retraite la langue' ['Parents, children, uncles, sons-in-law in retreat. Morals, ideas, morality, love in retreat. Language in retreat, language in retreat, language in retreat'], declares the narrator.[19]

Meanwhile, reminders of the traumatic dispersal affecting Bédros/Pierre's community are frequent throughout. It is his Armenian companion, the intellectual Souren, who most forcefully articulates the young men's experience of their statelessness, speaking of their *patrie* [fatherland] as 'un nœud gordien impossible à défaire' ['a Gordian knot that it is impossible to untie'].[20] 'Chez nous' ['With us'], he says, 'il n'y a pas de terrain, il n'y a pas de mouvement, il n'y a pas de champ d'action' ['there is no land, there is no movement, there is no sphere of action'].[21] The Armenians' forced displacement is experienced, as is indicated by the book's title, as retreat, but, as is suggested by Souren's allusions to voids or intractable spatial figures in these quotations, this is not retreat in spatial terms. To quote this character once more:

> Non qu'il y ait aujourd'hui bataille et lutte pour la vie, mais parce qu'il y a quelque chose de plus fatal, de plus implacable, il y a

quelque chose de terrible, d'irrésistible, qui hurle son nom à tous les carrefours: c'est la retraite. La retraite, la retraite des Arméniens. ... Elle efface. Fait fondre, disparaître toute chose.[22]

[Not because there is striving and struggle of life, but because there is something more inevitable, more relentless, there is something awful, something irresistible that yells its name at every street corner: it is retreat. Retreat, the retreat of the Armenians ... It wipes things out. Makes everything dissolve and disappear.]

Retreat, then, is understood not in terms of pulling back to secure territory, but as a movement of withdrawal inwards, even of self-erasure. As befits the legacy of an event which retreats from designation and narrativisation, the emphasis here is on the disintegration of the very apparatus of language itself: the operative locus of a culture devastated at its core.

Hospitals and sanitoria: scenes of witnessing

From 1936, Kerestedjian's life changed dramatically when he became chronically infected with tuberculosis of the bones and began a lengthy stay at la Salpêtrière hospital in Paris. At the outbreak of World War II, his condition was compounded by a surgeon's failed attempt to complete a bone graft on unhealed tissue, leading to a serious deterioration of his health, and giving rise to an abiding embitterment towards medical personnel on his part.[23] There followed a period of invalidity characterised by numerous relapses and periods of respite. From 1939 to 1959, he made numerous stays in regional sanatoria – notably at Berck, Bidart and Pessac. Treatment by penicillin from 1959 brought about a major improvement in his health, and from that year onwards he was accommodated at the Home Arménien in St Raphael. As he confided in his correspondent Louise Servicen in 1959: 'L'atmosphère de la maison est triste, forcément, mais j'ai l'avantage très appréciable d'y posséder une chambre personnelle. Depuis vingt ans que je me trouvais relégué dans des salles à dix ou à vingt lits, la vie en commune m'était devenue un enfer' ['The atmosphere in the home is dreary, of course, but I have the great advantage of having an individual room here. Over the twenty years that I have spent confined to rooms with ten or twenty beds, life on the ward has become hell for me'].[24] He remained there for another 14 years, until his death in 1974.[25]

By the mid-1930s, Kerestedjian had already begun to compose poetry in French under the name Armen Lubin, and he produced a number of collections, bearing titles such as *Le Passager clandestin* ['The stowaway'] (1946) and *Sainte Patience* ['Blessed patience'] (1951)[26] which point to the acute persistence of themes of non-belonging and physical suffering in his work. Of all Lubin's work, it is perhaps his prose text *Transfert nocturne* ['Night transfer'] for which he is most renowned, and it is for this work that he was awarded the Prix Rivarol in 1955.[27] The book can be situated within a post-war literary and philosophical context distinguished by radically diminished conceptions of humanity rooted in experiences of suffering and hardship. Just as Hannah Arendt, as we have seen in the introduction to this study, casts the plight of stateless persons as a mass experience of territorial dispossession and privation of rights, Robert Antelme, in his concentration camp narrative *L'Espèce humaine* ['The human race'], reveals how detainment, cold, hunger and forced labour engender a form of life defined by irreducible, radical need.[28] As for the author of *Transfert nocturne*, it was the many years he spent on communal wards which led Lubin to reflect on the effective dehumanisation of the gravely ill within medical institutions. In terms of genre, the text can be said to belong to an 'autopathographic' literature, that is, a genre of writing 'dans lequel l'auteur évoque, de façon centrale ou périphérique, des faits, des idées ou des sentiments relatifs à sa propre maladie' ['in which the author evokes, centrally or peripherally, facts, ideas or feelings relating to his or her own illness'].[29]

A work in two parts, *Transfert nocturne* firstly recalls the author's experience at la Salpêtrière hospital in a style characterised by realism and dark humour, while the book's second half offers an extended meditation on the nature of suffering. In one chapter, Lubin considers various literary responses to extreme physical suffering, by authors such as André Gide, Arthur Rimbaud and Alfred de Vigny. Here, he dismisses both an attachment to an ideal of stoicism present in a poetic couplet by Vigny and a preference for extravagant romantic sighs[30] which he attributes to Gide. For Lubin, both of these approaches are inadequate to appreciate what he sees as the brutishly ego-destructive nature of the ravages wrought by severe illness:

> En effet, si Gide avait cette coutume-là (assurément excellente), c'est que ses souffrances étaient, elles aussi, d'excellente qualité : des souffrances obéissantes qui se laissaient envelopper. Mais au-delà du fait qu'un mal particulier peut très bien bâillonner l'homme et rendre impossible les gros soupirs adoucissants … quel

> parti doit-on prendre lorsque la douleur inhumaine dépasse de loin notre cri et se refuse aux enveloppements ? ... Tant que la vie coulait sans souffrance physique, l'homme faisait-il autre chose que justifier l'axiome avec plus ou moins de « bonheur » : *Homo homini lupus* ? Désormais isolé de ses semblables et resté seul avec son loup personnel, ne sera-t-il pas obligé de lui jeter en pâture sa propre personne intérieure ?[31]
>
> [Indeed, if Gide did have that (undoubtedly excellent) custom, it is because his suffering was itself of excellent quality: obedient suffering which is easily encompassed. But beyond the fact that a particular illness can very well stifle a man and make great soothing sighs an impossibility ... which side should we take when human suffering goes far beyond the volume of our cries and does not yield to attempts to encompass it? ... For as long as his life went by without physical suffering, did man not more or less 'happily' justify the axiom *homo homini lupus* [man is a wolf to his fellow man]? Now that he is isolated from his fellow man and left alone with his wolf, will he not be forced to toss his very own inner person to the jaws of the beast?]

Noteworthy here is the way the customary animalistic aggression of the physically able towards their fellow humans becomes altered fundamentally in the life of the invalid. For those who experience physical suffering, such aggression – which is supposedly fundamental to the social constitution of the self – instead deflects back upon the invalid's intimate life, which becomes the object of contestation. As we shall see later in this chapter, it is against just such a set of concerns that we can approach a poem such as 'L'Ombre à deux couleurs' ['The two-coloured shadow'], a piece dramatising a violent internalised contestation which takes the subject position as its terrain, fragmenting it and setting it against itself. Ultimately, however, at the close of his reflections on the literary treatment of suffering, Lubin insists on his own status as an involuntary witness, powerless to account for the spectacle of suffering and death which surrounds him in the common space of the ward:

> À la fin de chaque tragédie, je pensais invariablement, à ces gens qui passent leur vie sans connaître la souffrance physique, à ces gens qui s'éteignent dans un sommeil angélique, à ces gens qui ignorent jusqu'à leur mort. À la fin de chaque tragédie, moi, témoin involontaire, j'étais contraint de rapprocher ces deux mondes

> étrangers l'un à l'autre : le malheur inconcevable et le bonheur qui l'est davantage. Si d'autres témoins les trouvent concevables, et si, de l'union de ces deux mondes ils tirent des *Illuminations* (gravures coloriées), tels que le Paradis et l'Enfer, chez moi les choses se passent un peu différemment. De l'opposition en moi de ces deux mondes, il ne résulte qu'une annulation. Et faute de toile de fond, la question de gravure ne se pose même pas. Il se peut que, dans ces moments-là, j'aie l'air d'un illuminé.[32]
>
> [At the end of each tragedy, I invariably thought of those people whose lives go by without experiencing physical suffering, those who pass away in heavenly sleep, those who dwell in a state of ignorance until their death. At the end of each tragedy, I was, like an involuntary witness, forced to bring together two worlds that were foreign to each other: unimaginable misfortune and an even more inconceivable happiness. If other witnesses find them conceivable, and if from the union of these two worlds they bring forth *Illuminations* (coloured engravings), such as Heaven and Hell, with me things happen a little differently. What comes about as a result of the opposition of these two worlds within me is nothing other than a cancellation. And because there are no background scenes, the idea of making engravings does not even arise. At times like this, it may be that I look like a man enlightened.]

The choice of the term 'annulation' ['cancellation'] in this passage is significant, not least because it is brought into contrast with Arthur Rimbaud's notion of 'illumination' and that term's connotation of enlightenment. Employed in legal discourse to designate an action or deed which has been declared null or void, or in everyday usage to denote the calling off of a meeting, 'annulation' in this passage evokes the idea of a mental representation which has no grounds for being. So overwhelming is the obstacle posed by extreme suffering to writing (figured here as 'gravure' ['engraving'] by way of an extended reference to the subtitle of Rimbaud's *Illuminations*: 'painted plates') that it leads Lubin into an attitude of renunciation, rhetorically speaking, at least. This posture of renunciation, motivated by the poet's perception of the inadequacy of his own speech, cannot be separated from his medical construction as patient.

Lubin suggests that it is not sufficient merely to account for the phenomenological experience of suffering; as both *Transfert nocturne* and much of his poetry intimate, literature has to get to grips with the administrative frameworks that construct the individual as a medical or legal object. Indeed, it may be argued that one of the more original features of the poet's contribution to the literature of suffering is how his prose reflects as much – perhaps even more so – on the medical fact of his hospitalisation as on his experience of his illness.

The sanatorium as it figures in Lubin's prose and poetry is quite distinct from that place of intellectual ferment or romantic encounter to be found in Thomas Mann's *Der Zauberberg* ['The magic mountain'] or in *Vizuina luminată: Jurnal de sanatoriu* (published in French as *La Tanière éclairée: journal de sanatorium* ['The illuminated den: sanatorium diary']), a work by another resident of Berck, the Romanian writer Max Blecher.[33] As noted by Roland Barthes, himself a one-time tuberculosis sufferer, the space of the sanatorium enabled distinctive networks of sociability to form: 'tandis que les autres maladies désocialisent, la tuberculose, elle, vous projetait dans une petite société ethnographique qui tenait de la peuplade, du couvent et du phalanstère : rites, contraintes, protections' ['while other diseases lead to social exclusion, tuberculosis thrust you into a tiny ethnographic community which, with its rites, constraints and security measures, had something of the tribe, the convent and the phalanstery'].[34] The medical establishments frequented by Lubin, by contrast, shared little of that rarefied atmosphere: for much of his life, he was a patient in a public health system where illiteracy and poverty were the norm for many, and where he seems to have had minimal or no contact with patients of the opposite sex, thus furthering his perception of isolation from the social body. While his personal correspondence offers some suggestion of what he perhaps saw as a kind of *déclassement intellectuel* [declining intellectual status] given his circumstances as a published author in this context, he nonetheless shows a strong affinity with his fellow patients. Moreover, his own flair in capturing the rhythms peculiar to Armenian popular speech rendered him exceptionally receptive to the various witticisms and retorts which circulated around him in the common space of the ward. This is shown, for instance, by the following anecdote related in a letter to Jacques Brenner dated 23 January 1950:

> Il m'a fallu déménager hier, pour abandonner ma chambre aux ouvriers, qui s'y livrent à des travaux de réfection. Maintenant je me trouve à la 55, avec un clochard « né natif », de l'île d'Oléron et un Algérien de 19 ans, qui vendait des tapis dans les rues de Béziers. J'ai fait donner à l'Algérien des romans de Delly, car ce jeune homme n'aime rien tant que les romans d'amour. Malheureusement il ne

> comprend pas le quart de ce qu'il lit. Ce matin il demandait à son voisin, le clochard, le sens de ces mots : *sans doute* ; *indolore* ; *malheur*. Le clochard qui ne parvenait pas à trouver une définition franco-algérienne, gesticulait comme un beau diable. Finalement exaspéré, il a dit au jeune homme, « Le malheur ? le malheur ? mais tu es dedans, mon pauvre vieux ! » Alors, l'autre : « Ah ! compris, c'est *le lit*. »[35]
>
> [I had to move yesterday and give my room over to the workmen who are carrying out repairs there. Now I'm at number 55, with a 'native-born' tramp from the île d'Oléron and a 19-year-old Algerian who used to sell carpets in the streets of Béziers. I made sure some novels by Delly were given to the Algerian because this young man loves nothing so much as romance novels. Unfortunately, he doesn't understand a quarter of what he reads. This morning he asked his neighbour, the tramp, the meaning of these words: *no doubt*; *painless*; *misfortune*. Unable to find a Franco-Algerian definition, the tramp was waving his hands about like a demon. Eventually, out of exasperation, he says to the young man, 'Misfortune? Misfortune? It's right where you are right now, my poor chap!' And the other one replies: 'Ah! Understood, it's *the bed*.']

Here, the sanatorium emerges as a fragmented linguistic and social space in which misunderstandings, linguistic accidents and bitter ironies are frequent. Yet if Lubin was attentive to the possibilities of popular speech as a source of subjective colouring in this context, he was equally alert to what he saw as the objectifying logic of the clinical encounter.

Illness and statelessness

A keen perception is thus maintained throughout *Transfert nocturne* of the hospital or sanatorium as a space wherein a disciplinary gaze is directed unremittingly towards the life of the invalid, radically depriving that individual of agency: 'Le Corps Soignant joue une comédie soigneusement mise au point, dans le seul but d'obtenir la soumission du malade – qu'on appelle justement le *patient*' ['The medical staff put on a carefully rehearsed act, with the sole purpose of forcing the sick person – who is aptly called the *patient* – into submission'].[36] In biographical terms, there was a very pressing connection between the medical and legal domains for Lubin because it was his ill health which rendered him unfit for military service and thereby obstructed his attempts to secure naturalisation as a French citizen.[37] This is a factor which underscores the extent to which the latter concept is bound up with normalising strategies directed towards the body.[38]

As Jacques Brenner writes, Lubin saw himself as 'l'objet d'une « incompréhensible loi »' ['the object of an "incomprehensible law"'].[39] The law in question in Lubin's case is arguably not only that obscure law that governs individual destinies but the immigration legislation which surrounded Chahnour Kerestedjian's repeated applications for naturalisation. He does not appear ever to have succeeded in these applications, and, as is shown by a letter to his close friend Madeleine Follain on 9 January 1953, with no small degree of cynicism with regard to the medical profession, he became largely resigned to his situation:

> Ne vous tracassez pas trop pour ma naturalisation. J'estime que la qualité de réfugié arménien apatride ne messied pas à un misérable que l'on traîne vers les asiles infâmes, dans l'espoir que, après la rechute inévitable, on l'enverra en sana, où il pourra encore longtemps nourrir les gros patrons qui vivent de l'exploitation des tuberculeux.[40]
>
> [Don't worry too much about my naturalisation. I believe that the status of stateless Armenian refugee is not unbecoming for a man who is being dragged into notorious asylums, in the hope that, after his inevitable relapse, he will be sent to a sanatorium, where he can go on for a long time making a living for the big bosses who keep themselves going by exploiting tuberculosis patients.]

As the letter confirms, Lubin saw a form of connection between his refugee status and his own self-conception as invalid, a notion which is also taken up in the pages of *Transfert nocturne*: amid scatological asides on daily rituals such as the changing of bedpans, the poet reflects on the effectively diminished existence of some of the more gravely ill fellow patients with whom he shared the common space of the ward. Thrown back by the force of their suffering on the givenness of their physical condition, these individuals are described as follows:

> Ceux d'entre eux qui avaient conscience de leur déchéance, ceux-là vivaient une tragédie, puisqu'ils se trouvaient dans l'obligation de changer de race, à leur corps défendant. De Français qu'ils étaient, ils devenaient des Arméniens promis à tous les massacres. Pis encore :

Arménien de l'espèce « apatride ». Ces malades-là n'avaient plus qu'une seule patrie : la douleur. Dans cette patrie aussi vaste qu'inhumaine, les gens formaient une race à part, avec leur propre mentalité, leurs mœurs et leurs coutumes. Bien entendu, leur langage aussi se transformait, pour se réduire à un idiome quasi incompréhensible et incommunicable. Le malade devenu « personne déplacée » dans sa propre patrie se trouvait exclu du monde sans que son isolement fût possible. Car plus il s'isolait et se renfermait, plus il exposait des crevasses, des fentes et des fêlures en nombre croissant. À travers tous ces trous grandissait sa vulnérabilité.[41]

[Those who were aware of their decline experienced a tragedy because they found themselves obliged to change race against their will. They went from being Frenchmen to Armenians destined for massacre. Worse still, they were Armenians of the 'stateless' kind. From then on, those patients in particular only had one homeland: pain. In that homeland as vast as it is inhuman, these people formed a race of their own, with their own mentality, morals and customs. Needless to say, their language also underwent a transformation, degenerating into an almost incomprehensible and incommunicable idiom. The patient who had become a 'displaced person' in his own homeland found himself excluded from the world without actually being able to isolate himself from it safely. Because the more he cut himself off from it and withdrew, the more he laid bare a proliferation of cracks, fissures and rifts. Through each of these gaps, his vulnerability grew.]

The passage above is one of the few in the whole of Lubin's poetry and prose in French that allude directly to the historical contexts of genocidal massacre and forced displacement.[42] It is significant here, moreover, that the return to an originary scene which might have been thought to be forgotten or repressed occurs in the context of the poet's hospitalisation, for it is in this setting that the effective dehumanisation of the sufferer is staged as a kind of becoming stateless (indeed, the choice of the term 'déchéance' – connoting either physical degradation or a withdrawal of rights – is particularly apt in this respect). For Lubin, the abject suffering of the gravely ill effectively precipitates their descent into the ranks of the 'exterminables', to adapt a term used by Janine Altounian (the 'non-exterminables', namely those who are not at threat of genocidal persecution).[43] Taking up an analogy which entwines the geopolitical and the pathological, the poet casts the plight of these invalids as that of habilitated citizens reduced to the status of 'Arméniens promis à tous les massacres' ['Armenians destined for massacre'].

In this analogy, the invalid, like the stateless Armenian, undergoes a painful and debilitating withdrawal from a world held in common. Both figures find themselves the object of a force of expropriation or perceive the effective effacement of their individuality, at least in terms of how that individuality may be underwritten by the State, by norms of health or by the ability to participate in a common language. As powerful as that force of expropriation might be, however, the body – now thinkable only in terms of a lingering vulnerability – remains as testimony to a human presence through the emphasis placed on enduring suffering. Moreover, the paradox of 'exclusion without isolation'[44] conveys a sense that as well as being excluded from a meaningful world beyond the walls of medical institutions, the invalid has been placed in common with others similarly dispossessed of their individuality by dint of illness. It is this set of perceptions, formulated sporadically throughout the pages of *Transfert nocturne*, that tacitly informs Lubin's poetry, allowing it to intimate a form of experience configured at the intersection of disciplinary gazes, both medical and legal.

In the disciplinary gaze

Throughout the poetry of Lubin, there is an underlying sense of the writing subject as a 'world-poor' individual, insofar as the world of phenomena extends itself to him in a mode that is contingent on neither possession nor belonging,[45] but rather is experienced as that 'primary severity' alluded to in the poem 'Aventures' ['Adventures']. In these lines, the theme is underscored by the isolation of three nouns connoting exclusion and constraint:

> Rien que la terre, rien que cette sévérité première,
> Refus, défense, interdit
> Qui s'opposent à toute concession[46]
>
> [Nothing but the earth, nothing but that primary severity
> Refusal, prohibition, interdiction
> Where no claim can be staked]

Consistent with this (customary) perception of a fundamental resistance of the world to assimilation is a sense that the subject becomes consigned to various *non-lieux* [non-places] with which the individual Kerestedjian was himself familiar; these included the shady Montparnasse hotels of his early years in Paris. Occupied by sex workers and fellow refugees, these establishments were 'tous bâtis sur des terres plus ou moins légales' ['all built on more or less legal land'][47] in the terms of the poem 'Les Logis provisoires' ['Temporary lodgings']. Likewise, a dog 'au regard d'interdit de séjour' ['with a banned-from-entering look'][48] encountered on the street in the poem 'Faubourg' ['Suburb'] is a reminder that Lubin's awareness of his refugee status shadows his textual evocation of these locales. As if to suggest that even the experience of time and physical space alters in response to the migrant condition, many of the catechrestic tropes present in the poems written during or inspired by these Parisian years allude to sudden, furtive movements ('En emportant ses filles larguées, l'hôtel se glisse' ['As it bears away its ditched demimondaines, the hotel slips'], from 'Luxe' ['Luxury'];[49] 'le printemps s'insinue comme une forfaiture' ['spring creeps in like a felony'], from 'Hôtel borgne'[50]) or to moments of sustained idleness ('Sur des poubelles tordues les dialectes se penchaient' ['on twisted dustbins dialects leaned', from 'L'Exode' ['Exodus']).[51]

Similarly, the setting of the poem 'Monsieur Arnaud, bachelier' ['Monsieur Arnaud, school leaver'] is a *hôtel borgne* [shady hotel] occupied by a group of refugees, with a *glissement* [slippage] on the word 'borgne' (meaning 'having one eye only' or 'being poorly lit') serving ironically to introduce the notion that these individuals constitute objects of surveillance. As in the previous example from 'L'Exode', what renders the refugees suspicious is the speaking of foreign languages ('dialectes' ['dialects'], in a telling rhyme here with 's'infecte' ['gets infected']):

> Hôtel borgne dont l'œil valide s'infecte,
> Hôtel où les réfugiés et leurs dialectes
> Se glissent par une vieille porte noircie,
> La police reconnaît en elle l'objet de ses soucis.[52]
>
> [Shady hotel with one infected working eye
> Hotel into which the refugees and their dialects
> Sneak through a darkened old doorway,
> The police have it in their sights.]

However, the most abiding imagery of Lubin's poetry was to be provided by the environment of medical establishments, and the sand dunes and maritime landscapes which featured in his regular perambulation of the grounds of the sanatorium at Bidart along the Atlantic coastline.[53]

No doubt due to the poet's isolation and exclusion from the social body in these spaces, it is these texts which are most strongly invested with that same creeping sense of disquiet affecting place and self. In 'L'Ombre à deux couleurs' ['The two-coloured shadow'], the invasive effects of the surgeon's scalpel are assimilated to an expropriating force:

> Du haut en bas une ligne axiale me divise,
> Me divise sans disjoindre les deux volets
> De l'échelle double et de la double identité
> L'homme qui se divise s'enténèbre cependant.
>
> Et la nuit qui me porte atteinte en montant,
> Côté ombre qui se ramifie et côté sang,
> C'est l'ombre à deux couleurs, la pâle et la sombre,
> L'hésitante d'une part, et celle qui me surprend.
>
> L'hésitante fièvre ira bien rattraper l'autre
> Quelque part vers le sommet, lieu de rencontre,
> Quelque part où se dissipent erreurs et méprises.
>
> Ô les graves ouvrières nuitamment requises
> Pour la démolition lente de notre double
> Devant l'entrée haute ![54]
>
> [From top to bottom a line divides me along my axis
> Divides me without separating the two parts
> Of the dual ladder and of dual identity,
> Yet a shadow casts over a man sawn in two.
>
> Night harms me as it rises,
> On the shadow side branching out and on the blood side,
> Behold the two-coloured shadow, pale and dark,
> One that hesitates, and one that surprises me.
>
> The hesitant fever will get ahead of the other
> Somewhere near the summit, that meeting place,
> Somewhere where errors and misunderstandings fall away.
>
> O the solemn working women required nightly
> For the gradual demolishment of our double
> Before the supreme gates!]

If we consider this irregular sonnet as a whole, the poem presents, at least provisionally, a hope of sorts: that of suspending the drive towards disintegration, and of imagining another temporality and another place, that vague 'quelque part où se dissipent erreurs et méprises' ['somewhere where errors and misunderstandings fall away']. Yet ultimately, even this afterlife does not bring consolation, the poet being aware that he cannot reach the afterlife without an intensification of care and without being surrounded by the 'graves ouvrières' ['solemn working women'] who denote the medical staff. The shortened line 'Devant l'entrée haute' ['Before the supreme gates'] therefore arguably marks a certain disappointment, and a collapse back into disintegration. In a manner similar to the characterisation of the invalid offered in an earlier quotation from *Transfert nocturne* ['Night transfer'], this image of 'division without separation' suggests the fundamental incompleteness of the surgical action through the persistence of a consciousness of the violence of that action in the body of the patient.

This, therefore, is a self which articulates an acute sensibility of its own dividedness, both linguistically and culturally. In this respect, Lubin's poetry follows squarely in the wake of the Rimbaldian 'JE est un autre' ['I is another']; however, in Lubin's case, the reader is presented with, as Pierre Brunel writes, 'un *je* qui n'ose plus se dire que comme objet, et comme victime d'une agression' ['an *I* who no longer dares to speak of itself other than as an object and as the victim of aggression'].[55] In 'Minuit' ['Midnight'], nightmare and nocturnal angst merge in the surreal image of removal men carrying furniture out of the hospital at night:

> Le vent bouscule les plus gros déménageurs
> Dont les meubles sortent en tumulte de la forêt.
> A l'hôpital le silence s'étale plus qu'ailleurs
> Quand l'homme se démeuble au dernier degré.
>
> L'arrière-pays n'est plus pour l'homme,
> Pour l'homme étalé. [...][56]
>
> [The wind shakes up even the burliest of the removal men
> Hauling furniture that comes rattling out of the forest.
> In hospital, silence fans out more than elsewhere
> When man unravels to the last degree.
>
> The hinterland is no place for man any more,
> For a man scattered.]

Lubin's self-styled *homme étalé* ['scattered man'] exists bereft of any hinterland and is construed here in terms of the very impossibility of possession and belonging. This abiding sense of the invalid body as a kind of matter for exploitation and of the consequent loss of any holistic conception of the self is perhaps what emerges most strongly from much of Lubin's work.

In a 1949 letter to Jean Paulhan, Lubin writes that 'Mes dialogues imaginaires … restent, surtout la nuit, très décousus, toujours entortillés, ou d'une longueur lassante' ['The dialogues that go on in my imagination … especially at night, are always very disjointed, always twisted, or of a tiresome length'].[57] Just as it is the *medical* gaze which is enacted in many of Lubin's poems, in a similar manner, a number of the sanatorium poems which dramatise the poet's night-time 'dialogues imaginaires' are themselves overlaid with *legal* imagery, marking out that space of indistinction between the punitive and the palliative which the poet believed he had come to occupy. Thus, in the following quotations from the poems 'Partie adverse, souffrance physique' ['Opposing party, physical suffering'], 'Les Deux Accusés' ['The two defendants'] and 'Les Hautes Terrasses' ['The heavenly platforms'], just as in the title of the text 'Le Témoin avancé' ['The advanced witness'], there is a notable pattern of references to deliberations, opposing sides, defendants and supporting evidence:

> 'Partie adverse, souffrance physique'
>
> Dans la salle où les ombres délibèrent
> La partie adverse obtient la parole.[58]
>
> ['Opposing party, physical suffering'
>
> In the room where the shadows deliberate
> The opposing party is granted the right to speak.]
>
> 'Les Deux Accusés'
>
> L'accusé du jour était brûlé de fièvre
> Et celle de la nuit saisie par le froid.[59]
>
> ['The two defendants'
>
> The day's defendant was burning with fever
> And the night's was stricken with cold.]

'Les Hautes Terrasses'

Quel colloque pourrait se tenir entre moi et la nuit
Quand je suis seul à parler avec preuves à l'appui ?[60]

['The heavenly platforms'

What colloquium shall be had between the night and me
When it is I alone who speak, with proofs to support me?]

Noticeable within each of these couplets is how they designate the harried efforts towards speech of a subject whom a punitive disciplinary logic strives to construe as speechless, senseless or unreliable. What is marked out here is an enunciating presence, but one whose utterances do not accede to any properly affirmative or declarative quality, being instead marked by hesitation and cancellation, as the subject is obliged repeatedly to self-justify, pressured to offer an account of his self. Such couplets are frequent within the poems, and, as Philippe Jaccottet suggests in an essay on Lubin, their presence may indicate the way the poet's ill health also affected his approach to versification: 'peut-être parce que cette forme naît d'une respiration qui s'efforce d'être régulière, mais qui a vite besoin d'un repos ; elle parvient à prononcer une longue phrase soutenue, puis elle retombe, s'interrompt, d'où une solennité comme fatiguée, sans aucune emphase' ['perhaps because this form is born of a breath which makes every effort to be regular, but very quickly needs to take rest; it manages to utter a long sustained phrase, then it falls away, breaks off, hence its solemn and seemingly exhausted character, lacking any affectation'].[61]

Solemn attestation

In 'J'ai un couple d'amis' ['I have a couple of friends'], the poet walks along the edge of a wood bordering the sanatorium at sunrise, next to a row of pine trees which obscure the light of dawn. In this piece, the hesitation alluded to above is intimated via a rather opaque – and, to a certain extent, self-pitying – dialogue with the self (here, in the self-directed rejoinder 'Si, la femelle, je le sais' ['Yes, the female one, I know']):

À moi qui ne dispose que du mauvais versant
D'impénétrables barreaux : rien que des mots,

Rien que mes syllabes plus ou moins parés,
L'envers d'une haie d'honneur, presque ses regrets
Et pas d'issue ! Si, la femelle, je le sais.[62]

[For me, acquainted only with the wrong side
Of impenetrable bars: nothing but words,
Just my more or less dapper syllables,
The very opposite of a guard of honour, almost its regrets
And no way out! Yes, the female one, I know.]

The puncturing, dilatory effects produced by this example can be considered an instance of what André Dhôtel identifies in Lubin's poetry as 'une parole prolongée, se perdant parfois, se repliant avec de soudaines détentes' ['a kind of protracted speech that sometimes loses its way, folding in on itself and abruptly falling slack'].[63] In these lines, the image of a 'mantle' of words is intended not so much to suggest a guard of honour through which a poetic subject might be borne along – intact – towards his triumphant revelation beyond the physical barriers separating him from the world, but to figure a subjectivity in suspension, and the illusory compensations of his command of language. Despite a venturesome enjambment, this remains a walled-in consciousness ('pas d'issue' ['no way out']), albeit one which advertises its condition eloquently in presenting a kind of speech which seems to have become neglectful of its addressee and is instead directed back towards itself. This injection of spontaneous, hesitant orality moreover suggests a form of provisionality, and is thereby a device by which the poem may achieve the effect of underplaying its status as construction or composition.[64]

Likewise, the piece 'Bonheur et tourment' ['Pleasure and torment'] supplies a further instance of this kind of involuted speech. Amid a sequence of couplets which oscillate between exhilaration and despair, the reader encounters the following peculiar use of the neutral demonstrative pronoun:

Et puis on s'était dit : « Exil c'est débris. »
Sans savoir qu'après ceci venait ceci.

Et ceci : l'éblouissement comme une alerte,
Rien d'autre après, rien qu'une mer entrouverte.[65]

[And then we thought, 'Exile is debris'
Without knowing that after this came this.

And this: a shimmer that comes as a warning,
Nothing else after that, nothing but a parted sea.]

While 'ceci' ['this'] often announces what will follow later in the order of syntax, by multiplying it and ultimately suspending its referent here, the text ultimately points to a weakening of affirmation, thus offering a subtle commentary on exile and the loss of origins.

As these examples show, the singularity of the poem for Lubin is not solely that it serves to register the traumas of hospitalisation or exile or to rehearse the symbolic dispossession of speech they effect. In addition, his writing evinces a sharp alertness to the possibilities inherent in poetry as a discourse reflexively aware of its own lack of grounding. In this perspective, it is worth considering a section from 'La Note' ['The note'], a poem which engages the question of witnessing. As the poet watches, another patient on the ward passes away, and his corpse is illuminated by a ray of sunlight. In one of the starker parallels drawn in his poetry, Lubin compares the withered finger ('griffe') emerging from tangled sheets to the 'x' placed by an illiterate person on official documents (otherwise known as a 'signature à la griffe'). Within this morbid parallel, which is very much consistent with the poet's critique of the medical establishment, the patient's death, cast here as a 'disparition des archives' ['disappearance of/from the archives'], equates to the accomplishment of an administrative procedure:

Ainsi qu'on trouve le total des totaux
Tout à fait vers la fin tout à fait vers le bas
Ainsi je trouve dans tous mes hôpitaux
Un lit placé bien bas un lit plat

Où l'homme s'en va laisser sa peau.
Il est toujours gradué par la température
Ce lit laissé en blanc qui ressemble à
« Place-réservée-pour-la-signature ».

Il en est qui se signent à l'approche du trépas
Ensuite leurs bras s'ouvrent tous les deux
Comme la signature de l'illettré, cette croix
Qui arrête le corps dans un compte mystérieux.

« Il a eu son compte », dit le troupeau
Mais la signature succédant au total des totaux

N'est qu'une simple griffe qui émerge
Des draps enchevêtrés couleur de cierge.

Absolument indéchiffrable croit-on
Mais tout se simplifie lorsqu'il tonne
Et l'éclair parfait à lui seul
Forme l'entourage immédiat de la mort.

Plus parfaite que le cercle laissé en blanc
Sa vérité impose un total aveuglement
En vue de la disparition des archives,
Tout est résolu d'avance dans sa lumière vive.

dans la note

Quand reviennent porteurs de lance
Les novembres pluvieux
Un chien savant chien immense
Fait des comptes mystérieux.

Il compte il compte il recommence
Tous les chagrins s'appellent absence
Tous les chagrins porteurs de lance.[66]

[Just as one finds the grand total
Right the way down, down towards the end,
So in every one of my hospitals I find
A bed placed quite low down, a flat bed

From which a man slips away, leaving only his skin.
It is always graded by temperature
This bed left blank that resembles
'Space-reserved-for-signature'

At their final hour, some make the sign of the cross
Then their arms lie open.
That cross, like an illiterate person's signature,
That brings the body to a halt in a mysterious calculation.

'He's out for the count,' say the herd ...
But the signature that comes after the grand total

Is just a simple mark left by a finger that comes forth
From tangled sheets the colour of candles.

It's absolutely indecipherable, so they say
But it all becomes clearer when thunder rumbles
And a perfect flash of lightning alone
Stands in as the next of kin.

More perfect than the circle left blank
Its truth causes total blindness
In view of the disappearance of the archives,
Everything is resolved ahead of time in its bright light.

in the note

When spear bearers return
Rainy Novembers
A trained dog a huge dog
Does mysterious calculations.

He's counting he's counting he's doing it again
All sorrows are called absence
All sorrows spear bearers.]

The poem's play on the multiple connotations of the word 'note' in French (be that, for instance, as official communication, as written account or as bill) is telling. Here, it underscores the framework that these different verbal accounts create around the event of the man's death, whether via the colloquial parlance of other patients ('il a eu son compte' ['he's out for the count']) or by means of administrative procedures or archives. In this connection, the allusion to a '« Place-réservée-pour-la-signature »' ['"Space-reserved-for-signature"'], that formula present on administrative forms, elicits a connection to attestation, that formal declaration which affirms that something exists or is the case.

A series of comments by Jacques Derrida in an essay on Michel Deguy prove particularly suggestive in this context. Derrida raises the question of poetic testimony, describing it in relation to Deguy's work as an 'attestation secrète et sans vérité hors de sa propre performativité, hors de sa propre attestation, hors de ce qui fait exception de son œuvre propre' ['secret attestation and one with no truth outside of its own performativity, outside of its own attestation, outside of what makes an exception of its own work']. What is at issue here is not a truth held up to external verification; attestation does not deal primarily in the factual and the substantial. Rather, its locus is the provisional, and precisely what it attests to or discloses is its own unfolding as language. As Derrida elaborates in the same passage:

> ... le témoignage poétique ... ne rapporte pas autre chose, autre chose que soi, en son acte. Il ne dit rien d'autre mais rien de moins que son acte qui à la fois s'agit et s'archive, opère, s'opère et s'enregistre. Opère de façon inaugurale ... Il ne se rapporte pas à autre chose que lui-même, il n'est pas narration, reportage ou procès de connaissance, information ou culture.[67]
>
> [... poetic witnessing ... does not report anything different, other than itself, in its act. It says nothing other than, and nothing less than, its own act, which at the same time acts upon itself and archives itself, carries itself out and records itself. ... It does not refer to anything other than itself, it is not a narrative, a report or a process of knowledge, information or culture.]

Although, then (or, indeed, precisely since), as Paul Ricœur notes in *Soi-même comme un autre* ['Oneself as another'], attestation carries all the 'vulnérabilité d'un discours conscient de son défaut de fondation' ['vulnerability of a discourse conscious of its own lack of foundation'],[68] it is through that reflexive awareness of its absence of foundation that the poem attests to its own singularity within the arena of language.

'La Note', in attending to the accounts offered of the man's death, thus advertises its own form of vigilance, its own account distinct from those of medical records and anecdotal observations. The nature of this vigilance can be inferred from the list of actions in the quotation from Derrida above, all of which entail an analytical treatment of – or indeed an attitude of conspicuous care towards – language itself. This may offer a possible way to appraise the curious figure of the 'chien savant' ['trained dog'] which features in the closing stanzas, along with his continually renewed 'comptes mystérieux' ['mysterious calculations']. The poem's concern is neither informational legitimacy nor narrative validity; its specificity lies rather in the potential it offers to observe language in the act of producing and preserving itself, and thereby to deflect back on the propositions which gain currency around a given event. That this is not a neutral or disinterested pursuit for Lubin becomes clear when we consider the extraordinary resonance this text establishes between the poet's present situation, as repeated witness to the death of his peers, and the labour of memorialisation of the victims of the Armenian genocide which he conducted as a teenager in Istanbul in the company of his uncle Teotig. In this context, 'La Note' reflects a conviction that that event and its ongoing legacy resist conscription into the order of the explicitable.[69] Elaborating its own discursive regime, its own archive and its own forms of attestation, poetry here offers itself as that provisional but no less foundational 'document of a crisis', described by Paul Celan in a letter to Ingeborg Bachmann.[70]

Poetry's vigilance

Like 'La Note', the text 'Sous la loupe' ['Under the magnifying glass'] underscores poetry's capacity to deflect back critically on the experience of hospitalisation. Evoking the light cast by the moon on the darkened forms of the poet's fellow patients as they lie in bed at night, the poem alludes to the imaginary mastery of the medical gaze over the bodies of the infirm. That gaze is figured here in terms of a 'loupe savante' ['erudite magnifying glass'] which passes over the patients' exposed skin:

> À l'hôpital où tous les maux sont nocturnes
> Le malade remonte le rideau couleur de lune,
> Il laisse entrer l'air pur et le ciel étoilé
> En leur disant avec rancune :
> Nous ne sommes pas rancuniers !
>
> La lune filtrée par des branchages
> Promène des loupes savantes sur les lits,
> Déchiffrant le rêve, fouillant l'agonie
> Et en révélant sur des peaux jaunies
> L'étrange parchemin d'un apocryphe.
>
> Est-ce bien vrai ? Qu'est-ce qui est faux ?
> Comme l'apocryphe aussi a ses sanglots,
> Qu'il a ses râles également douteux,
> Le doute régit le cœur blême de l'hôpital
> Comme une loupe qui se concentre et puis s'étale.[71]
>
> [In the hospital, where illness strikes at night
> The patient raises the moon-tinted curtain,

Letting in the fresh air and the starry sky
He says to them grudgingly:
We don't hold grudges!

Moonlight filtering through the branches
Casts erudite magnifying glasses over the beds,
Deciphering dreams, delving into agonies
And revealing on jaundiced skin
The strange parchment of an apocrypha.

Is this true? What is false?
Just as the apocrypha too has its sobs,
And groans that are equally dubious,
Doubt governs the pale heart of the hospital
Like a magnifying lens that homes in, then blurs out.]

In a study of the meanings attributed to skin in literature and culture, Steven Connor writes: 'Exposure suggests the condition of being reduced to an object for sight. The objectifying power of sight, which comes from its unique reliance on distance and separation, is capable of separating me from myself, of painfully dissociating the visualizable portion of me from the rest.'[72] The medical ward is, classically, the space of medical observation, and, here, the invalid's gesture of opening the curtains to usher in the moonlight at first encourages the deciphering, excavating operations of analytical reasoning and the reduction of the patient's body to an 'object for sight'. However, the focus soon shifts to a different, altogether less decisive regime of seeing, since, in the moon's pale, uncertain light, motifs of truthfulness or authenticity found wanting come to the fore. These include the resentment which the invalid feels despite claims to the contrary, the 'dubious' groans and the mention of apocrypha. Although the diurnal, clinical gaze may proceed straightforwardly from skin to text, here, the 'étrange parchemin' ['strange parchment'] denotes obstacles to legibility, while the biblical reference infers an inauthentic or illegitimate kind of writing. From the perspective of metre, the more expansive qualities of the final quintet (its last four lines pairing two lines of eleven syllables, followed by two of thirteen syllables, thus toying with the classical metre of the alexandrine) mirror the final blurring effect connoted by the image of the magnifying glass. Emerging here is a form of observation which does not achieve certainty over its object, but rather attests, ultimately, to the eclipse of intellectual or moral certainties: 'Est-ce bien vrai ? Qu'est-ce qui est faux ?' ['Is this true? What is false?'].

Poems such as 'Sous la loupe' ['Under the magnifying glass'] are thus marked by a preoccupation with the objectifying logic of the gaze. While this theme, and related ones of witnessing and vulnerability, are present also in the pages of *Transfert nocturne* ['Night transfer'], it is Lubin's verse, with its delicate alternation of tone, perspective and scale, which is more apt to infer the possibility of a form of observation distinct from that of the medical gaze. In 'Feux contre feux' ['Fire against fire'], another poem which features a similar nocturnal setting, the poet is caught between the night sky's invitation to transcendent thought and the unbearable experience of his own embodied condition. Combining refrains together with elliptical constructions which proceed by inversion and juxtaposition in the opening and closing stanzas, the poem suggests a fundamental volatility of emotional attitude:

> Deux surfaces, mêmes dimensions :
> Mon front et le ciel étoilé.
> Deux surfaces, feux contre feux.
>
> Gâchis contre gâchis mais exaltés
> Par la fusion des nuits à hautes cimes,
> Mais chute aussi qui me corrige,
> L'écart rétabli, fini le prestige.
>
> Comme on est malhabile, convalescent,
> Rejeté ainsi, hors de l'élément !
>
> Froidement vidé je me sentis
> Quand retomba ma dépouille,
> Poches retournées je me sentis.
>
> Par la fusée et la fusion lointaines,
> Dans les hauteurs où tout est urgent,
> J'ai vu le ciel, il livrait le domaine.
>
> J'ai vu le point nul du sacre :
> Absorption, déchirement, simulacre
>
> De tout ce qu'ici-bas
> Nous ne pouvons pas posséder,
> Ici-bas et en ces lieux
> Où fuse l'amour: feux contre feux.

Gâchis contre gâchis mais exaltés
Jusqu'à la plus haute source des larmes,
Mais chute aussi qui me corrige,
L'écart rétabli, fini le prestige.

Comme on est vain, presque mort,
Poches retournées, dedans dehors.[73]

[Two surfaces, same dimensions:
My forehead and the starry sky.
Two surfaces, fire against fire.

Waste against waste but exalted
By the merging of the nights' lofty peaks,
But a fall too that chides me,
Once the gap is restored, prestige is no more.

How clumsy one is as a convalescent,
Relegated thus, out of the element!

Chilled, drained, I felt
When my skin fell away,
Pockets turned outwards, I felt

Through distant fireworks and fusion,
High above, where everything is urgent,
I saw the sky, relinquishing its estate.

I saw the consecration at its zero point:
Absorption, heartbreak, simulacrum

Of everything down here on earth
That we cannot possess,
Here on earth in these places
Where love rings out: fire against fire.

Waste against waste but exalted
To the highest source of tears,
But a fall too that chides me,
Once the gap is restored, prestige is no more.

How vain we are, almost dead,
Pockets turned outwards, inside outside.]

Here, the insistent 'j'ai vu … j'ai vu' ['I saw … I saw'] midway through the piece and the more syntactically expansive accompanying constructions are together suggestive of the hallucinatory drive of Rimbaldian *voyance*, yet the return to halting ellipses arguably points to the ultimate non-coalescence of imaginative vision and communicates something of language's resistance to falling in with the designs of the 'I' in recounting what it has witnessed. Indeed, despite its sudden affirmative stance, the 'I' ultimately recedes as the locus of articulation and is superseded by the more anonymous 'nous' ['we'] and 'on' ['we'/'one'], terms more appropriate to convey the condition of being one patient among others. While they connote material poverty, and also, more gruesomely, a kind of evisceration, the 'poches retournées, dedans dehors' ['pockets turned outwards, inside outside'] of the closing line also suggest a poetic construction inhabited by a kind of vacancy at its core, and thereby subtly play into the characterisation of Lubin's poetry as eschewing 'depth' or 'substance'.

If 'La Note' testifies to a poetry which, to recall Derrida above, 'fait exception de son œuvre propre' ['makes an exception of its own work'], the poem 'Sans rien autour' ['With nothing around it'] similarly attends to the imaginative possibilities of a discourse apprised of the vulnerability of its own proposition. From its opening lines, this poem foregrounds a 'homeless' writing subject who claims to have neither house nor room nor other resting place. Taking stock of this absence of any place from which to articulate a point of view, through the metaphor of a paneless, frameless window, the poem offers a philosophically tinged reflection on the possibility of seeing in a world where the external conditions that validate an individual perspective have been removed. This provisional aspect is underscored by a hesitant, irregular rhyme pattern which at points stretches from one stanza to the next ('autour'/'amours'; 'étonnant'/'blanc' ['around'/'loves'; 'incredible'/'white']). Although it tends to cluster around lines of 10 syllables, the poem also displays a high degree of metrical irregularity. Nonetheless, the regular pairing of feminine and then masculine rhymes in the more expansive final stanza suggests a more affirmative conclusion:

> N'ayant plus de maison ni logis,
> Plus de chambre où me mettre,
> Je me suis fabriqué une fenêtre,
> Sans rien autour.
>
> Fenêtre encadrant la matière
> Par le tracé tendre de son contour,

Elle s'ouvre comme la paupière,
Se ferme sans rien autour.

Se sont dépouillées les vieilles amours,
Mais la fenêtre dépourvue de glace
Gagne les hauteurs, elle se déplace,
Avec son cadre étonnant.

Qui n'est ni chair ni bois blanc,
Mais qui conserve la forme exacte
D'un œil parcourant sans ciller
L'espace soumis, le temps rayé.

Et je reste suspendu au cadre qui file,
J'en suis la larme la plus inutile
Dans la nuit fermée, dans le petit jour,
Ils s'ouvrent à moi sans rien autour.[74]

[Having neither home nor abode,
No room where I could go,
I made myself a window,
With nothing around it.

Window framing matter
By the tender trace of its outline,
It opens like an eyelid,
Closes with nothing around it.

Old loves worn thin
But the window with no pane
Makes for the heights, it moves,
With its incredible frame.

Which is neither flesh nor white wood,
But which maintains the exact shape
Of an unblinking eye that passes through
Arrested space, annulled time.

And I hang from the frame as it flows on,
I am its most useless tear
Closed in the night, at the break of day,
They open to me with nothing around.]

Although, as will be apparent in the next chapter, the conceit of 'Sans rien autour' ['With nothing around it'] is not as conceptually elaborate as that of Jabès's *Aely*, it is striking that the theme of a disembodied eye should have appealed to both poets in the context of their respective meditations on statelessness and non-belonging. Just as Jabès's treatment of this figure focuses on his subversion of the objectifying logic of the gaze in *Aely*, Lubin's poem similarly centres on the possibility of seeing outside the habitual conditions which govern perception. Retaining as it does the shape of a pupil, the curious detached gaze invoked here is not that of a starkly impersonal, clinical objectivity; what is implied is not a movement outside of a human reality, but, as the allusions to tears suggest, a paradoxically enhanced and affect-laden one. All acts of viewing are subject to external forces which centre and legitimise perspective; Lubin's conceit here, emerging from the hypothesis of a reversal of frame and window ('Fenêtre encadrant la matière' ['Window framing matter']), is that, once abstracted from the order of objectivity, poetic seeing establishes its own precarious truth, acknowledging the exceptionality of the proposition it elaborates.

Conclusion: cultivating 'slightness'

As noted previously, Lubin's verse typically invites characterisations which underscore its 'slightness' or 'meagreness'. Philippe Jaccottet, for instance, argues that Lubin's poems 'ne sont riches en rien, sinon en vérité intime' ['are rich in nothing, other than in inner truth'],[75] while André Dhôtel comments that they neither develop an 'idée générale' ['general idea'] nor explore depth of feeling or belief but offer 'simples notations' ['simple observations'] of the real. In the same passage, Dhôtel states, tellingly, that 'sa singulière ressource n'est autre que de s'exercer en chaque notation à rester *en suspens*, à constater *le suspens* de toute expression, de toute donnée' ['in each one of his observations, his singular ingenuity consists entirely of striving to retain an *unresolved* quality, to note the *unresolved* quality of any form of expression, of any given thing'].[76]

Indeed, a central preoccupation of Lubin's poetics is precisely to 'watch over' a weakening of the structures of affirmation, as if the condition of detachment and watchfulness in which the poet found himself by dint of genocidal trauma, statelessness and a chronic, lifelong medical condition made him especially receptive to language's own malaise. Lubin's elevation of the cognate condition of 'patience', with its etymological link to suffering, is telling in this respect, for the poet's vigilance with respect to the word does not primarily evoke an effort of the will, but rather something suffered or undergone. Vigilance does not produce comfort or consolation for the watcher; rather, it renders the perception of separation ever more acute, as the poem 'À la nuit venue' ['At nightfall'] relates: 'lorsqu'on est en terre d'exil et exilé, / Plus on est éveillé plus on est exilé' ['Exiled, in the place of exile, / The more alert one is, the more exiled one is'].[77]

Though Lubin's vigilance may evoke a condition of passivity, it is a paradoxically active passivity which operates both broadly within, but simultaneously at the margins of, both the norms of affirmation and the strictures of poetic convention. For an author inured by his experience of medical institutions to listening to 'cette lamentation qui n'ose pas prendre de l'ampleur, toute cette plainte qui n'ose pas s'élever et s'affirmer' ['that lament that does not dare to raise its voice, that whole complaint that does not dare to rise up and assert itself'],[78] it would seem that Lubin adopts a posture which comes to terms with the weakening of the act of utterance, and which develops a range of textual means to exploit that weakening. In the later collections *Sainte Patience* ['Blessed patience'], *Les Hautes Terrasses* ['The heavenly platforms'] and *Feux contre feux* ['Fire against fire'], the poet's imagery is primarily limited to the few spaces with which he was physically acquainted, namely, the hospitals and sanatoria along with their grounds and surroundings; this pointedly restricted repertoire of images is but one aspect that contributes to the 'slightness' that is taken to characterise his work. Others include his predilection for the brevity of the couplet, for metrical irregularities and the *vers boiteux*; his episodic use of rhyme; and his periodic exploitation of spoken utterance to produce effects of provisionality. As Armand Robin notes in an essay on Lubin:

> Il y a ... une « retenue » volontaire, qui interdit qu'on puisse trouver en ces poèmes un quelconque appui pour une compréhension « utilisable » ; c'est sans doute ce qui explique que les « critiques littéraires », qui ont justement tant besoin de ce genre de compréhension, ont de la peine à « trouver quelque chose à dire », devant cette œuvre, qui ne se prête pas au traitement ordinaire. Ici le lecteur est contraint à une démarche agile où les pieds ne se posent jamais tout à fait nulle part.[79]
>
> [There is ... a deliberate 'restraint' that prevents us from detecting any kind of basis for a 'usable' understanding of these poems; this is

> probably why 'literary critics', who are so much in need of this kind of understanding, find it difficult to 'find something to say' when faced with this *oeuvre* that does not lend itself to the standard treatment. Here, the reader is forced to adopt an agile step and has the sensation that his or her feet never quite land in any particular place.]

As Robin suggests, a special kind of vigilance is required of the reader confronted with the shifting terrain of Lubin's verse, so indisposed is it to critical construal. Moreover, this is a quality which is underscored by the poet's own propensity for rewriting and by the deep anxiety over the need to improve his work which he reveals in his correspondence. For instance, although the editorial matter of the most recent complete edition of his poetry indicates that some of the poems (namely those featuring in *Feux contre feux*) are presented in their 'version nouvelle' ['new version'],[80] the revised version may differ so substantially from the original that it may be considered as a separate text in its own right. Lubin's revisions range from changes or substitutions of title to more substantial reprisals of syntactical elements or reworking of whole stanzas or poems. In passing, it is worth noting that this is also an essential trait of the late work of the author in the Armenian language, especially concerning a collection of texts dating from before World War II, *Թերթիկս կիրակնօրյա թիվը*, published in 1958 in Beirut in revised form, and whose title translates into French as *Le Numéro de dimanche de mon journal* ['My newspaper's Sunday edition'].[81] As Krikor Beledian argues in a recent article on exile and the poetics of rewriting in these texts, it is as if Lubin/Chahnour identifies the moment of first inscription with an originary loss which is then taken up and re-actualised with each instance of rewriting.[82]

In the work of other poets considered in this study, many of the characteristics outlined here in the work of Lubin undergo an undeniably more radical formulation than in his poems. For instance, the work of Ghérasim Luca engages in what is effectively a stuttering denudation and suspension of syntax in the host language. Similarly, as we shall see in the next chapter, in the fragmentary compositions of Edmond Jabès's *Livre des questions* ['Book of questions'], a form of metapoetic discourse develops in which the very possibility of affirmation is periodically deferred, pushing beyond speech into the white borders of the page. Yet, despite his poetry's rather conventional formal character, Lubin contrives to attach extraordinary existential and philosophical weight to some ostensibly 'light' constructions. His work offers a compelling insight into how statelessness can be figured as a diminished kind of participation in a language and a world held in common. Tentatively emerging from these texts is a sense of the inadequacy of medicalised or national-juridical conceptions of the individual in accounting for that diminished, yet irreducible life. Where the formal logics of medicine or the law function inadvertently to silence their disciplinary objects, a finite enunciating presence, or at least a trace thereof, nonetheless attests to itself in their wake.[83] The task which falls to Lubin, then, is to elicit a residual enunciating presence operative at a level below the affirmative structures of the host language, indeed of *all* language, even if this labour marks the elegiac loss of the security and integrity of the subject of enunciation.

Notes

1 Émil Cioran, *La Tentation d'exister* (Paris: Gallimard, 1956), 66.

2 Quoted in Krikor Chahinian, 'Écartèlement', *Cahiers bleus* 33 (1984): 16.

3 'Le nom propre est l'attestation visible de l'identité de son porteur à travers les temps et les espaces sociaux, le fondement de l'unité de ses manifestations successives et de la possibilité socialement reconnue de totaliser ces manifestations dans des enregistrements officiels, *curriculum vitae*, *cursus honorum*, casier judiciaire, nécrologie ou biographie qui constituent la vie en totalité finie par le verdict porté sur un bilan provisoire ou définitif' ['The proper name is the visible attestation of the identity of its bearer through time and social spaces, the foundation of the unity of his successive manifestations and of the socially recognised possibility of producing a total account of these manifestations in the official records, *curriculum vitae*, *cursus honorum*, criminal records, obituaries or biographies that constitute life as a finite totality by a definitive judgment cast on a provisional or final assessment']. Pierre Bourdieu, *Raisons pratiques: sur la théorie de l'action* (Paris: Seuil, 1994), 85.

4 'L'immigré est *atopos*, sans lieu, déplacé, inclassable. Rapprochement qui n'est pas là seulement pour ennoblir, par la vertu de la référence. Ni citoyen, ni étranger … il se situe à la frontière de l'être et du non-être social' ['The immigrant is *atopos*, placeless, displaced, unclassifiable. It is a comparison the aim of which is not simply to make the figure seem noble, based on the virtuousness of the reference. Neither citizen nor foreigner … he is at the border of social being and non-being']. Pierre Bourdieu, preface to *La Double Absence: Des illusions de l'émigré aux souffrances de l'immigré*, by Abdelmalek Sayad (Paris: Seuil, 1999), 6–7.

5 Armen Lubin, 'Trois lettres à Jean Paulhan', *Grandes largeurs* 12 (1987): 6–7.

6 Armen Lubin, 'À travers champs', *Cahiers des saisons* 19 (Winter 1960): 470.

7 See: George A. Bournoutian, *A Concise History of the Armenian People (From Ancient Times to the Present)* (Costa Mesa, CA: Mazda, 2003), 258. Given that 'Kereste' designates 'timber' in Turkish, the poet's ancestor may have been a timber merchant.

8 Quoted in: Téotig, *Mémorial du 24 avril*, trans. by Alice Der Vartanian and Houri Varjabédian (Paris: Parenthèses, 2016), 9.

9 Շահան Շահնուր, *Զոյգ մը կարմիր տետրակներ* (Beirut: Chirak, 1967).

10 Rita Soulahian Kuyumjian, *Teotig: Biography & monument to April 11* (London: Gomidas Institute, 2010), 37.

11 Named after the Norwegian diplomat and explorer Fritjof Nansen, who was appointed by the League of Nations to aid in the resettlement of stateless persons displaced by the Russian Revolution across Europe, the document afforded the holder a limited degree of state protection. The Nansen scheme was additionally opened to refugees displaced by the Armenian genocide in 1924, prior to which Armenian refugees in France had no valid entitlement to stay in the country. For more on issues relating to Armenian asylum in France at this period, see: Maud S. Mandel, *In the Aftermath of Genocide: Armenians and Jews in twentieth-century France* (Durham, NC: Duke University Press, 2003), 32, and Greg Burgess,

Refuge in the Land of Liberty: A history of asylum and refugee protection in France since the Revolution (Basingstoke: Palgrave Macmillan, 2008), 47–8.

12 It also further underscores the author's attentiveness to the nationality effect of certain names, since it marks a repudiation of the Turkish-derived family name Kerestedjian. The author's Armenian *nom de plume* is typically romanised in English as Shahan Shahnur, but for the sake of consistency with the predominantly French-language sources cited here, I have opted to use the French version.

13 Շահան Շահնուր, *Նահանջը առանց երգի* (Paris: Haratch, 1933) / Chahan Chahnour, *La Retraite sans fanfare: histoire illustrée des Arméniens à leur arrivée à Paris suite au génocide*, trans. by Krikor Beledian (Paris: L'Act Mem, 2009). It should be noted that the title of the Armenian original does not feature the words '*à leur arrivée à Paris suite au génocide*' ['on their arrival in Paris following the genocide'].

14 Particularly scandalous was the diatribe against the tenth-century poet and theologian Gregory of Narek, revered as a founding father of Armenian literature. For a discussion of Chahnour/Lubin's work and other literary responses to the Armenian genocide in this period, the reader may refer to Krikor Beledian's excellent history of Armenian-language literature in twentieth-century France: Krikor Beledian, *Cinquante ans de littérature arménienne en France: du même à l'autre* (Paris: CNRS Éditions, 2001).

15 Chahnour, *La Retraite sans fanfare*, 104.

16 Marc Nichanian, 'Catastrophic mourning', in *Loss: The politics of mourning*, ed. David L. Eng and David Kazanjian (Berkeley: University of California Press, 2003), 113. For a survey of Armenian literary responses to the Catastrophe, see: Krikor Beledian, 'L'Expérience de la catastrophe dans la littérature arménienne', *Revue d'histoire arménienne contemporaine* 1 (1995): 127–97.

17 Michael Pifer, 'The forgetful figure: Armenian representations of trauma in Arakel of Tabriz and Shahan Shahnur', *Journal of Literature and Trauma Studies* 5 (2016): 83.

18 Chahnour, *La Retraite sans fanfare*, 9.

19 Chahnour, *La Retraite sans fanfare*, 129.

20 Chahnour, *La Retraite sans fanfare*, 128.

21 Chahnour, *La Retraite sans fanfare*, 174.

22 Chahnour, *La Retraite sans fanfare*, 129.

23 Kerestedjian's deteriorating health and uncertain civil status is charted in detail in Krikor Chahinian, 'Drame et poésie de l'exil dans l'œuvre d'Armen Lubin en particulier et d'écrivains arméniens en France en général' (unpublished doctoral thesis, Université de Paris-Sorbonne, 1979). Kerestedjian's unhappy condition can be compared to that of the Romanian Jewish writer and fellow tuberculosis-sufferer Max Blecher.

24 Armen Lubin to Louise Servicen, 24 December 1959. The poet's correspondence, manuscripts and personal papers are held at the Bibliothèque littéraire Jacques Doucet, Paris (henceforth, 'BLJD') in the Fonds Lubin ('LBN'). I wish to acknowledge the kind assistance of the late Arpik Missakian in granting access to the Fonds Lubin. During his lifetime, Lubin's correspondents included the painter Madeleine Follain, and the writers and poets Jean Follain, Philippe Jaccottet, Jean Paulhan and Henri Thomas.

25 Hélène Gestern's recent work *Armen* singularly interweaves biography and autobiography and is one of the most authoritative and extensive treatments of Lubin's life available to readers to date. See: Hélène Gestern, *Armen* (Paris: Arléa, 2020).

26 The works were published separately: *Le Passager clandestin* (Paris: Gallimard, 1946); *Sainte Patience* (Paris: Gallimard, 1951). However, they are collected (in partially revised editions) in a later Gallimard volume: *Le Passager clandestin. Sainte Patience. Les Hautes Terrasses et autres poèmes*, pref. by Jacques Réda (Paris: Gallimard, 2005).

27 Armen Lubin, *Transfert nocturne* (Paris: Gallimard, 1955).

28 Robert Antelme, *L'Espèce humaine* (Paris: Gallimard, 1957).

29 Stéphane Grisi, *Dans l'intimité des malades: de Montaigne à Hervé Guibert* (Paris: Desclée de Brouwer, 1996), 25.

30 A comparable avoidance of such Romantic posturing is suggested in the early poem 'L'Ô', in which a prostitute who occupies the same hotel as the poet is observed as she returns from her night's work; on her arrival she retrieves from the street the letter 'ô' which has fallen from the hotel's signage: 'Des égards à celle-là qui est toujours battue, / Qui paye régulièrement sa chambre contre reçu, / Qui cherche la confiance, cherche la sympathie / Et rentrant à l'aube, elle rapporte / L'Ô de l'HÔTEL tombée dans la rue.' ['Consideration for the one who's always

getting battered / Who routinely pays her board in exchange for a receipt / Who is seeking trust, seeking compatibility / And who on the way home at sunrise, gathers up / the O of the HOTEL which had fallen into the street']. Lubin, *Le Passager clandestin. Sainte Patience. Les Hautes Terrasses et autres poèmes*, 28. With its symbolic casting off of the 'Ô', this image signals a posture characteristic of Lubin's *oeuvre* more generally: the determined rejection of a certain variety of poetic hyperbole in favour of an aesthetic of ironic detachment and understatement.

31 Lubin, *Transfert nocturne*, 94.

32 Lubin, *Transfert nocturne*, 98–9.

33 Max Blecher, *Aventures dans l'irréalité immédiate* suivi de *La Tanière éclairée*, trans. by Marianne Sora, Georgeta Horodinca and Hélène Fleury (Paris: Maurice Nadeau, 1989).

34 Roland Barthes, *Roland Barthes par Roland Barthes* (Paris: Seuil, 1975), 39.

35 Lubin to Jacques Brenner, 23 January 1950, LBN, BLJD.

36 Lubin, *Transfert nocturne*, 89.

37 As reported by Jacques Brenner in 'Présentation d'Armen Lubin', *Cahiers André Dhôtel* 6 (2008): 13.

38 Indeed, it is interesting to note how the very disease from which the poet suffered itself focalises the issues of statelessness and naturalisation outlined in this analysis, for it points to a problem encountered more broadly by the Armenian community to which the poet belonged: 'In the late 1920s, the French Armenian population was particularly susceptible to contagious diseases such as tuberculosis. The standard French response to the disease was to house those afflicted in a sanitorium, but the government refused to subsidize the same care for foreigners. Fortunately, most of those infected with the disease could return to their own country, where they were eligible for medical care or at least could rely on their own consulate for financial or medical assistance; Armenians could not': Mandel, *In the Aftermath of Genocide*, 34. The situation described by Mandel shows the extent to which naturalisation may be considered to be contingent upon normative biological factors as well as on the more obvious formal procedures in relation to citizenship.

39 Jacques Brenner, *Mon histoire de la littérature française contemporaine* (Paris: Grasset, 1987), 168.

40 Lubin to Madeleine Follain, 9 January 1953, LBN, BLJD.

41 Lubin, *Transfert nocturne*, 72–3.

42 Indeed, it is interesting to consider in this context the trope of involuntary witnessing deployed in the earlier cited passages from *Transfert nocturne* ['Night transfer']. It is worth noting that the author's illness is not mentioned in his Armenian writing.

43 In a study which addresses the ways in which post-genocidal generations undertake the 'working through' of the historical trauma experienced by their forebears, Altounian has recourse to the term 'non-exterminables' to designate those who are unaffected by the legacy of trauma. 'Pour réellement exister et acquérir une voix politique, le témoignage requiert un déplacement dans les générations, mais aussi dans l'espace des autres, c'est-à-dire un transfert dans l'espace de ceux que nous appellerons les « non-exterminables » du moment' ['In order to genuinely exist and acquire a political voice, witnessing requires a shift between generations, but also into the space of others, that is, a transfer into the space of those we will call the "non-exterminables" of a given moment']. Janine Altounian, *De la cure à l'écriture : l'élaboration d'un héritage traumatique* (Paris: PUF, 2012), 118.

44 See above: 'Le malade ... se trouvait exclu du monde sans que son isolement fût possible' ['The patient ... found himself excluded from the world without actually being able to isolate himself from it safely'].

45 Patrick Reumaux writes that 'Tout est d'abord obstacle dans la poésie de Lubin, depuis les choses les plus lointaines, l'océan déchiqueté comme un poumon qui vomit le cœur en avant de ses remparts, les pins qui montrent leurs cicatrices, la voûte du ciel qui s'ouvre mais ne tient jamais ses promesses, jusqu'à l'environnement immédiat (sana ou hôpital à la dérive) et aux objets les plus proches, veilleuse, fiole, broche réduite entre les doigts de la main' ['Everything is first encountered as an obstacle in Lubin's poetry, from the most distant things, such as the ocean shattered like a lung spewing its heart before it reaches the shoreline, the pines displaying their scars, or the vault of the sky that opens up but never keeps its promises, to the immediate environment (the sanatorium or hospital drifting past) and those objects that lie close by, whether they be a night light, a phial, or a brooch under the fingertips']. Patrick Reumaux, 'Une poésie sans rien autour', *Études* (May 1975): 719–20.

46 Lubin, *Le Passager clandestin. Sainte Patience. Les Hautes Terrasses et autres poèmes*, 218.

47 Lubin, *Le Passager clandestin. Sainte Patience. Les Hautes Terrasses et autres poèmes*, 43.
48 Lubin, *Le Passager clandestin. Sainte Patience. Les Hautes Terrasses et autres poèmes*, 165.
49 Lubin, *Le Passager clandestin. Sainte Patience. Les Hautes Terrasses et autres poèmes*, 32.
50 Lubin, *Le Passager clandestin. Sainte Patience. Les Hautes Terrasses et autres poèmes*, 40.
51 Lubin, *Le Passager clandestin. Sainte Patience. Les Hautes Terrasses et autres poèmes*, 95.
52 Lubin, *Le Passager clandestin. Sainte Patience. Les Hautes Terrasses et autres poèmes*, 171.
53 Lubin's verse, often centring almost wholly on the lingering visual impressions gathered on these walks, has often led to characterisations of his poetry in terms of its 'slightness'; as André Dhôtel writes, 'Lubin n'écrit rien qui ne vienne d'une expérience immédiate. Ni idée générale, ni sentiment, ni croyance. De simples notations concernant des objets, prises dans la vie au jour le jour' ['There is nothing that Lubin writes that doesn't come from an immediate experience. No general ideas, no feelings, no beliefs. Just simple observations of objects, taken from life one day to the next']. J. de Bourbon-Busset, André Dhôtel, Jean Follain, Jean Mambrino and Patrick Reumaux, 'Entretiens du Polyèdre: Armen Lubin, l'étranger', *Cahiers bleus* 32 (Summer–Autumn 1984): 14.
54 Lubin, *Le Passager clandestin. Sainte Patience. Les Hautes Terrasses et autres poèmes*, 222.
55 Pierre Brunel, 'Le Double Langage d'Armen Lubin', *Francofonia* 5 (Autumn 1983): 24.
56 Lubin, *Le Passager clandestin. Sainte Patience. Les Hautes Terrasses et autres poèmes*, 127.
57 Lubin to Jean Paulhan, 18 September 1949, LBN, BLJD.
58 Lubin, *Le Passager clandestin. Sainte Patience. Les Hautes Terrasses et autres poèmes*, 48.
59 Lubin, *Le Passager clandestin. Sainte Patience. Les Hautes Terrasses et autres poèmes*, 116.
60 Lubin, *Le Passager clandestin. Sainte Patience. Les Hautes Terrasses et autres poèmes*, 195.
61 Philippe Jaccottet, *L'Entretien des muses: chroniques de poésie* (Paris: Gallimard: 1968), 201.
62 Lubin, *Le Passager clandestin. Sainte Patience. Les Hautes Terrasses et autres poèmes*, 210.
63 'Dans ses écrits Armen Lubin ne fait jamais que des remarques en passant. ... Rien que des détails notés et puis considérés à l'endroit, à l'envers, en diagonale. Cela fait des poèmes qui ne sont pas des chants ni des compositions, mais une parole prolongée, se perdant parfois, se repliant avec de soudaines détentes' ['In his writings, Armen Lubin never makes anything but remarks in passing. ... Nothing but details noted and then considered the right way up, upside down, diagonally. This results in poems that are not songs or compositions, but a kind of protracted speech that sometimes loses its way, folding in on itself and abruptly falling slack']. André Dhôtel, 'L'Œuvre d'Armen Lubin', *Cahiers bleus* 33 (1984): 9.
64 For another example, see the following lines from 'Courte éclaircie' ['Sunny interval']: 'C'était l'orage. Précédé de son souffle aigu / L'averse approchait. Mais rien qu'une courte pluie, / Non, pas de pluie. Rien. Si, de la petite pluie / Dans la lumière rasante de l'horizon / Quand soudain ce furent de joyeux grêlons' ['There was a storm. Preceded by a sharp breeze / The downpour was approaching. But nothing more than a brief shower, / No, no rain. Nothing. Yes there was, just a little rain / In the oblique light on the horizon / When suddenly sparkling hailstones fell']. Lubin, *Le Passager clandestin. Sainte Patience. Les Hautes Terrasses et autres poèmes*, 213.
65 Lubin, *Le Passager clandestin. Sainte Patience. Les Hautes Terrasses et autres poèmes*, 242–3.
66 Lubin, *Le Passager clandestin. Sainte Patience. Les Hautes Terrasses et autres poèmes*, 242–3. See also: Armen Lubin, *Le Passager clandestin* (Paris: Gallimard, 1946), 69–70.
67 Jacques Derrida, 'Comment nommer', *Le Poète que je cherche à être*, ed. by Yves Charnet (Paris: La Table ronde, 1996), 200.
68 Paul Ricœur, *Soi-même comme un autre* (Paris: Seuil, 1990), 45
69 As Nichanian notes, 'Le génocide n'est pas un fait. Ce n'est pas un fait parce que c'est la destruction même du fait, de la notion de fait, de la factualité du fait' ['Genocide is not a fact. It is not a fact because it is the very destruction of fact, of the notion of fact, of the factuality of fact']. Marc Nichanian, *La Perversion historiographique: une réflexion arménienne* (Paris: Lignes & Manifestes, 2006), 9.
70 'Das Dokument einer Krise, wenn Du willst – aber was wäre Dichtung, wenn sie nicht auch das wäre, und zwar radikal?' ('The document of a crisis, you might say – but what would poetry be if it were not this as well, and, indeed, radically so?'). Cited in: Gert Hofmann et al., introduction to *German and European Poetics after the Holocaust: Crisis and creativity* (Rochester, NY: Camden House, 2011), 7.
71 Lubin, *Le Passager clandestin. Sainte Patience. Les Hautes Terrasses et autres poèmes*, 112.
72 Steven Connor, *The Book of Skin* (London: Reaktion, 2004), 67–8.
73 Lubin, *Le Passager clandestin. Sainte Patience. Les Hautes Terrasses et autres poèmes*, 206.
74 Lubin, *Le Passager clandestin. Sainte Patience. Les Hautes Terrasses et autres poèmes*, 137.

75 Philippe Jaccottet, *L'Entretien des muses: chroniques de poésie* (Paris: Gallimard: 1968), 199.
76 André Dhôtel, 'L'Œuvre d'Armen Lubin', *Cahiers bleus* 33 (1984): 13.
77 Lubin, *Le Passager clandestin. Sainte Patience. Les Hautes Terrasses et autres poèmes*, 204.
78 Lubin, *Transfert nocturne*, 90.
79 Armand Robin, *Écrits oubliés*, I, 2 vols., ed. by Françoise Morvan (Rennes: UBACS, 1986), 260.
80 Lubin, *Le Passager clandestin. Sainte Patience. Les Hautes Terrasses et autres poèmes*, 268.
81 For a full bibliography of works by Chahnour, see Beledian, *Cinquante ans*, 453.
82 Krikor Beledian, 'L'Écriture comme réécriture chez Chahan Chahnour/Armen Lubin', *Modern Languages Open*, 1 (2019): 9, accessed 26 January 2021, http://doi.org/10.3828/mlo.v0i0.222.
83 That diminished form of existence is perhaps best conceived of as a supplementary, residual quality of the *homme étalé* ['scattered man'], to whom the security of possession or belonging is denied. 'Enlevez, supprimez tout ce que vous voudrez : vous ne viendrez pas à bout de l'exposition commune. Car, de par la soustraction que celle-ci y introduit, l'humain persiste comme trace ou vestige de son propre passage : ce rien qui en reste par impossible lorsque tout lui a été enlevé. Finissant, évanouissant – à jamais' ['Remove, delete all you want: you won't be able to overcome this common exposure. For, through the subtraction that it ushers in, the human lingers on as a trace or vestige of its own passage: that nothing that remains of it against all possibility when everything has been taken away from it. Ending, vanishing – eternally']. Martin Crowley, *L'Homme sans: politiques de la finitude* (Fécamp: Nouvelles éditions Lignes, 2009), 27.

Bibliography

Primary material

Chahnour, Chahan. *La Retraite sans fanfare: histoire illustrée des Arméniens à leur arrivée à Paris suite au génocide*, translated by Krikor Beledian. Paris: L'Act Mem, 2009.

Շահնուր, Շահան. *Զոյգ մը կարմիր տետրակներ*. Beirut: Chirak, 1967.

Շահնուր, Շահան. *Նահանջը առանց երգի*. Paris: Haratch, 1933.

Lubin, Armen. 'À travers champs', *Cahiers des saisons* 19 (Winter 1960): 464–70.

Lubin, Armen. Fonds Armen Lubin, Bibliothèque littéraire Jacques Doucet, Paris.

Lubin, Armen. *Le Passager clandestin*. Paris: Gallimard, 1946.

Lubin, Armen. *Le Passager clandestin. Sainte Patience. Les Hautes Terrasses et autres poèmes*. Preface by Jacques Réda. Paris: Gallimard, 2005.

Lubin, Armen. *Sainte Patience*. Paris: Gallimard, 1951.

Lubin, Armen. *Transfert nocturne*. Paris: Gallimard, 1955.

Lubin, Armen. 'Trois lettres à Jean Paulhan', *Grandes largeurs* 12 (1987): 6–7.

Secondary material

Altounian, Janine. *De la cure à l'écriture: l'élaboration d'un héritage traumatique*. Paris: PUF, 2012.

Antelme, Robert. *L'Espèce humaine*. Paris: Gallimard, 1957.

Barthes, Roland. *Roland Barthes par Roland Barthes*. Paris: Seuil, 1975.

Beledian, Krikor. *Cinquante ans de littérature arménienne en France: du même à l'autre*. Paris: CNRS Éditions, 2001.

Beledian, Krikor. 'L'Écriture comme réécriture chez Chahan Chahnour/Armen Lubin', *Modern Languages Open* 1 (2019). Accessed 26 January 2021. http://doi.org/10.3828/mlo.v0i0.222.

Beledian, Krikor. 'L'Expérience de la catastrophe dans la littérature arménienne', *Revue d'histoire arménienne contemporaine* 1 (1995): 127–97.

Blecher, Max. *Aventures dans l'irréalité immédiate* suivi de *La Tanière éclairée*, translated by Marianne Sora, Georgeta Horodinca and Hélène Fleury. Paris: Maurice Nadeau, 1989.

Bourdieu, Pierre. Preface to *La Double Absence: Des illusions de l'émigré aux souffrances de l'immigré* by Abdelmalek Sayad, 9–13. Paris: Seuil, 1999.

Bourdieu, Pierre. *Raisons pratiques: sur la théorie de l'action*. Paris: Seuil, 1994.

Bournoutian, George A. *A Concise History of the Armenian People (From Ancient Times to the Present)*. Costa Mesa, CA: Mazda, 2003.

Brenner, Jacques. *Mon histoire de la littérature française contemporaine*. Paris: Grasset, 1987.

Brenner, Jacques. 'Présentation d'Armen Lubin', *Cahiers André Dhôtel* 6 (2008): 12–16.

Brunel, Pierre. 'Le Double Langage d'Armen Lubin', *Francofonia* 5 (Autumn 1983): 21–6.

Burgess, Greg. *Refuge in the Land of Liberty: A history of asylum and refugee protection in France since the Revolution*. Basingstoke: Palgrave Macmillan, 2008.

Cermakian, Stéphane. 'Armen Lubin: Exil, langue et littérature', *Acanthe: Annales de Lettres françaises de l'Université Saint-Joseph* 28 (2010): 11–25.

Cermakian, Stéphane. 'Le devenir-étranger de la poésie d'Armen Lubin', *Carnets: revue électronique d'études françaises* 2.1 (2014): 108–23.

Chahinian, Krikor. 'Drame et poésie de l'exil dans l'œuvre d'Armen Lubin en particulier et d'écrivains arméniens en France en général'. Unpublished doctoral thesis, Université de Paris-Sorbonne, 1979.

Chahinian, Krikor. 'Écartèlement', *Cahiers bleus* 33 (1984): 15–28.

Chessex, Jacques. 'Dans les demeures d'Armen Lubin', *Nouvelle Revue française* 191 (November 1968): 652–8.

Cioran, Émil. *La Tentation d'exister*. Paris: Gallimard, 1956.

Connor, Steven. *The Book of Skin*. London: Reaktion, 2004.

Crowley, Martin. *L'Homme sans: politiques de la finitude*. Fécamp: Nouvelles éditions Lignes, 2009.

De Bourbon-Busset, J., André Dhôtel, Jean Follain, Jean Mambrino and Patrick Reumaux, 'Entretiens du Polyèdre: Armen Lubin, l'étranger', *Cahiers bleus* 32 (Summer–Autumn 1984): 12–27.

Derrida, Jacques. 'Comment nommer'. In *Le Poète que je cherche à être*, edited by Yves Charnet, 182–206. Paris: La Table ronde, 1996.

Dhôtel, André. 'L'Œuvre d'Armen Lubin', *Cahiers bleus* 33 (1984): 9–13.

Gestern, Hélène. *Armen*. Paris: Arléa, 2020.

Grisi, Stéphane. *Dans l'intimité des malades: de Montaigne à Hervé Guibert*. Paris: Desclée de Brouwer, 1996.

Hofmann, Gert, Rachel MagShamhráin, Marko Pajević and Michael Shields. Introduction to *German and European Poetics after the Holocaust: Crisis and creativity*, edited by Gert Hofmann, Rachel MagShamhráin, Marko Pajević and Michael Shields, 1–16. Rochester, NY: Camden House, 2011.

Jaccottet, Philippe. *L'Entretien des muses: chroniques de poésie*. Paris: Gallimard, 1968.

Mandel, Maud S. *In the Aftermath of Genocide: Armenians and Jews in twentieth-century France*. Durham, NC: Duke University Press, 2003.

Nichanian, Marc. 'Catastrophic mourning'. In *Loss: The politics of mourning*, edited by David L. Eng and David Kazanjian. Berkeley: University of California Press, 2003.

Nichanian, Marc. *La Perversion historiographique: une réflexion arménienne*. Paris: Lignes & Manifestes, 2006.

Pifer, Michael. 'The forgetful figure: Armenian representations of trauma in Arakel of Tabriz and Shahan Shahnur', *Journal of Literature and Trauma Studies* 5 (2016): 65–94.

Reumaux, Patrick. 'Une poésie sans rien autour', *Études* (May 1975): 719–21.

Ricœur, Paul. *Soi-même comme un autre*. Paris: Seuil, 1990.

Robin, Armand. *Écrits oubliés*. Edited by Françoise Morvan. 2 vols. Rennes: UBACS, 1986.

Soulahian Kuyumjian, Rita. *Teotig: Biography & monument to April 11*. London: Gomidas Institute, 2010.

Téotig, *Mémorial du 24 avril*, translated by Alice Der Vartanian and Houri Varjabédian. Paris: Parenthèses, 2016.

2
No grounds for looking: Edmond Jabès and the questioning of the image

Je suis à la recherche
d'un homme que je ne connais pas,
qui jamais ne fut tant moi-même
que depuis que je le cherche.
Edmond Jabès, 'Chanson de l'étranger'

[I am in search
of a man I do not know,
who has never been more myself
than since I have been looking for him.
Edmond Jabès, 'Song of the stranger']

The preceding chapter explored statelessness in relation to the work of Armen Lubin primarily as a lived experience, one marked by a placing of individual speech *in extremis* and the emergence of a subject position sharply abstracted from categories of place and political selfhood. However, as we saw in the latter stages of that chapter, in relation to the difficulty of establishing any definitive 'genetic' account of Lubin's *oeuvre*, it is also the very integrity of the literary object that is at stake where the questions of statelessness and non-belonging are concerned. The present chapter develops a more metatextual focus on this issue in relation to the writings of Edmond Jabès. In poems and prose which dwell at length on the uncertainties produced by the experience of exile, Jabès marks a radical break with those protocols which habitually govern the production of meaning in and by the text (among them referentiality, narrative progression and principles of coherence), at times signalling a radical estrangement from the very system of writing itself. Over the course of

Jabès's *oeuvre*, poetry is increasingly less operative as a stable generic category and more as an elusive quality or disposition of language. Developing the significance of these paradigms throughout the work of this writer, the present chapter argues that it is Jabès's treatment of the image and the visual which focalises many of the uncertainties associated with the condition of non-belonging.

Jabès is a figure of central importance for this study, not least by dint of his enduring meditation on his enforced exile from his native Egypt and his highly distinctive exploration of the status of writer and book within the diasporic community of Judaism. Discussing Jabès's *Livre des questions* ['Book of questions'] in his selection of essays *L'Amitié* ['Friendship'], Maurice Blanchot argues that the Egyptian writer's work melds 'cette écriture qui est la difficulté du poète' ['that writing that is the difficulty proper to the poet'] with 'la justice difficile, celle de la loi juive, la parole inscrite avec laquelle on ne joue pas, et qui est esprit parce qu'elle est le fardeau et la fatigue de la lettre' ['that difficult justice of Jewish law, the inscribed word that cannot be played with, and which is spirit, because it is the burden and fatigue of the letter'].[1] Jabès's writing is, according to Blanchot, marked by two ruptures, the first designating the historical experience of the unspeakable chaos and persecution of the Shoah or Holocaust. The second rupture identified by Blanchot 'est comme antérieure à l'histoire, non plus subie, mais exigée et qui, exprimant la distance prise à l'égard de toute puissance, délimite un intervalle où le judaïsme introduit son affirmation propre' ['is as if anterior to history, not suffered but demanded, and which, expressing distance in regard to every power, marks out a space where Judaism introduces its own affirmation'];[2] this more immemorial kind of break concerns the particular status of the written word and the responsibility attributed to the act of writing within Judaism. In the *Livre des questions*, Jabès interprets motifs of absence, silence and withdrawal as the means by which the Jewish covenant is secured; in turn, these same motifs are understood to shadow both writer and book, supplying their very conditions of possibility, and signalling the advent of a 'parole … qui invite l'homme à ne plus s'identifier avec son pouvoir' ['speech … which invites man to no longer identify with his power'].[3]

A substantial body of criticism has already explored how the *Livre des questions* and other works by Jabès disclose the exilic qualities of writing.[4] Through a lexicon of absence and erasure, what emerges in his work is a kind of text constituted by numerous discursive ruptures and hesitations, persistently eluding the reader's attempts to identify it in terms of centres or origins, or as the expression of a unitary self. Drawing broadly on Jabès's poetry, on his *Livre des questions* and other later works, this chapter will argue that Jabès's writings offer a privileged site within which questions of exile, especially as they concern visuality and the image, are engaged. In its emphasis on the Jew as a figure historically condemned to a life of homelessness and wandering, the *Livre des questions* sets out to '[destabilise] all the identificatory mechanisms that support our notions of nationhood, of the individual subject, and of his language', as Joan Brandt argues.[5] In Jabès's treatment of the image, it is the mimetic basis of those mechanisms, that is, a mimetic conception of the image as the basis of *identification*, that itself comes under scrutiny. Through a focus on the image, then, we stand to appreciate the enduring force of Jabès's interrogation of belonging, subjectivity and the written word.

The image: groundless central ground

If a traditional conception of the image is of a feature which centralises and organises literary language, articulating the relationship between literal and figurative levels of discourse and between signifiers and signifieds, Jabès is determined to unsettle that paradigm. Inviting as he does the reader of the text *Aely* to 'apprendre à voir où le monde n'est plus' ['to learn to see where the world is no more'],[6] Jabès aims to abstract writing from the image's binding efficacy and the mimetic assumptions that accrue to it. Through a thematic orientation away from personalised experience and all but the most featureless of topographies, and via an interruptive spacing of textual matter, he inscribes silence and the unsayable at the heart of his texts. Indeed, a feature of Jabès's writing, which situates itself in an order other than that of being and presence, is that it is oriented towards a set of preoccupations (among them death, the desert and the unsayable) which it is problematic to cast in visual terms. In a related fashion, Jabès expresses anxiety about the figurative dimension of the poetic image (as present in surrealist literary practices to which his own youthful poetry is indebted), and reflects on the proscription of image-making in Judaism. While he responds to a long tradition of reflection on the image within modern poetry in French, ranging from Stéphane Mallarmé to Pierre Reverdy to the surrealists to René Char, Jabès's writings offer a unique understanding of the place of the image within the framework of exile.

According to Brian Glavey and W. J. T. Mitchell, 'the concept of the poetic image in all its ambivalence holds part of the central ground of poetics'.[7] Such ambivalence in part derives from the fact that the term is habitually invoked to account for so many of the distinct ways in which the literary text generates meaning: the image is 'variously, a metaphor, simile, or figure of speech; a concrete verbal reference; a recurrent motif; a psychological event in the reader's mind; the vehicle or second term of a metaphor; a symbol or symbolic pattern; or the global impression of a poem as a unified structure'.[8] While Jabès's poetic practice and comments on the image relate necessarily to this extended set of concerns, as well as to the prohibition on graven images within Judaism, it is useful to situate them also in relation to the treatment of the literary or philosophical image by Maurice Blanchot. Writing in the essay 'Les deux versions de l'imaginaire' ['The two versions of the imaginary'] which appears in *L'Espace littéraire* ['The space of literature'], Blanchot notes that according to the classical understanding, the image comes after the object in the order of representation: the image holds the object at a distance, so that it can be grasped formally and conceptually, thereby creating the presence of an absence. Blanchot then proposes an alternate reading, one which he elucidates by recourse to an analogy between the image and the body of a dead person. The corpse, he explains, complicates the relationship to place that structures the classical model of representation. This is because the corpse is present both here and nowhere, its strangeness issuing from the fact that the dead one is neither completely *of* the world, nor wholly absent from it:

> La mort suspend la relation avec le lieu, bien que le mort s'y appuie pesamment comme à la seule base qui lui reste. Justement, cette base manque, le lieu est en défaut, le cadavre n'est pas à sa place. Où est-il ? Il n'est pas ici et pourtant il n'est pas ailleurs ; nulle part ? mais c'est qu'alors nulle part est ici.[9]
>
> [Death suspends the relation to place, even though the deceased one leans heavily on it as if upon the only basis that is left to him. Indeed, this basis is lacking, the place is missing, the corpse is not in its place. Where is it? It is not here, and yet it is not elsewhere. Nowhere? But then nowhere is here.]

It is thus as if, according to Blanchot, by analogy with the corpse, the image introduces just such a kind of distancing into the thing itself, absenting it from itself:

> L'éloignement est ici au cœur de la chose. La chose était là, que nous saisissons dans le mouvement vivant d'une action compréhensive,

– et, devenue image, instantanément la voilà devenue l'insaisissable, l'inactuelle, l'impassible, non pas la même chose éloignée, mais cette chose comme éloignement, la présente dans son absence ...[10]

[Here distancing is at the heart of the thing. The thing was there, we grasp it in the vital movement of an act of comprehension and, having become image, instantly it has become the elusive, no longer of its time, the impassive. It is not the same thing at a distance, but this thing as distance, the present thing in its absence ...]

The image comes to be possible therefore on the basis of this absenting, since, as Gerhard Richter notes, reading Blanchot, it is 'inscribed into a kind of groundless ground, a terrain in which it can neither affirm nor negate, neither articulate nor disarticulate'.[11] It is to this paradoxical status of the image, as that which both entails a radical groundlessness and yet supplies the central ground of poetics, that we now turn.

This chapter argues that what begins as a questioning of the function of the image in Jabès opens onto an exploration of image's capacity to question, as it becomes the agent of a perennial uncertainty over what is beholden to the eye (or indeed veiled from it). That uncertainty, introducing disruption into the very mechanisms of affirmation, frequently bears also upon the latter's elusive relation to the poetic and converges upon questions of word and image in Jabès's work. A focal point for these issues in Jabès's writing is his theory of the 'vocable', originally a term belonging to the field of linguistics, and one which he sees as eliciting the unique qualities of the written word. By distinction with the acoustic 'mot' ['word'], the term 'vocable' belongs only to the order of the written. As what Warren Motte calls 'a purely orthographical artifact',[12] the 'vocable' thus speaks only to the eye, according to Jabès:

On peut dire un mot; on ne peut que lire un vocable. ... Le vocable apporterait, avec lui, cette précision : le mot se fait vocable où le livre se fait. En d'autres termes, le mot se métamorphose en vocable à mesure qu'il prend conscience, à travers la phrase, de son appartenance au livre et que croît son désir de s'y intégrer ...[13]

[A word can be spoken; a vocable can only be read. ... The vocable would bring with it this specific quality: the word becomes vocable where the book is made. In other words, the word is transformed into a vocable as it gains awareness, through the sentence, that it belongs to the book and as its desire to become part of the book grows ...]

Following this shift of emphasis from the audible to the visible, one of the aims of the present chapter is to emphasise the written word and the image in Jabès as privileged sites of a periodic estrangement from (and elusive re-engagement with) the system of writing itself, at least where writing assumes an identification with affirmation and the will to power.

Egyptian years and exile

Edmond Jabès was born into a Francophone[14] Jewish family in Cairo in 1912. For a writer whose work '[inhabits] a space that eschews subjectivity and intentionality',[15] it is fitting that ambiguity surrounds the official record of his birth and the moment of his entry into the apparatus of identification:

> Né le 16 avril au Caire, mon père par inadvertance, aux autorités consulaires chargées d'établir mon acte de naissance, me déclara né le 14 du même mois. Dois-je inconsciemment à cette erreur de calcul, le sentiment que quarante-huit heures m'ont toujours séparé de ma vie ? Les deux jours ajoutés aux miens ne pouvaient être vécus que dans la mort. Ainsi ... la première manifestation de mon existence fut celle d'une absence qui portait mon nom.[16]
>
> [Although I was born on the 16th of April in Cairo, my father inadvertently stated to the consular authorities responsible for drawing up my birth certificate that I was born on the 14th of that month. Do I subconsciously owe the feeling that 48 hours have always separated me from my life to this miscalculation? The two days added on to my life could only be experienced in death. And so ... the first manifestation of my existence was that of an absence that bore my name.]

Daniel Lançon notes the existence of several historical variations on the transcription of the writer's Hebrew surname (among them Jabez, Yabez and Yavetz), and suggests potential ancestors or distant relations in fifteenth-century Spain and sixteenth-century Istanbul.[17] Jabès's forebears had been present in Ottoman Egypt since the first decades of the nineteenth century, and probably adopted French as their first language in the years 1880–90.[18] Following an 1882 revolt led by the nationalist leader Ahmed 'Urabi against European colonial involvement in the country, a social crisis emerged 'qui menaçait la sécurité des

« apatrides » qu'étaient alors les juifs égyptiens' ['that threatened the security of the "stateless persons" which Egyptian Jews then were'].[19] It was in this climate that Jabès's grandfather obtained Italian nationality, thus bringing his family under the jurisdiction of the Italian consulate in a country that would henceforth come under de facto British control. Jabès was thus in the peculiar position of being doubly estranged, by language and by citizenship, from the country of his birth.[20]

Jabès received a French-language education at the Collège Jean-Baptiste de la Salle and the Lycée français de la Mission laïque, and was particularly active throughout his youth in Cairo's Francophone cultural scene, entering into correspondence with writers associated with French surrealism, such as Paul Eluard and Max Jacob, and forming a friendship with the French author Gabriel Bounoure, then resident in Cairo.[21] Acutely heedful of the unfolding events in Italy following Mussolini's March on Rome, he was also a signatory to an open letter published by the Comité des groupes d'action antifasciste et italiens libres [Committee of Free Antifascist Italian Action Groups].[22] After a period of study at the Sorbonne in the early 1930s, he returned to Cairo, where he worked as a stockbroker and married Arlette Cohen in 1935. In 1940, when Italy entered World War II, as an Italian citizen he was arrested by British forces in Cairo, and imprisoned for one month, only to be released once proof of his earlier antifascist publications could be supplied.[23] During this period, he published numerous volumes of poetry. With titles such as *Les Mots tracent* ['Words trace'] (1943–51), *La Voix d'encre* ['The ink voice'] (1949) and *L'Absence de lieu* ['The absence of place'] (1956), these works deal in such themes as desire, death, exile and the nature of poetry itself, and are marked by the influence of surrealism.[24]

With the continuing rise of Egyptian Arab nationalism and the coming to power of Gamal Nasser in the 1950s, however, the author was forced, with tens of thousands of other members of the Jewish and other foreign communities of Egypt, to leave the country altogether. Jabès's wife and children went into exile, moving to Paris in 1955, and he joined them in 1957, 'à la suite de tracasseries, de séquestre de ses biens et de risque d'emprisonnement' ['following harassment, confiscation of his property and the risk of imprisonment'].[25] Jabès continued to reside in France until his death in 1991.

It was the experience of forced displacement which prompted Jabès, following his arrival in France, to develop a much more radical reflection on the connections between Judaism, exile and writing. Although he had been born into a secular family and possessed minimal religious knowledge of Judaism before leaving Egypt, Jabès began to read the Talmud and the Kabbalah, not so much in the spirit of religious discovery, but through a fascination with these textual sources' connection to Jewish history and thought and their specific features of commentary and dialogue. If the history of Judaism was one of persecution and exile, it was the religious text, or what Jabès refers to as 'the book', that became the repository of that culture.

It was in France that Jabès to a large extent left behind the poetry of his Egyptian years and began to develop a new mode of writing through the *Livre des questions*. This series of alternating meditations, dialogues, aphorisms, poems, fragments, narrative interludes and letters in its first three volumes presents the reader with an account of the love affair between a young wartime Jewish couple, Yukel (a writer) and Sarah, whose lives are profoundly marked by the experience of deportation, the Shoah and Sarah's descent into madness. Subsequently, in the concluding four volumes, published in collected form as the second *Livre des questions*, the 'récit éclaté' ['shattered narrative'][26] of the two lovers gives way to an even more fragmented form of narration; the books *Yaël*, *Elya*, *Aely* and *• El, ou le dernier livre* ['• El, or The last book'] deal successively with a woman murdered by her lover; the woman's stillborn child; a figure who lacks all character attributes with the exception of the gaze; and the Kabbalistic theme of God's deliberate self-contraction, that originary act of creation which allowed space and time to come into being, and which Jabès sees as linked to the act of writing.

Although it appears at times to situate itself within a Jewish tradition of rabbinical commentary, and although the name of God is repeatedly invoked throughout, the *Livre des questions* repeatedly signals its own post-religious bent, positing God not as final origin, but as ultimate void. In Jabès's 'Judaism after God', all textual values are to be articulated paradoxically in respect of the vacancy left by the withdrawal of the divine, an event which is echoed in the absenting or occlusion of the image. Jabès's is a curious posture marked by a radical break from theological tenets, on the one hand, and by a re-engagement with Kabbalistic sources, on the other. As regards those sources, it is the doctrine of *Tzimtzum* originating in the Kabbalah of the sixteenth-century mystic Isaac Luria that appears to contribute to Jabès's understanding of the act of creation as fundamentally characterised by negativity.[27] According to this tradition, the universe came into being through God's contraction of his own infinite light, thus giving rise to a realm in which finite entities could exist. Just as this divine paradigm privileges a contraction or concealment of presence as the originary creative act, for Jabès, writing thus does not articulate a presence, but rather is articulated in respect of a void which inflects it in movements of negation and rupture:

> Le monde s'exile dans le nom. À l'intérieur, il y a le livre du monde.
>
> Écrire, c'est avoir la passion de l'origine ; c'est essayer d'atteindre le fond. Le fond est toujours le commencement. Dans la mort, sans doute aussi, une multitude de fonds constitue le tréfonds ; de sorte qu'écrire ne signifie pas s'arrêter au but, mais le dépasser sans cesse.[28]
>
> [The world goes into exile in the name. Within it, there is the book of the world.
>
> To write is to have a passion for origins; it is an attempt to reach to the depths. The depths are always the beginning. In death, no doubt also, a multitude of depths forms the innermost depths; so that writing does not mean stopping at the goal, but forever moving beyond it.]

Since this is a kind of writing which will attempt to defy the metaphysical logic of being and presence, we in turn find that it renders suspect the representative dimension of literature.[29] In Jabès's work, the proscription of the idolatrous image present in the second commandment transfers to a posture which would deny writing representational value in any conventional sense and would lead writing and image-making away from the mimetic appropriation of the world. It is in this perspective that we can understand the citation often attributed to Jabès, 'J'ai peu de goût pour les images' ['I have little fondness for images'].[30]

The image in the youthful poetry

To set out in more detail the implications of this attitude towards the representational function, it is possible to trace a shift in Jabès's practice of the poetic image, from the surrealist-influenced poetry of his Egypt years to the fragmentary compositions of the *Livre des questions*. In the 1949 poem 'L'Auberge du sommeil' ['The inn of sleep'], the refrain 'Avec mes poignards / volés à l'ange / je bâtis ma demeure' ['With my daggers / stolen from the angel / I build my dwelling'] punctuates a series of dream images which coalesce around a desired female 'tu' ['you']. Some early evocations of this figure's beauty and genealogy give way to more expansive stanzas like the following:

> Tibet lointain où nul ne t'atteint où tu retrouves intacte
>   ton âme verte et belle
> échappée aux églises parmi les bâtons de réglisse que savourent
>   nonchalamment les sages
> les frêles crayons d'ennui avec lesquels tu illumines d'éclairs
>   la nuit
> Tu joins la mort à l'amour le désir des roses
> à la terre terrible du passé l'araignée à la pie insupportable.[31]
>
> [Faraway Tibet where no one reaches you where you find intact
>   your soul green and beautiful
> escaped from the churches amid the liquorice sticks that the sages
>   lick nonchalantly
> the fragile pencils of boredom with which you brighten the night
>   with bursts of light
> You join death to love the desire of roses
> to the terrible terrain of the past the spider to the unbearable magpie.]

Here the reader is confronted initially with what Joseph Guglielmi calls 'salves d'images' ['salvos of images'][32] seemingly bereft of their conventional symbolic value when considered individually and lacking logical connection with other images in the same sequence. Yet in the apparent absence of logical links between distant Tibet, wise men eating liquorice, and magpies, an organising principle is suggested through recurrent properties of sound: 'lointain', 't'atteint'; 'églises', 'réglisse'; 'ennui', 'nuit'; 'la mort à l'amour'; and so on. In characteristically surrealist fashion, as will be familiar to readers of André Breton's *Nadja*, it is the desired female 'tu' in whose orbit these chance-determined psychological connections are forged. Each of these processes within the Jabès poem is anchored within a surrealist practice of the poetic image, one which had been familiar to readers of French poetry ever since the celebrated formulation of Pierre Reverdy:

> L'image est une création pure de l'esprit. Elle ne peut naître d'une comparaison mais du rapprochement de deux réalités plus ou moins éloignées. Plus les rapports des deux réalités rapprochées seront lointains et justes, plus l'image sera forte – plus elle aura de puissance émotive et de réalité poétique.[33]

[The image is a pure creation of the mind. It cannot be born from a comparison but from a juxtaposition of two more or less distant realities. The more the relationship between the two juxtaposed realities is distant and accurate, the stronger the image will be – the greater its emotional power and poetic reality.]

This surrealist theory therefore implies a rejection of the poetic image considered as a point of relay between two levels of discourse, the literal and symbolic. Such a collapsing of discursive hierarchies is a feature of the dream imagery in 'L'Auberge du sommeil'. It is significant that the adoption of this model affirms the irreducible presence of these images to the unconscious mind, regardless of their lack of verifiable basis in any externally convened reality. The surrealist practice of the image would seem therefore to display a *presentative* if not *re-presentative* quality, but in either case, it is still underpinned by a sense of the *thereness* of the object of vision.

Jabès himself was mindful of this, and as his writing evolved, he sought to distance himself from what he saw as a surrealist understanding of the image as an autonomous component of discourse:

> En fait, je suis visuel: je regarde les mots qui sont déjà une sorte d'image. Faisant corps avec le texte, l'image ne fonctionne plus pour moi comme une image. Ancrée dans la pensée, dans le développement, elle est un raccourci dans le discours, comme si elle n'était pas là pour elle-même mais par souci de précision. L'image surréaliste nous séduisait, nous frappait mais elle était autonome comme quelque chose d'« ajouté ».[34]
>
> [I'm actually a visual person: I look at the words which are already a kind of image. Being of one body with the text, the image no longer functions for me like an image. Rooted in thought, in development, it is a shortcut in discourse, as if it were not there for its own sake but for that of precision. The surrealist image seduced us and was striking to us, but it had an autonomous quality, like something 'added in'.]

As a further instance of this sense of Jabès's anxiety over the image in its figurative dimension, we might briefly consider the treatment of the figure of the sun in two lines of a 1956 poem, 'L'Absence de lieu': 'Terre d'outre-nuit que le soleil arrache à / la méditation et aux épines du doute' ['Land beyond night torn by / the sun from meditation and the thorns of doubt'].[35] The sun here figures in respect of a poetic subject for whom it connotes familiar properties of subjective illumination and enhanced knowledge.

Yet if it is the sun which has the capacity to elevate the subject above doubt in this poem, the sun figures in quite a different way in a citation typical of the second *Livre des questions*. In the *Livre des questions*, it is but a '*[...] soleil, cercle incendié dans le refus du cercle. / Le centre est-ce, alors, la négation du centre ; ce point précis où il est contesté par la courbe que le doute a stoppé* [sic] *en pleine ascension ?*' ['*[...] sun, incinerated circle in the refusal of a circle. / Is the centre, then, the negation of the circle; that precise point where it is contested by the curve that doubt brought to a halt just as it was on the ascent?*'].[36] Here the sun is effectively denied positivity; in any sense, it is that which does not bear looking at. The figure consumes itself instead in a burning spectacle of which the only trace is a circular outline, signalling a trajectory interrupted by doubt, self-interrogation and negative being. No longer possessed of the limitative function it displays in the earlier poem wherein its meaning is circumscribed, the sun devolves into the limit figure of the circle, a shape which seems primarily constituted by two kinds of void – the void within its boundaries and that which lies without – and which, rather than affirming the subject, provoke renewed interrogation.

Visibility and resemblance

What can account for the shift in Jabès's evolving practice with respect to the image? Crucially, Jabès eschews conventional aesthetic or representative approaches to the question and brings the image instead into the service of a distinctive project which draws on and develops aspects of the structural framework of Jewish ethics and law, albeit in an implicitly atheist perspective. To approach the question of the image in this perspective, it is necessary to draw on the particular significance that Jabès attaches to issues of visibility and to examine his theory of resemblance.

While the story of Yukel and Sarah dominates the first three books of the *Livre des questions* cycle, it is in the volumes published together as the second *Livre des questions* that Jabès's distinctive treatment of visibility emerges. The volume entitled *Aely* is about an instance of seeing, although the gaze elicited in this book is not even that of an incarnate self: Aely is 'l'œil de ce qui ne fut pas' ['the eye of what was not'].[37] With the withdrawal of phenomenological experience and the positive attributes of character, it becomes apparent that for Jabès, vision, as evoked in this work, is no longer construed along familiar poles of subjectivity and objectivity which would organise it according to patterns of perception or reception. The new paradigm is hypothesised in a fragmentary dialogue which draws out its latent ethical dimension:

> « Est-ce parce qu'un être, une chose nous voient que nous les voyons, demandait-il ? En ce cas, toute découverte ne serait que le point de jonction de deux regards.
>
> « Voir serait, alors, mieux que recevoir ; bien plus que percevoir l'objet par les yeux ; ce serait reconnaître, à son secret désir, un appel et y accourir. »[38]
>
> ['Is it because a being, a thing sees us that we see them?' he asked. 'In that case, any discovery would only be the connecting point of two looks.
>
> 'To see would then be better than to receive; much more than seeing the object through the eyes; it would be, following one's secret desire, to recognise a call and come running.']

According to Jabès, the law is inherent in the gaze of the other: 'Dans le mot *œil*, il y a le mot *loi*. Tout regard contient la loi' [In the word *eye* [*œil*], there is the word *law* [*loi*]. Every look contains the law'.[39] Here, it should be noted that Jabès's distinctive understanding of 'la loi', as Beth Hawkins argues, relates to a 'system of law and, likewise, a universally applicable covenant' which predates the Abrahamic covenant; Jabès appears to hark back to the Talmud's Noahide laws, promoting a universally binding conception of the law that is not exclusive to any one religious community.[40]

In *Aely*, the link between observance of the law and the condition of being observed is developed further: 'Une loi, tel un œil de la loi, l'œil incorruptible de la lettre. – Observer la loi à la lettre, n'est-ce pas se tenir fermement dans son champ de vision ?' ['A law, like an eye of the law, the incorruptible eye of the letter. – To observe the law to the letter, is that not to hold oneself firmly in its field of vision?'].[41] Here, 'observer la loi à la lettre' signals an emerging link between vision, observance of the law, and the act of writing. Vision is not aligned with consciousness of an object but with submission to the other's authority and vigilance: 'Un œil me surprend et m'égare. Je suis vu, mais ne peux me voir' ['An eye surprises me and leads me astray. I am seen, but cannot see myself'].[42]

To place oneself in the gaze of Aely thus requires that we refrain from the impulse to make the law an object of our knowledge; the law's contents are destined to remain unknown – even though it requires that we acknowledge it formally and structurally despite their effective absence. It is thus, as Gary D. Mole writes, by surrendering subjectivity and becoming 'the object of the law's scrutiny rather than attempting to scrutinize the law itself'[43] that the writer contributes to the law's re-inscription: 'L'écrivain, à son insu, est le rédacteur élu de la loi' ['The writer is, without his knowledge, the chosen writer of the law'].[44] In this sense, through assuming his own ignorance of the law's object, the writer, as a kind of unwitting legislator, participates in the extension and reformulation of that which cannot be known (and by which he is bound, paradoxically).

Considering this as a model of subjectivity contingent upon the subject's relation to a universal law, we might argue that Jabès presents a distinct variation on what Michel Deguy views as a proclivity of the subject of speech to except itself from the (linguistic) law which it is brought to observe by dint of its accession to language. For Deguy, subjectivity is ineluctably split, between a socialised version of the self and what the subject perceives to be its own exceptional quality.

> La figure du souverain comme exception à la loi qu'il fait régner en identifiant le principe de sa subjectivité au fondement de la loi est celle où se reconnaît le sujet moderne. … Pour pouvoir parler vrai, et par exemple énoncer des vérités sur la vérité, le sujet de la parole se scinde en sujet d'exception (celui pour lequel ne vaut pas la proposition universelle qu'il fonde) et en *ce moi* qui fait partie des autres, des « gens ». A la faveur de cette scission, le sujet, profitant de cette susceptibilité infinie de la subjectivité de s'excepter de la loi qu'il reconnaît, en est un qui : *a)* prend pour maxime de son action : « Ce que je fais, personne d'autre ne doit le faire » ; *b)* pose comme condition pour réassujettir son privilège à la Loi que l'*autre* « commence par s'y soumettre ».[45]
>
> [The modern subject recognises himself in the figure of the sovereign who, by equating the principle of his subjectivity with the basis of law, can be understood as an exception to the law which he himself enforces. … In order to be able to speak truly, and for example to state truths about the truth, the subject of speech splits into an exceptional subject (one for whom the universal proposition that he himself founds is an invalid one) and into *that self* that is one of the others, the 'people'. By dint of this split, the subject, taking

advantage of subjectivity's infinite susceptibility to exclude itself from the law which it recognises as legitimate, is one who: *a)* takes as the maxim of his actions: 'No one else must do as I do'; *b)* once again submits to the Law on condition that the *other* 'must be first to submit to it'].

Although the structural comparison is warranted here, in so far as both models address the particular relation of the writer or the subject of speech to the law, they differ in one significant respect. By contrast with Jabès's withdrawal of subjectivity, Deguy's model is contingent on the subject's cognitive appraisal of the law, as well as on transgressive acts which, by placing it beyond social experience. and beyond the law's reach, contribute to linguistic variation and accrue to this split subject its own institutive power. This indicates a useful point of comparison, because it appears that what follows a logic of the exception in Deguy might, in the case of Jabès, more properly be thought of as an *in*-ception, that is, as an internalised exception which returns what is new to a point within the boundaries of the same. In this sense, observance of the law re-emerges as an inceptional act, having a foundational aspect. The internalised exception is one which can leave no trace in the Jabesian book but the spacing which marked its occurrence. A constitutive power, negatively inscribed, thus emerges in instances of blankness:

> « Dans le livre, disait-il, l'écriture est absence et la page blanche, présence.
> « Ainsi Dieu qui est absence est présent dans le livre. »
>
> Blancheur passée en loi.
> Le livre ouvert.
>
> [...]
>
> Nous faisons, en écrivant acte de soumission à la loi, acte de soumission à Dieu, acte de soumission au néant.[46]
>
> ['In the book,' he said, 'writing is absence and the blank page is presence.'
> 'So God who is absence is present in the book.'
>
> Whiteness passed into law.
> The open book.

[…]

By a written act of submission to the law, we make an act of submission to God, an act of submission to nothingness.]

Here, that which we intuitively assign to absence (the blank) re-emerges as the very principle of the book; the blank materialises absence, both formally and structurally. By analogy with the figure of the absent God, it follows that what is made visible – imaged – is here effaced by the very gesture which makes it apparent.

In *Le Livre des marges* ['The book of margins'], incorporating and moving beyond the ethical framework sketched in the passages from *Aely* above, the motifs of the eye and the law are taken up again, this time as Jabès develops a poetics of the fragment, notably in the following passage:

> C'est dans la fragmentation que se donne à lire l'immensurable totalité. Aussi est-ce toujours par rapport à une totalité controuvée que nous affrontons le fragment ; celui-ci figurant, chaque fois, cette totalité dans sa partie reçue, proclamée et, en même temps, par sa contestation renouvelée de l'origine, devenant, en se substituant à elle, soi-même origine de toute origine possible, décelable.
>
> De cette fertile « déconstruction » qui opère dans les deux sens – de la totalité afin de déboucher sur l'ultime fragment et de l'infime fragment afin, en s'annulant au fur et à mesure dans le néant du fragment prépondérant, de reconstituer, à travers son effacement, cette totalité – l'œil est le guide, le phare. Il fait – Il est – la loi. L'invisible nous requiert derrière tout ce qui est vu et comme s'il n'était, dans son absence, que ce qui se cache au sein de ce qui se montre – ou encore ce qui nous cache ce qui, pourtant, se montre – et le silence, ce qui est tu dans une parole proférée.[47]
>
> [It is in fragmentation that the immeasurable totality can be read. So it is always in relation to a fabricated totality that we face the fragment, which always figures only the accepted, proclaimed part of this totality, and which, at the same time, by contesting the idea of origins, by taking the place of origin, becomes itself the origin of all possible origins, one which can be traced.
>
> The eye is the guide or beacon for this fruitful 'deconstruction' which works in both directions – from totality leading to the ultimate fragment and from the tiniest fragment, which gradually

> cancels itself out in the nothingness of a greater fragment, and through its obliteration, gives this totality form once more. The eye lays down – it is – the law. The invisible places a demand on us behind everything that is seen, as if it were, in its absence, only what is hidden at the heart of what is shown – or even what hides from us the very thing that is shown – and silence, which is what is unsaid in a word that has been spoken.]

As Jacques Derrida argues in his study of Jabès, in writing there is a '*lapsus* essentiel entre les significations' ['essential *lapse* between meanings']: 'Prétendre le réduire par le récit, le discours philosophique, l'ordre des raisons ou la déduction, c'est méconnaître le langage, et qu'il est la rupture *même* de la totalité. Le fragment n'est pas un style ou un échec déterminés, c'est la forme de l'écrit' ['To claim to be able to reduce it through narrative, philosophical discourse, the order of reasons or deduction is to misconceive language, and the fact that it is the very *rupture* of totality itself. The fragment is not a determined style or failure, but the form of the written word'].[48] It is just this sense of the fragment as neither an effect of style nor a lack of accomplishment, but as the very condition of writing itself, that is at issue in the long citation from Jabès above. While visibility is explicitly thematised in this passage, references to figuration, fragmentation and erasure further underscore that it is their visual, visible quality which enables the different modalities of the book to be discerned.

In its charting of the passage from totality to fragment, and vice versa, Jabès's valorisation of the eye in the passage from the *Livre des marges* is curious, nonetheless. As he elides the distinction between seeing and seen, in other words, between that which sees and that which is available to apprehension by the gaze, it is as if the very act of seeing which attempts to constitute an object extrinsic to the eye comes to erase the specificity of perspective. It is notable here that looking, often construed as a passive function, is invested with a power of *doing*, or perhaps, in reality, of un-doing. Indeed, it is by dint of this power that the law is actualised ('il fait – il est – la loi' ['the eye lays down – it is – the law']), not in so far as something is produced through the action of looking, but because it is the look which bears witness to that 'deconstructive' dynamic which becomes the regenerative principle of the book. There are, as such, no grounds for looking in the framework hypothesised by Jabès (for the act is inseparable from a loss of perspective), and yet it is an eye, albeit a disembodied one, which maintains vigilance over the 'dividing and redoubling'[49] which characterises the book's economy.

The links suggested here between visibility and the image are taken up once more in the *Livre des ressemblances* ['Book of resemblances'], that later book which 'ressemble à un livre – qui n'était pas, lui-même, un livre; mais l'image de sa tentative' ['resembles a book – which was not, itself, a book; but the image of an attempt at the book'].[50] The *Livre des ressemblances* is thus a revisiting of the *Livre des questions* insofar as 'chaque livre est le prolongement ou l'accomplissement contestés du livre, écrit ou à écrire, auquel l'écrivain est rivé' ['each book is the controversial extension or accomplishment of that book, whether written or yet to be written, to which the writer is bound'].[51] Early in the text, a rabbinical dialogue underscores the connection between resemblance, the image and the withdrawal of the divine: 'Peut-on rassembler à Celui qui, par essence, est sans ressemblance ? demandait reb Eliav. Il lui fut répondu ceci : « Ne sommes-nous pas l'image du vide qui est sans image ? »' ['Can we resemble He who, by essence, is without resemblance? asked Reb Eliav. He was answered thus: "Are we not the image of the void that is without image?"'].[52]

Thus, even as it is associated with likeness or analogy, the particular understanding of resemblance which develops in Jabès's writing simultaneously overturns the principle of identity, problematising essence and eliciting the very difference which we might intuitively assume it to suppress: 'toute ressemblance marque la différence dont on souhaitait l'abolition' ['every resemblance signals the difference which it had been hoped would be abolished'].[53] Resemblance thus comes into play with every effort of thought to apprehend otherness. In fact, thought demands it: only that which is unthought is unmarked by resemblance, having neither identity nor non-identity: 'Penser l'autre, c'est perpétuer la ressemblance. Il n'y a pas d'impensé ressemblant' ['To think otherness is to perpetuate resemblance. There is no unthought thing that resembles another'].[54]

Jabès, however, posits a point of rupture in the logic of resemblance: 'Le cri est déchirure de ressemblance' ['The cry is the tearing of resemblance'].[55] Thus the interruptive charge is attributed to the cry, as that which is heard, without any more precise meaning for those who utter it or hear it than an opaque expression of suffering which breaks the continuity of speech. In a recent study, Lucie Taïeb explores the status of the cry in Jabès's writing, developing its importance for Jabès's approach to the unnameable suffering of the victims of the Shoah through the story of Sarah and Yukel. Moving from speech to book, Taïeb argues that the *cri* can be aligned with the interruptive qualities of the textual blank. It is in this sense that the blank is understood as the formless imprint of an absence: 'le « tracé » de ce qui ne laisse pas de trace' ['the "outline" of that which leaves no trace']. [56] The blank is a marker of lack, signalling rupture and the sudden inoperativity of resemblance, and yet, by dint of its interruptive force, it bears singularly adventitious qualities.

A poetics of spacing

It follows that the blank occupies a central importance within Jabès's poetics, just as it had done for other writers he admired, among them Stéphane Mallarmé and René Char. Although at times he gives focus to the materialised typographic space between letters or words, his preoccupation with the blank infers a more wide-ranging praxis placing primacy on the activity of *spacing* of the printed word, an activity that may be alternately oriented towards fragmentation or combinatory in character. In a citation from the aphoristic text 'Les Rames et la Voile' ['Oars and sails'], Jabès takes up this theme, moving from a typographic frame of reference to an ethical one: 'En supprimant, avec les signes de ponctuation, les zones franches, le poète aggrave, entre les mots, les causes de conflits ou multiplie les chances d'une intime entente' ['By removing free zones through the use of punctuation marks, the poet increases the causes of conflict between words or multiplies the opportunities for an intimate harmony']. [57] If, as this citation suggests, space can be viewed as a kind of notional liminal 'free zone' of contact without liability, then it is notable that what is designated by 'punctuation' in this citation alludes not to the extension of such a space, but to its contraction or maximal limitation. Indeed, exposure and encounter are the conditions of the Jabesian poem at the expense of space.

Frequently, in Jabès's work, word and letter are held to possess an impassive, inscrutable quality, one which recalls distinctly those characteristics imputed to the written law in the passages from *Aely* cited earlier: the text 'L'Appel' ['The appeal'], cited below, for instance, evokes 'ces mots qui ne disaient rien' ['these words which said nothing']; in 'Portes de secours' ['Emergency exits'], they are 'étrangers à l'homme' ['foreign to man']. Indeed, an epigraph to the latter text underscores this potential resistance of the word; here, Jabès appears to caution against constituting poetry itself as an object of knowledge, warning that such an approach will lead only to vain self-torment: '*Je cherche, avec des mots, à saisir la poésie; mais déjà, elle s'est réfugiée en eux. De la poursuivre là où elle est devenue ma voix, c'est moi seul, alors, que je tourmente*' ['*I try to grasp poetry with words, but it has already taken refuge within them. Through pursuing it to the point where it has become my voice, I alone am the one I torment*'].[58] However, if word and letter may seem at a profound level impervious to poetic design or scrutiny, by contrast spacing – understood in terms of a paradigm of contraction or withdrawal – is invested with a paradoxical agency.

Offering a variation on the etymological understanding of poetry as something made or created, the poem arguably possesses a quite specific sense in the work of Jabès, for whom the gesture of creation is one characterised by self-contraction or withdrawal, in a gesture which re-actualises the *Tzimtzum* or divine contraction of space present in the Lurianic Kabbalah. If, according to some modern understandings, poetry might be thought of as that which possesses a power to except itself from a prevailing discursive regime,[59] and thereby to found an autonomous field of practice, it may not be productive to conceive of the poem as a discursively distinct regime within the Jabesian book. For Jabès, it is not so much that the poem inaugurates a *sui generis* space within the book but that poetry is internalised, or brought into the book. This is not in so far as the book 'contains' poetry, but in the sense that the poetic inheres in paradigms of fragmentation, in periodicity, and in a number of performatively charged instances which rupture the regular alternation of aphorism and dialogue.

As an example of such rupturing, we might consider a passage from the *Livre des questions* in which the sign-seeking activity of the eye is perpetually invoked and solicited in the very absence of its object. This poem-like passage from the second volume dramatises the circular nature of Jabesian questioning:

> Un cercle
> et, dans ce cercle, un autre
> cercle
> et, dans ce nouveau cercle, un cercle
> nouveau
> et ainsi de suite
> jusqu'à l'ultime cercle devenu un point
> assujettissant,
> puis un imperceptible point ;
> mais incroyablement présent ; mais majestueusement absent.
> Une femme et une parole.
> Une femme tournant en rond,
> autour d'une parole tournant en rond ;
> lentement d'abord, puis vite ;
> incroyablement vite
> jusqu'à n'être plus, dans l'espace où elles furent soulevées

qu'un cercle,
à la poursuite d'un cercle plus petit,
de plus en plus petit,
grotesquement, à présent, petit.
Un trou, un œil vide ;
un œil de nuit ;
un œil crevé.
Et quoi ? On y regarde.
On s'y enfonce.
Est-ce cela qu'on appelle : Unité ?
Un cercle désagrégé ?
Un cri, un pas, un aveu
circulaires ?[60]

[A circle
and within the circle another
circle
and in this new circle a further
circle
and so on
until the last circle, which has become a forceful
point,
then an imperceptible point
so unbelievably present, so majestically absent.
A woman and a word.
A woman turning
around a word turning
first slowly, then faster,
unbelievably fast
until they are no longer anything but a circle
in pursuit of a smaller circle
one growing ever smaller,
now a tiny circle, grotesquely so.
A hole. A vacant eye.
An eye of night.
A shattered eyeball.
And then what? You look into it.
You sink into it.
Is this what is called Unity?:
a circle gone to pieces?
A cry, a step, an avowal,
all circular?]

Here, the expansion and contraction of line lengths in regular succession appear to mirror the movement of a writing absorbed by its own conditions of possibility. Amid multiple accelerations and repetitions, a succession of circles is alluded to, each circle containing the next in perpetual succession, until all that can be discerned is a point – a point, which, although it would seem to be the origin to which all these successive accretions tend, is rather simply a threshold or limit point between presence and absence, something that is no longer purely of the order of being. Indeed, the absence of the locative in French (that is, the words 'il y a' ['there is']) here tends to dispel any sense that these things *are*. And yet, although the point connotes an end-stop to language, an effective silence, it is also the minimal discursive trace. Although it hints towards that which cannot be expressed, it is also not possible to empty it of meaning. A vacillation, a hesitation ensues, as meaning is posited and retracted; perhaps this is how to account for the evanescent image of the woman encircling the word. Other images feature too – a shattered eye, an empty socket and an eye at night – but these would seem to connote a blocking of vision. Similarly, when taken together, temporal and spatial indicators such as 'puis' ['then'], 'jusqu'à n'être plus' ['until they are no longer'], 'à présent' ['now'], 'Un cercle plus petit' ['A smaller circle'] and 'de plus en plus petit' ['growing ever smaller'] lead us to think that description is a compromised activity, for the object whose presence it strives to register at no point seems to be the same as itself. That it should even belong to the realm of extension is in question, for it seems to become available to the gaze only at the very moment of its rupture and dissolution *as* object.

Spacing: combination, erasure, lineation

In these conditions, an evolved understanding of the image emerges, one which is linked to the central importance of the blank. Just as in the above example, for Jabès, it falls to the writer to suspend the becoming-apparent of things in the book; the image is not an image of some object, but of that suspension. In turn, his concern with the blank does not so much designate a space within which something occurs or a neutral surface on which inscription takes place, but rather characterises what happens *to* writing as the object of a displacement.

While *Aely* emphasises the necessity for the writer to consent to a paradoxical form of submission to the written law, the subsequent volume • *El, ou le dernier livre* ['• El, or The last book'] by contrast elicits a transgressive quality of the act of writing which can be grasped in terms of such a displacement. Even in its title, which features a point or full stop, the volume offers further evidence of Jabès's preoccupation with the written trace at the limits of presence and absence. '*(« Le mot se lit dans l'éclatement solaire de ses limites telle, à travers le geste de colère de Moïse, la Loi dans la brisure des céleste Tables », disait-il)*' ['*("The word is read through the solar shattering of its limits just like the Law in Moses's angry gesture of breaking the heavenly Tablets", he said)*']:[61] following a paradigm established by Moses's destruction of the tablets which symbolised the breaking of the covenant between God and the Israelites, the shattering of the word thus acquires a generative potency.[62] This power becomes apparent only as the affirmative function of the word recedes, exposing the risk that inheres in any arrangement of language, as the letters composing the written word become available to endless recombination:

> Le mot *aérien* est menacé, dans son propre sein, par le mot *rien*.
> [...] Otez *l* à voile et vous lirez : voie.
> Une aile dévoilait le jour.
>
> « *Aérien* peut se lire *A et Rien*, ou bien *A est rien*.
> « Dans le premier cas, il y aurait A – lettre, comme on sait, qui contient toutes les autres – et puis *Rien*.
> « Dans le second cas, *A* qui ne serait que *Rien*.
> « Que pouvons-nous en conclure sinon que *A* est *Rien* et *Tout* à la fois, disait-il.
> « Ainsi le point. »[63]
>
> [The word *aerial* ['*aérien*'] is threatened, at its core, by the word *nothing* ['*rien*'].
> [...] Lift off 'l' / the sail ['*l* à voile'] and you will read: way ['voie'].
> A wing unveiled the day.
>
> '*Aérien* ["Aerial"] can be read as *A* and *Rien* ["Nothing"], or as *A est rien* ["A is nothing"].
> In the first case, there would be A – a letter which, as we know, contains all other letters – and then *Nothing*.
> In the second, *A* would be merely *Nothing*.
> What can we conclude from this other than that *A* is *Nothing* and *Everything* at once, he said.
> Thus it is of the point.']

Instances abound in *Aely* in which this apparent 'threat' deriving from inside language itself becomes manifest, and they can be seen in the context of Hebrew letter combination practices known as *Tzeruf*, which were devised for divinatory or exegetical purposes; the point here is not to isolate any one meaning but to underscore the principle that inheres in language of its necessary transformation and recombination.[64]

The device is deployed once more in a sequence of couplets contained in *Le Livre des ressemblances* which plays on the components of the words 'désert' ['desert'] and 'infini' ['infinite']:

> Ici, la fin
> Ici, la fin de la parole, du livre, du hasard.
>
> Désert !
> Jette ce dé. Il ne sert à rien.
>
> Ici, la fin du jeu, de la ressemblance.
> L'infini, par le truchement de ses lettres, nie la fin.
>
> Ici, la fin ne peut être niée. Elle est infinie.
>
> Ici n'est pas le lieu,
> ni même la trace.
>
> Ici est sable.[65]

> [Here, the end
> Here, the end of the word, of the book, of chance.
>
> Desert !
> Cast aside this dice ['*dé*']. It is useless ['*ne sert à rien*'].
>
> Here, the end of the game, of resemblance.
> The infinite, by the interpretation of its letters, denies the end.
>
> Here, the end cannot be denied. It is infinite.
>
> Here is not the place,
> Nor even the trace.
>
> Here is sand.]

It is noticeable here that Jabès's conception of the infinite is not that which extends indefinitely in space ('place' is, after all, negated here) but that which is endlessly incomplete, partial or fragmentary, and thereby analogous with desert sands. The desert, this space where no return is possible, and where the very attributes of place are lost, is in this way aligned to a paradigm of un-working of language in its referential capacities. The very repetition of the term intimates that 'ici' ['here'] is never identical with itself, nor is it the scene in which something can be said to take place.[66] Just as the 'here' eludes definition, gestures of linguistic erasure and variation come to predominate, as is conveyed in the trope of casting a die. In this sense, the 'dé' of the word 'désert' is cast aside, yet in throwing out this word, a homophone to 'dé', a die, is cast or 'jeté', in an acknowledgment of Mallarmé's *Un Coup de Dés jamais n'abolira le Hasard* ['A throw of the dice will never abolish chance']. The momentary recourse to verse form in this passage, combined with the reference to a foundational text of poetic modernity in French, arguably suggests a persistent attachment on Jabès's part to the poem as a privileged means to interrogate the mechanisms of affirmation itself.

Just such an approach informs a late text, 'L'Appel' ['The appeal'], dating from the period of Jabès's 'return' to poetry in the mid-1980s:

Il avait – lui semblait-il – mille
choses à dire
à ces mots qui ne disaient rien ;
qui attendaient, alignés ;
à ces mots clandestins,
sans passé ni destin.
Et cela le troublait infiniment ;
au point de n'avoir, lui-même, plus
rien à dire,
déjà, déjà.[67]

[He had – it seemed to him – a thousand
things to say
to these words which said nothing;
which waited, in a line;
to these stowaway words,
without past or destiny.
And that troubled him infinitely;
To the point that he himself no longer had
anything to say,
already, again.]

Again, in this poem, the impetus appears to derive from within language itself: words wait, 'lined up', apparently anticipating their division and redeployment. For Jabès, the experience of language is that of an *égarement* [leading astray] always already repeated (and underscored here by anaphora: 'à ces mots' … 'à ces mots'…'déjà'…'déjà' ['to these words' … 'to these words'…'already'… 'again']), one whose effect is to silence the subject (the perennially anguished 'il' ['he']), but paradoxically also, to make the poem speak. In this way, the text's contrasts and anaphoric effects are brought to the fore as Jabès exploits devices of lineation and indentation.

In passing, a passage from 'Le Pacte du printemps' ['The pact of spring'] of 1957 offers a point of comparison with 'L'Appel'. As the last text published in the volume *Je bâtis ma demeure* ['I build my dwelling'], it marks the beginning of the 'hiatus' in Jabès's poetic production and the commencement of the cycle of works beginning with the *Livre des questions*. 'Le Pacte du printemps' adopts a different formal approach from 'L'Appel', but arguably in pursuit of a similar effect, underscoring what yasser elhariry in a valuable article on this collection sees as indicative of 'a tension inherent in Jabès's construction of poetic place: a full assumption of impasse, and the impossibility of an easy dwelling of any sort, whether in the world, or even in the words forged by the poet himself'.[68] From the first stanza, phrase and line are out of step, and norms of line-initial capitalisation are jettisoned, just as the writing subject's encounter with words is evoked as akin to being led astray along a perilous path:

> Les mots se sont engagés dans
> le sentier des mines mpyais ont
> perdu ma voix Silence encrier
> renversé La plume est l'épave[69]
>
> [The words have set out on
> the path through the mines but have
> lost my voice Silence overturned
> inkwell The pen is the wreck]

Here, just as in 'L'Appel', the focus is not so much the expressive intent harboured by a writing subject, but the drama of the erasure of that intent.

The letter and the para-graphic

As Jacques Derrida has argued, the tradition of logocentricism establishes speech in the Western tradition as the locus of significance, with writing considered as secondary to, and representative of, speech.[70] Consistent with his theory of the 'vocable', however, Jabès encourages a renewed engagement with the graphic, written qualities of the word over its phonetic counterpart. Taken together with his theory of the 'vocable', features such as letter combination and spacing in Jabès's poetic output, and in the cycle beginning with the *Livre des questions*, point to the existence in his work of what we might call a para-linguistic, or more specifically, a para-graphic imaginary, active in the margins of the written word. In this way, emphasis is transferred away from word and sentence and instead towards the relationship between the individual grapheme and peripheral components or devices such as blanks, lineation, letter combination and punctuation. Even textual brevity can be considered in this vein, as is unsurprising from a writer whose choice medium is the aphorism, and who habitually wrote on the backs of Parisian metro tickets.[71] While these components and devices do not belong strictly to the system of writing itself, they nonetheless produce an enhanced readerly awareness of the letter, as the minimal operative unit within that system. As Frédéric Marteau notes, the deployment of these devices in the Jabesian text draws the reader's attention persistently back to 'la visibilité de la lettre, résultat (reste) de l'érosion du nom, de sa brûlure ou de sa crémation' ['the visibility of the letter, which is the result of (or what is left over after) the erosion of the noun, its incineration, or its cremation'] .[72]

Charts and diagrams

• *El, ou le dernier livre* ['• El, or The last book'] offers one of the most salient examples of Jabès's concern with this para-graphic dimension. In this final volume, the *Livre des questions* cycle culminates in an extended meditation on the act of writing. As is announced by an epigraph to the volume originating in the Kabbalah, the Hebrew word 'El' (intimating 'God') is awarded particular focus: 'Dieu, *El*, pour se révéler, Se manifesta par un point' ['God, *El*, to reveal himself, manifested Himself as a point'].[73] Indeed, it is around the figure of this minimal trace, both origin and end, that the text revolves, eliciting a parallel between God's deliberate self-contraction or cancellation in *Tzimtzum* and the writer's withdrawal of subjectivity. While it dwells both on the figure of the point as punctuation mark, •, and 'El', considered as the unit common to so many of the proper names which feature within the *Livre des questions*, *El* also contains a number of visually striking diagrams and charts. Figures 2.1 and 2.2, for instance, underscore the persistence of 'El' throughout the seven volumes of the cycle.

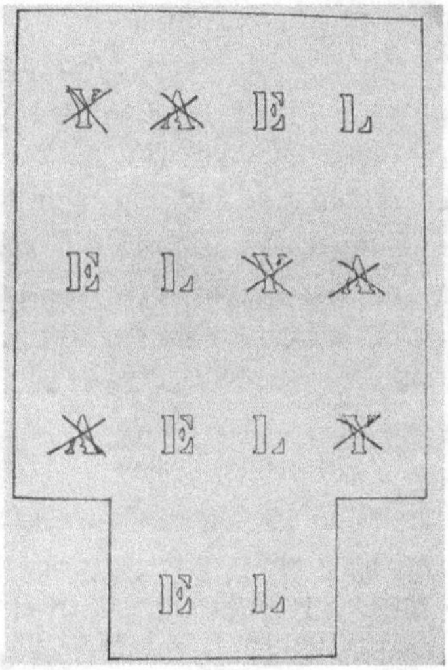

Figure 2.1 Diagram from: Edmond Jabès, *Le Livre des questions, II: Yaël; Elya; Aely; • (El, ou le dernier livre)*, Paris: Gallimard, 2008: 503. By permission of Editions Gallimard, France.

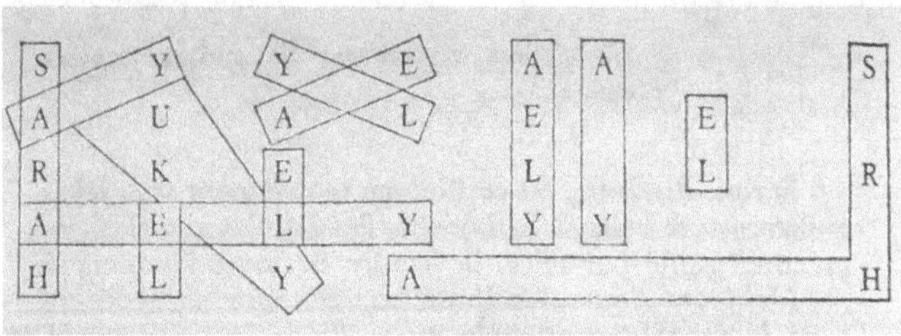

Figure 2.2 Diagram from: Edmond Jabès, *Le Livre des questions, II: Yaël; Elya; Aely; • (El, ou le dernier livre)*, Paris: Gallimard, 2008: 526. By permission of Editions Gallimard, France.

In a passage which appears below the diagram shown in Figure 2.2, we read the following:

> Fragmenter le nom de Dieu qui est formé de tous les mots de la langue afin de le réduire à un mot, à une syllabe, à une lettre. Ainsi avions-nous abordé au bout de la nuit, l'alphabet.
>
> Avec leurs morceaux épars, rétablir dans leur parenté nouvelle les Tables exemplaires.

La clé c'est, peut-être, *Aely*.

Visibilité de la mort.
Tu écris : *mourir*. Tu sais, désormais, que tout sera vu.[74]

[To fragment the name of God which is formed of all the words in language in order to reduce it to one word, to one syllable, to one letter. Thus, at night's end, we reached the alphabet.

With their scattered pieces, to restore the exemplary Tables to their new relation.

The key is, perhaps, *Aely*.
Visibility of death.
You wrote: *die*. You know, from this moment forth, all will be seen.]

This passage offers an example of what Joseph Guglielmi calls 'la promotion de la lettre en tant que moteur de la *production du sens* et en même temps comme propagateur de l'inconnu et exemption du sens' ['the promotion of the letter as the motor of the production of meaning and at the same time as the proponent of the unknown and the exemption of meaning'].[75] Presenting combinatory patterns and paradigms of contraction and substitution, the diagrams enable the viewer to visualise erasure at work within the word in an instance of what Beth Hawkins calls 'a representation that makes visible without fixing'.[76] It is significant here that the disembodied eye of *Aely* is invoked as the 'key' to the new relations which are brought about as the result of fragmentation, for the 'morceaux épars' ['scattered pieces'] manifest themselves visually.[77] Offering perhaps a distant allusion to diagrammatic representations such as the Tree of Life in Kabbalah mysticism (which enable the viewer to apprehend visually the relations between key spiritual concepts within that tradition), the gaze solicited by the second diagram is markedly non-linear and non-totalising. By dint of this, it allows for novel possibilities of detecting oppositions, analogies and otherwise undisclosed relations as the reader 'moves laterally on the surface of the text', to borrow the terms of Sydney Lévy.[78]

Drawings on paper

Although such experiments in word and image are relatively rare in his writing, and while he ordinarily adopts a highly classical syntax, Jabès denies his reader the comfort of what we might call the literate eye, that is, the eye that enjoys familiarity with language's signified content. Some abstract ink drawings by Jabès himself, shown in Figure 2.3, play upon this indeterminacy. These drawings are in addition to a further series of spontaneous drawings or doodles in the margins of Jabès's manuscripts, works which Aurèle Crasson and Anne Mary argue may be considered as having either a preparatory or cathartic function; that is, they may be understood either in terms of an 'entraînement à l'écriture' ['a way of practising for writing'] or as 'aides à l'extériorisation d'événements traumatisants' ['aids in the externalisation of traumatising events'][79] relating to themes such as the plight of Sarah, the Shoah and anti-Semitism. The four drawings shown in Figure 2.3, on the other hand, seem to possess an alternately incipient or vestigial quality, suggesting a move towards or away from some state, whether graphic or alphabetic.

This unstable semiotic status derives from the fact that they gesture towards writing without having the status of formally recognised signifiers within a system of writing or script. In *Par des traits*, Henri Michaux explores this ambiguous space between writing and drawing, speculating on how the 'traits' ['dashes/lines'] of which the characters of written language are composed might originate in what he terms a 'préécriture pictographique' ['pictographic prewriting']. Hypothesising a kind of mythical time when the graphic components of written language were first laid down, Michaux suggests that this prewriting is largely motivated by chance, having its origins primarily in gesture and play:

> La préécriture pictographique, elle, probablement une curiosité quand d'abord on la vit, avec des tâtonnements, avec bien des hésitations quand on la fit. Que de bouts de langues furent inventés, et sans idée d'avenir ou d'en faire une collection, encore moins une collection gardée précieusement. Évocations un peu au hasard, tels furent leurs « gestes » plus ou moins heureux, ceux du temps où l'on glissait un à un avec incertitude les signes qui peut-être n'allaient pas prendre, ne seraient pas adoptés, d'abord jeux familiaux, pour rester entre soi, en petits groupes à l'écart.[80]

> [Pictorial prewriting, probably a curiosity when first glimpsed, tentatively, with much hesitation when it was produced. So many bits of language were invented, and without any intention towards their future or of making a collection out of them, much less a preciously guarded collection. Their more or less fortuitous 'gestures' were somewhat chance evocations, those of the time when one by one we hesitantly gave shape to signs that might not be taken up, adopted. Family games above all, to keep oneself occupied, in small groups away from others.]

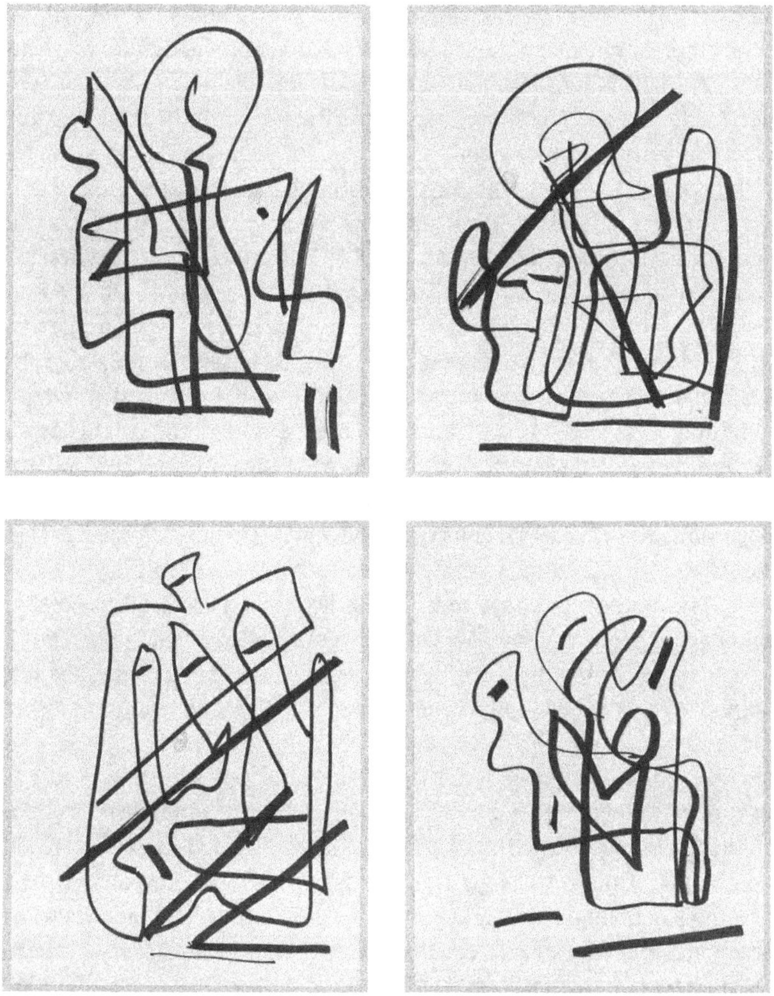

Figure 2.3 Edmond Jabès, drawings. Source: Bibliothèque nationale de France. By permission of Viviane Jabès Crasson.

While the fact that they do not strictly belong to his manuscripts means that it is difficult to conclude with certainty as to their precise purpose or function for Jabès, the four drawings by the writer shown in Figure 2.3 also offer a useful point of comparison with some artistic experiments conducted by Roland Barthes. These drawings are considered primarily in terms of their artistic qualities rather than in their relation to written signs. In a short piece entitled 'Le degré zero du coloriage' ['Colouring degree zero'] in which he offers a commentary on these experiments,

Barthes notes how they granted him 'le soulagement (le repos) de pouvoir créer quelque chose qui ne soit pas directement dans le piège du langage, dans la responsabilité fatalement attachée à toute phrase : une sorte d'innocence, en somme dont l'écriture m'exclut' ['the relief (or sense of restfulness) of being able to create something that does not fall directly into the trap of language, into an idea of responsibility that would inevitably attach itself to every sentence: all in all, a kind of innocence that is excluded by writing'].[81] To Barthes, such experiments offer the chance to explore the pleasure-inducing spontaneity and gesturality of graphic invention in a way that is free of the burden of affirmation ('the trap of language'). Indeed, absent-minded designs on paper of the type he describes would appear to suggest a way of subduing formalising intent, not to say a suspension of the will to power. Such drawings do not formalise a concept or idea, nor do they present an object for contemplation and interrogation; as Michaux remarks regarding his own experiments with drawing in 'Dessins commentés', 'un dessin ne s'ausculte pas' ['a drawing does not examine itself'].[82]

This relative freedom and creative licence experienced by Barthes when colouring and by Michaux in his drawings and 'prewritings' is a feature also of the drawings by Jabès, since they occupy a status somewhere between abstract artworks, doodles and experiments in calligraphy or hieroglyphics. Set against the recurrent themes and preoccupations of Jabès's writings, they also arguably testify to the author's awakening to a distinctive form of Jewish consciousness, since in their physical outline (if not in their elaborate composition) they recall something of the squareness characteristic of printed Hebrew script. If via their seemingly spontaneous composition they hint at a kind of freedom, that freedom is circumscribed by a supplementary concern with the necessity to respect the second commandment concerning the production of graven images. As such, responsibility paradoxically reattaches itself to Jabès's graphic work here if we consider that a function habitually ascribed to images is that of monstration or showing. In an interview in which he describes his fondness for abstraction in the plastic arts, he declares that '[on] voit mieux dans ce qui ne montre pas' ['you see better in what is not shown'].[83] In this respect, the abstractive nature of the works can be said to fulfil an iconoclastic function, one which is not destructive of the image per se, but of that intent to display. Led away from a function of representation, in these conditions, the image, and tentatively also the written sign, becomes an agent instead of entreaty, suggestion or uncertainty.

Art critical writing

This unfolding conception of the image also informs Jabès's aesthetic preferences, which are reflected in a selection of essays published in the posthumous collection *Un Regard* ['A look'], a volume dwelling on works by a wide range of contemporary artists. In a manner recalling his own artistic experiments, Jabès is drawn to bodies of work which are either removed from figurative intent or suggest a degree of commonality with some of the core concerns of his own writing. An essay on the Japanese painter Yasse Tabuchi, for instance, emphasises how Tabuchi's canvases exploit absence and emptiness:

> Ses toiles sont plaquées dans le vide dont elles s'approprient une part. Elles partent du néant pour déboucher sur lui. De la mort à la mort.
>
> En elles, le vide s'accorde au vide de l'univers. Le dehors se veut, ici, le dedans où nous nous enfonçons et qui exclut tout dehors arbitraire.[84]
>
> [His paintings are lodged in the void of which they appropriate a part. They start out from nothingness only to lead into it. From death to death.
>
> In them, the void resonates with the void of the universe. The outside is meant, here, to be the inside into which we sink and which excludes any arbitrary outside.]

Although a broad range of artists feature in the pages of *Un regard*, some trends are apparent. Jabès, for instance, notes that surrealist painting held little appeal for him.[85] However, an interest in artistic approaches to the body is apparent from a brief chapter on the diaphanous red nudes of Claude Garache, as well as the chapters on Francis Bacon and Antonio Saura, painters notable for the gnarled human figures featuring in their work. A further group of chapters clusters around artists belonging to the lyrical abstraction movement, such as Jean Degottex, Olivier Debré and André Marfaing. The lyrical abstractionists' combination of monochrome palettes and often quasi-calligraphic brushstrokes finds an affinity in Jabès's approach to the written text. The peculiar variety of uncertainty elicited by some of these works arguably concerns not so much the conditions in which viewing takes place (such as might occur through the fragmentation or multiplication of phenomenological perspective, in the manner of the synthetic phase of cubism), but more the nature or possibility of viewing itself.

Situated in or on the margins of writing, these images characterised primarily by combinations of hesitant strokes, dashes and lines suggest a wavering between word and image that invites the viewer to interrogate the boundary lines between reading and looking. Indeed, Jabès's comments in an essay on the monochromes of André Marfaing betoken a desire to evoke via his own writing a limit-position between the graphic qualities of letters ordained to be read and the fundamental alien opacity of the alphabetic, of black marks on a white surface:

> Un trait, une ligne fine, un coup de sabre dans le vide ?
>
> Cela a débuté avec des formes étranges, des lettres indécises ne marquant rien d'autre que cette indécision d'être, de signifier ; des idéogrammes difficiles à déchiffrer parce que mal à l'aise dans leur peau.
>
> Cela a débuté avec le premier regard, avec le premier geste de la main, surgis de la nuit opaque, surpris par l'éblouissante clarté du vide, du Rien, de l'espace blanc de la toile ou du papier, conscients, tout à coup, que c'est avec cet espace aveuglant qu'il fallait, désormais, compter.
>
> Lumière noire, intérieure, contre lumière blanche, environnante.[86]
>
> [A stroke, a fine line, a sword thrust in the void?
>
> It began with strange forms, uncertain letters marking nothing other than this uncertainty over being, over signifying; ideograms that are difficult to decipher because they are uncomfortable in their own skin.
>
> It started with the first glance, with the first gesture of the hand, rising up from the opaque night, startled by the dazzling clarity of the void, of the Nothing, of the white space of the canvas or of the paper, conscious, all of a sudden, that it is with this blinding space that we now have to come to terms.
>
> Black light, on the inside, against white light, all around.]

What appeals to Jabès in Marfaing is that his works invite but ultimately frustrate a desire to 'read' them as ideograms. What is striking here is how Jabès construes the artist's creative process as a struggle which in effect pits the pictorial and the alphabetic against each other. As the gestural and visual emphasis of the passage indicates, the irreducible tension between these poles is of foundational import. Although the viewer may receive the impression of being led away from the letter and towards the image, and vice versa, it is notable that Jabès insists that neither of these terms is ultimately secondary to the other; indeed, there is no possibility of *illustration* here, only of a paradoxical form of elucidation disengaged from epistemological certainties: 'Lumière noire, intérieure, contre lumière blanche, environnante' ['Black light, on the inside, against white light, all around'].

Another focus in the volume is the works of Spanish sculptor and lithographer Eduardo Chillida, with whom Jabès collaborated on a work featuring three of the writer's aphorisms. In a piece on Chillida, Jabès evokes that artist's signature exploration of the interplay of solid and void:

> Tout obstacle a son point faible. Celui-ci cède toujours au passage de l'inconnu.
>
> Et si ce point était, lui-même, un cercle ? Le vide serait dedans.
>
> Et si le cercle était le centre – vide infini – d'un hypothétique cercle qui l'aurait englouti ?
>
> Nul créateur ne peut travailler ce point imprécisable et, pourtant, précisé. *Il est travaillé par lui*. Juste assez pour se souvenir que le vide auquel l'œuvre, chaque fois, le renvoie pour se confronter à lui, est seul à soutenir l'univers. L'artiste ne saurait le maîtriser qu'en l'assumant, qu'en acceptant – mais est-ce une acceptation ? – de devenir, soi-même, ce vide dans lequel l'œuvre évolue et sur lequel elle s'appuie.[87]

> [Every obstacle has its weak point. This one always gives way to the unknown.
>
> What if this point was itself a circle? The void would be inside.
>
> What if the circle was the centre – the infinite void – of a hypothetical circle that would have swallowed it up?
>
> No creator can work on this point that resists definition and yet remains defined. *He is worked on by it*. Just enough to be able to remember that the void to which the work sends him back every time to confront it is the only one supporting the universe. The artist can only master it by coming to terms with it, by accepting it – but is that acceptance? – to become, oneself, that void within which the work evolves and on which it is based.]

Arguably, more than many of the aphorisms of the *Livre des questions*, this citation gives a succinct idea of Jabès's project. If we are to talk about a word–image relation here between literature and the visual arts, it is not so much through an exchange of substantial forms or structures, such as that which occurs earlier in the century between newspaper or advertising graphics, on the one hand, and practices of collage in modernist poetry, on the other, but more through a transfer of absences. For Jabès, the voids and elemental forms which dominate Chillida's image would tend to suggest that the uncertainty in the act of looking is inseparable from a retraction of the object and an accompanying anxiety over the subject position.

Just as is the case in the question posed near the end of a citation from the *Livre des questions* which appears earlier in the present chapter ('Et quoi? On y regarde / On s'y enfonce' ['And then what? / You look into it. / You sink into it'],[88] it would seem that to look at something in Jabès's universe is not to enact mastery over it as an object of knowledge, but rather to be rendered indistinct by it. The resulting dissolution of the subject's prerogatives and designs is not presented as fundamentally isolating in its effects, but paradoxically opens onto a more collective – and boldly abstract – frame of reference, no longer bound by the underpinnings of personhood; as we read in *Le Livre des marges*: 'Peut-être n'ai-je, dans mes livres, que tenté de me défaire du « Je » encombrant au profit du « Nous » presque anonyme. Écrire ne serait, à travers les mots, qu'accéder peu à peu à cet anonymat' ['Perhaps all I have attempted to do in my books is to get rid of the cumbersome "I" in favour of the almost anonymous "We". Writing would thus simply be, through words, the act of gradually attaining this state of anonymity'].[89] The image plays a central role in the accession to this anonymity, in essence neither utopian nor dystopian. On this note, the following exchange is found in the interview with Serge Fauchereau:

> S. Fauchereau : On lit dans *Le Livre de Yukel* : « Nous rassemblerons les images et les images des images jusqu'à la dernière qui est blanche et sur laquelle nous nous accorderons »…
>
> *Edmond Jabès* : Dans l'effacement. Devant ce qui est devenu rien, nous nous accorderons. On peut accepter et on peut, aussi, refuser quelque chose qui existe ; mais on s'accorde sur ce qui n'est plus rien, comme sur ce qui n'est pas encore ; sur ce Rien défunt ou à venir. Désespoir ou espérance.[90]

[S. Fauchereau: We read in *The Book of Yukel*: 'We will gather together images and images of images until the last image which is white and on which we will agree' …

Edmond Jabès: In erasure. We will agree in the presence of what has become nothing. We can accept and equally we can refuse something that exists; but we can agree on that which is no longer anything in the same way as we can on that which is not yet; on this Nothing that is deceased or yet to come. Despair or hope.]

Conclusion: drawing back from writing

Jabès is very much aware of the irony of his position, which requires the image at the same time as denying it, at least where it is conceived along figurative or representative lines. Although a statement imputed to him announces provocatively that '[j'ai] peu de goût pour les images' ['I have little fondness for images'],[91] his stance appears significantly more nuanced elsewhere: 'Il ne faut pas croire que l'absence soit dépourvue d'images. Sans elles, nous ne pourrions concevoir l'absence. Images d'images refoulées par l'omnipotente présence et qui, ô ironie, la propagent' ['It is not the case that absence is devoid of images. Without them, we could not conceive of absence. Images of images which are suppressed by almighty presence and which, ironically, are the force that transmit it'].[92] In this way the image re-emerges not as an agent of the formalisation of concepts and ideas, but rather as that which withdraws the object from cognisance, inhering instead in the non-conceptual and the elliptical. As Francis Wybrands notes, '[cette] destitution de l'image de la poésie n'est pas un thème de l'œuvre, elle est bien plutôt sa matière ou mieux encore le « comment » de son avancée' ['[this] destitution of the image of poetry is not a theme of Jabès's *oeuvre*, rather it is its substance, or, better yet, the thing that explains how it progresses'].[93]

With the Jabesian text, then, the reader is confronted with a literary object so shifting and elusive that it can feel misleading to qualify it as poetry. As a generic category privileged in the work of the early Jabès, poetry finds itself unseated; the poem as self-contained artefact is displaced or cast out of the genre-defying *Livre des questions* cycle. And yet paradoxically, the different kinds of rupture actualised through the latter writings can only be grasped, however provisionally, through reference to the forms and devices of poetry, or the vestiges thereof: poetry is 'ce mystère permanent dans lequel entrent tous les mystères' ['that permanent mystery into which all other mysteries enter'].[94] The writer himself lamented that the poetic dimension of his enterprise was neglected in scholarship devoted to his work during his lifetime.[95] In many ways, then, it is poetry, through features such as lineation, spacing, opposition, inference and analogy, which shadows Jabès's project as presented here.

Nonetheless, Jabès always stops short of adopting a posture which would make the text the object of a strategy; for a kind of writing which drifts continually towards metacommentary, it is arguably improper to insist on something so aestheticising as an avowed poetic design *sui generis*. As Jacques Derrida underscores in a telling passage of his essay on Jabès:

> Écrire, c'est se retirer. Non pas dans sa tente pour écrire, mais de son écriture même. S'échouer loin de son langage, l'émanciper ou le désemparer, le laisser cheminer seul et démuni. Laisser la parole. Être poète, c'est savoir laisser la parole. La laisser parler toute seule, ce qu'elle ne peut faire que dans l'écrit.[96]
>
> [To write is to withdraw. Not into one's tent in order to write, but to draw back from one's writing itself. To be stranded far from one's language, to free it or disable it, to allow it to make its way alone and impoverished. To leave speech. To be a poet is to know how to leave speech. To leave it to speak on its own, which it can only do in written form.]

Amid motifs of exile and errancy, Derrida argues that Jabès's writing is marked by a subdual of formalising intent and a leaving of language 'to make its way alone'. What Derrida understands as a drawing back from writing can be understood in terms of a visual and semantic hesitation that circles on the image as the groundless central ground of poetics and the visual qualities of the written word as 'vocable'.

This chapter has underscored the ethical dimension of the act of writing for Jabès and its role in securing the covenant of a 'Judaism without God': 'Écrire un poème fut toujours pour moi parachever un acte religieux' ['For me, to write a poem was always to accomplish a religious act'].[97] The figure of the Jew in Jabès ultimately overturns the mimetic logic of identification, as Joan Brandt writes, and instead 'forces us to confront the mimetic impropriety that resides at the heart of every being'.[98] This mimetic impropriety is integral to Jabès's non-representational understanding of the image as much as it is to his non-appropriative conception of the look or gaze, and to the exilic drive of his writing. If we are to follow Jean-Luc Nancy, such impropriety or non-self-identicality is in fact characteristic of poetry itself. As Nancy writes in his *Résistance de la poésie*:

> La poésie est par essence plus et autre chose que la poésie même. Ou bien: la poésie *même* peut fort bien se trouver là où il n'y a même pas de poésie. Elle peut même être le contraire ou le refus de la poésie, et de toute poésie. La poésie ne coïncide pas avec elle-même : peut-être cette non-coïncidence, cette impropriété substantielle, fait-elle proprement la poésie.[99]
>
> [Poetry is in essence more than or something other than poetry itself. Or rather, poetry itself may well be found where there is no poetry. It may even be the opposite or the rejection of poetry, and of all poetry. Poetry does not coincide with itself: perhaps this non-coincidence, this substantial impropriety, is what makes poetry itself.]

As a practice of language that draws back from itself and interrogates its own action in the space between writing and image-making, poetry's enduring appeal for Jabès is that of this characteristic impropriety.

Much as is the case in the excerpt from the poem 'Chanson de l'étranger' which serves as an epigraph to this chapter, the act of writing for Jabès is not the affirmative quest for identity we might have anticipated at the outset, when entering the *Livre des questions* and the various volumes which succeed it. As he claims in *Aely*: 'L'écriture n'est pas la projection de l'homme ; mais la délinéation de sa dévotion au vide, le devenir de l'inscription de sa négativité' ['It is not man that is projected through the act of writing; rather what it marks out is his devotion to the void, the future of the inscription of his negativity'].[100] What thus emerges is a kind of writing that does not see itself as bound to, or does not presuppose, a personalised identity of which it might be taken as the expression. The originality of this approach is, through various kinds of discursive rupturing, to confront us with the uncertainty of our knowledge. Disclosing the latent ethical dimensions of seeing and being seen, Jabès's writings open up a space for ethical engagement, as the 'I'/'eye' submits to the other's authority and vigilance. For Jabès, we are impelled to engage with this state, or rather, this absence of state. Exile is 'l'apprentissage de la blancheur' ['an apprenticeship in blankness'].[101] If the idea of learning is invoked paradoxically in the context of a failure of knowledge, it is because it is only in this atmosphere of uncertainty, amid the empty expanses of the blank page, that we may grasp the place from which the other speaks.

Notes

1 Maurice Blanchot, *L'Amitié* (Paris: Gallimard, 1971), 252.
2 Blanchot, *L'Amitié*, 252.
3 Blanchot, *L'Amitié*, 253.
4 Major works of Jabesian scholarship include: Didier Cahen, *Edmond Jabès* (Paris: Pierre Belfond, 1991); Adolfo Fernandez Zoïla, *Le Livre: Recherche autre d'Edmond Jabès* (Paris: Jean-Michel Place, 1978); Steven Jaron, *Edmond Jabès: The hazard of exile* (Oxford: Legenda, 2003); Daniel Lançon, *Jabès, l'Égyptien* (Paris: Jean-Michel Place, 1998); Gary D. Mole, *Lévinas, Blanchot, Jabès: Figures of estrangement* (Gainesville: University Press of Florida, 1997); Warren F. Motte, *Questioning Edmond Jabès* (Lincoln: University of Nebraska Press, 1990); Richard Stamelman, *Lost Beyond Telling: Representations of death and absence in modern French poetry* (London: Cornell University Press, 1990).
5 Joan Brandt, *Geopoetics: The politics of mimesis in poststructuralist French poetry and theory* (Stanford, CA: Stanford University Press, 1997), 211.
6 Edmond Jabès, *Le Livre des questions, II: Yaël; Elya; Aely; • (El, ou le dernier livre)* (Paris: Gallimard, 2008), 383. References to the *Livre des questions* appearing in this study are drawn from this collected volume, and from its counterpart *Le Livre des questions, I: Le Livre des questions; Le Livre de Yukel; Le Retour au livre* (Paris: Gallimard, 2010).
7 B. Glavey and W. J. T. Mitchell, 'Image', in *Princeton Encyclopedia of Poetry and Poetics*, ed. by Roland Greene et al. (Oxford: Princeton University Press, 2012), 660.
8 B. Glavey and W. J. T. Mitchell, 'Image', 662.
9 Maurice Blanchot, *L'Espace littéraire* (Paris: Gallimard, 1955), 269–70.
10 Blanchot, *L'Espace littéraire*, 268.
11 Gerhard Richter, *Afterness: Figures of following in modern thought and aesthetics* (New York: Columbia University Press, 2011), 149–50.
12 Motte, *Questioning Edmond Jabès*, 61.
13 Edmond Jabès, *Le Livre des ressemblances: Le Livre des ressemblances; Le Soupçon, Le Désert; L'Ineffaçable, L'inaperçu* (Paris: Gallimard, 1991), 91.
14 Daniel Lançon estimates the size of the Francophone community in Egypt to have been approximately 50,000 at the time of Jabès's childhood. Daniel Lançon, *Jabès, l'Égyptien* (Paris: Jean-Michel Place, 1998), 40.
15 Gary D. Mole, *Lévinas, Blanchot, Jabès: Figures of estrangement* (Gainesville: University Press of Florida, 1997), 1.
16 Jabès, *Le Livre des questions*, II, 254–5.
17 Lançon, *Jabès, l'Égyptien*, 21.
18 As Lançon notes, the linguistic profile of the Jewish community in Egypt was based on social divisions internal to the community, and evolved with the shifting political climate: 'En quelques générations, l'« acculturation » prédomine dans la communauté où s'opposent dès lors les arabophones des couches populaires en voie de prolétarisation et les italophones puis très vite francophones de l'élite bourgeoise du Caire et d'Alexandrie' ['Within the space of a few generations, the idea of "acculturation" came to prevail in the community which was divided between working-class Arabic speakers whose proletarianisation was already underway and members of the bourgeois elite of Cairo and Alexandria who spoke Italian before rapidly adopting French as their mode of expression']. Lançon, *Jabès, l'Égyptien*, 38.
19 Jean-Louis Joubert, 'Edmond Jabès', in *Dictionnaire de poésie de Baudelaire à nos jours*, ed. by Michel Jarrety (Paris: Presses Universitaires de France, 2001), 359.
20 Although Jabès had a strong command of spoken Egyptian Arabic dialect, he was unable to read standard written Arabic. Lançon, *Jabès, l'Égyptien*, 48.
21 For the correspondence with Jacob, see: Max Jacob, *Lettres à Edmond Jabès* (Pessac: Opales, 2003).
22 Jaron, *Edmond Jabès*, 83, fn. 47.

23 Cahen, *Edmond Jabès* (Paris: Pierre Belfond, 1991), 312.
24 Poems by Jabès are collected in the volume *Le Seuil; Le Sable; Poésies complètes 1943–1988* (Paris: Gallimard, 2009). Hereafter referred to as *Poésies complètes*.
25 Lançon, *Jabès, l'Égyptien*, 258–9. Ten years later, Jabès obtained French nationality.
26 Jabès uses this term in an interview with the author Paul Auster: Paul Auster, 'Book of the Dead: An interview with Edmond Jabès', in *The Sin of the Book: Edmond Jabès*, ed. by Eric Gould (Lincoln: University of Nebraska Press, 1985), 14.
27 For a discussion of Jabès, Isaac Luria and *Tzimtzum*, see: Przemysław Tacik, *The Freedom of Lights: Edmond Jabès and Jewish philosophy of modernity* (Oxford: Peter Lang, 2019).
28 Jabès, *Le Livre des questions,* I, 360.
29 'If the Judaic tradition proscribes the visual representation of God, so the Jabesian text swerves away from conventional representation, increasingly so, from the *Livre des questions* to the *Livre des ressemblances* to the more recent works. The main concerns of this body of work – death, loss, absence, emptiness, silence – defy visual representation and, in a broader sense, are extraordinarily resistant to other representational modes'. Motte, *Questioning Edmond Jabès*, 37–8.
30 See: Aurèle Crasson and Anne Mary, eds., *Edmond Jabès . ( )* (Paris: Hermann, 2012), 98.
31 Jabès, *Poésies complètes*, 99.
32 Joseph Guglielmi, *La Ressemblance impossible: Edmond Jabès* (Paris : Éditeurs français réunis, 1978), 34.
33 Pierre Reverdy, 'L'Image', *Nord-Sud* 2.13 (March 1918): 3.
34 Serge Fauchereau, 'Écrire, c'est le contraire d'imaginer: entretien avec Edmond Jabès', *Instants,* 1 (April 1989): 209.
35 Jabès, *Poésies complètes*, 27.
36 Jabès, *Le Livre des questions,* I, 375.
37 Jabès, *Le Livre des questions,* II, 297.
38 Jabès, *Le Livre des questions,* II, 297.
39 Jabès, *Le Livre des questions,* II, 308.
40 Beth Hawkins, *Reluctant Theologians: Franz Kafka, Paul Celan, Edmond Jabès* (New York: Fordham University Press, 2003), xx.
41 Jabès, *Le Livre des questions,* II, 309.
42 Jabès, *Le Livre des questions,* II, 306.
43 Mole, *Lévinas, Blanchot, Jabès*, 81.
44 Jabès, *Le Livre des questions,* II, 298.
45 Michel Deguy, *La Poésie n'est pas seule: court traité de poétique* (Paris: Seuil, 1987), 155–6.
46 Jabès, *Le Livre des questions,* II, 305.
47 Edmond Jabès, *Le Livre des marges* (Paris: Fata Morgana, 1984), 48–9.
48 Jacques Derrida, *L'Écriture et la différence* (Paris: Seuil, 1967), 107–8.
49 'The book, as a self-production (and hence also self-falsification) of the modalities of absence, as the child of the origin as cleavage, immediately divides or redoubles itself; it is at once a representation, a work, a reflective totality, and yet also an abyss, the "undulating surface of a breath" or, in the imagery of Jabès's provenance from Egypt, a desert of shifting sands.' Véronique M. Foti, 'Repetition/subversion: Derrida, Jabès and the language of difference', *Soundings: An Interdisciplinary Journal*, 68.3 (Fall 1985): 376.
50 Jabès, *Le Livre des ressemblances*, 15.
51 Jabès, *Le Livre des ressemblances*, 15.
52 Jabès, *Le Livre des ressemblances*, 35.
53 Jabès, *Le Livre des ressemblances*, 91.
54 Jabès, *Le Livre des ressemblances*, 46.
55 Jabès, *Le Livre des ressemblances*, 158.
56 'Jouant sur la double nature du poème qui à la fois se lit et s'entend, Jabès tente de donner entendre le reflet du cri, représentant une matière sonore inarticulée par une matière sonore silencieuse, un espace blanc parmi les mots. Le blanc est donc à lire comme le « tracé » de ce qui ne laisse pas de trace' ['Playing on the double nature of the poem which is both read and heard, Jabès tries to give voice to the reflection of the cry, representing inarticulate acoustic material by silent acoustic material, a white space among the words. The white is therefore to be read as the "outline" of that which leaves no trace']. Lucie Taïeb, 'Lire la présence de l'histoire dans *Le Livre des questions*', in *Les Poésies de langue française et l'histoire au XXe siècle*, ed. by Laure Michel and Delphine Rumeau (Rennes: Presses Universitaires de Rennes, 2013), 110.

57 Jabès, *Poésies complètes*, 303.
58 Jabès, *Poésies complètes*, 155.
59 'Poetry is still tethered to the norms of language, and thereby is still complicit in a "relation of force". Nonetheless, poetry does have a heightened ability to respond to the outside of discourse. … Poetry's uniqueness lies in the way it can straddle both the norm and the exception – both the inside and the outside of language – thus giving it a special force in the irreducibility of its hybridism.' Geoffrey Hlibchuk, 'The poetics of exception: contemporary North American poetry and the ghosts of relation' (doctoral dissertation, State University of New York at Buffalo, 2008), 20.
60 Jabès, *Le Livre des questions,* II, 23.
61 Jabès, *Le Livre des questions,* II, 505.
62 Indeed, as Beth Hawkins writes, it is the basis for a new covenant 'sealed by multiple acts of transgression' which 'carve open a space for interpretation, for commentary'. Hawkins, *Reluctant Theologians*, xv.
63 Jabès, *Le Livre des questions,* II, 547.
64 For a discussion of *Tzeruf* in the writings of the thirteenth-century Kabbalist Abraham Abulafia, see: Moshe Idel, *Language, Torah, and Hermeneutics in Abraham Abulafia* (Albany: State University of New York Press, 1989).
65 Jabès, *Le Livre des ressemblances*, 266.
66 Indeed, elsewhere, Jabès writes that: 'Le livre est, peut-être, la perte de tout lieu; le non-lieu du lieu perdu. Un non-lieu comme une non-origine, un non-présent, un non-savoir, un vide, un blanc' ['The book is, perhaps, the loss of all place; the non-place of the lost place. A non-place as a non-origin, a non-present, a non-knowledge, a void, a blank']. Jabès, *Le Livre des ressemblances*, 215.
67 Jabès, *Poésies complètes*, 396.
68 yasser elhariry, 'Demeure, Jabès', *French Forum*, 39 (2014): 139.
69 Jabès, *Poésies complètes,* 321.
70 Jacques Derrida, *De la grammatologie* (Paris: Minuit, 1967).
71 For an image of one of these metro-ticket manuscripts, see: Crasson and Mary, *Edmond Jabès. ( )*, 41.
72 Frédéric Marteau, 'L'Obsession grammatographique: Ponge, Perec, Jabès', *Textimage*, 3 (Summer 2009), accessed 19 January 2021, http://www.revue-textimage.com/04_a_la_lettre/marteau1.html.
73 Jabès, *Le Livre des questions,* II, 465.
74 Jabès, *Le Livre des questions,* II, 526–7.
75 Guglielmi, *La Ressemblance impossible,* 41.
76 Hawkins, *Reluctant Theologians*, 222.
77 In the interview with Paul Auster, Jabès draws an analogy between the fragments which constitute the book and the relationship of individual rooms to a house, underscoring this visual dimension: 'We know that we are in something immense, but at each moment we can only see what is in front of us … Totality is something we reconstitute ourselves through all these fragments, because these fragments provide visibility. In the same way, a book can be read because of the words'. Paul Auster, 'Book of the Dead: An interview with Edmond Jabès', 20–1.
78 'Rather than reducing Edmond Jabès to a known paradigm or rejecting him as incomprehensible, it is important to come to terms with his unreadability, to explore and exploit it, to move laterally on the surface of the text, tracing along the meanings and resonances.' Sydney Lévy, 'The question of absence', in *The Sin of the Book: Edmond Jabès*, ed. by Eric Gould (Lincoln: University of Nebraska Press, 1985), 147–59.
79 Aurèle Crasson and Anne Mary, 'L'Écriture hors frontières: dessins d'Edmond Jabès', *Genesis*, 37 (2013): 130.
80 Henri Michaux, *Œuvres complètes*, III, ed. by Raymond Bellour (Paris: Gallimard, 2004), 1282.
81 Roland Barthes, *Œuvres complètes*, III, ed. by Éric Marty (Paris: Seuil, 1995), 821.
82 Michaux, *Œuvres complètes*, I, 437.
83 Serge Fauchereau, 'Écrire, c'est le contraire d'imaginer: entretien avec Edmond Jabès', 216.
84 Edmond Jabès, *Un Regard* (Paris: Fata Morgana, 1992), 34–5.
85 Jabès, *Un Regard*, 61.
86 Jabès, *Un Regard*, 86.
87 Jabès, *Un Regard*, 65–6.

88 Jabès, *Le Livre des questions*, II, 23.
89 Jabès, *Le Livre des marges*, 130.
90 Serge Fauchereau, 'Écrire, c'est le contraire d'imaginer: entretien avec Edmond Jabès', 213–14.
91 Jabès, *Un Regard*, 9.
92 Jabès, *Le Livre des ressemblances*, 238.
93 Francis Wybrands, 'L'image imprévisible', in *Saluer Jabès: les suites du Livre*, ed. by Didier Cahen (Paris: Opales, 2000), 80.
94 'La poésie, ce mystère permanent dans lequel entrent tous les mystères'. Jabès, *Le Livre des marges*, 160–1.
95 'I was a bit disappointed that they don't speak about my writing itself, of a certain poetry that is in this form. Because if I wasn't a poet, I wouldn't have been able to write these books'. Jason Weiss, 'Edmond Jabès', in *Writing at Risk: Interviews in Paris with uncommon writers* (Iowa City: University of Iowa Press, 1991), 202.
96 Derrida, *L'Écriture et la différence*, 106.
97 Jabès, *Le Livre des questions*, I, 334.
98 'Indeed, the Jew in Jabès's texts forces us to confront the mimetic impropriety that resides at the heart of every being, for he shows that self-identity is dependent on the existence of an other, of an other's perception, or of an other's language without which no presencing, no manifestation of being would even be possible, but which at the same time sets in motion the processes through which that presence is also destroyed'. Brandt, *Geopoetics*, 211.
99 Jean-Luc Nancy, *Résistance de la poésie* (Bordeaux: William Blake & Co., 2004), 10.
100 Jabès, *Le Livre des questions*, II, 329.
101 Jabès, *Le Livre des ressemblances*, 261.

Bibliography

Primary material

Auster, Paul. 'Book of the Dead: An interview with Edmond Jabès'. In *The Sin of the Book: Edmond Jabès*, edited by Eric Gould, 3–25. Lincoln: University of Nebraska Press, 1985.
Fauchereau, Serge. 'Écrire, c'est le contraire d'imaginer: entretien avec Edmond Jabès'. *Instants*, 1 (April 1989): 209–17.
Jabès, Edmond. *Le Livre des marges*. Paris: Fata Morgana, 1984.
Jabès, Edmond. *Le Livre des questions, I: Le Livre des questions; Le Livre de Yukel; Le Retour au livre*. Paris: Gallimard, 2010.
Jabès, Edmond. *Le Livre des questions, II: Yaël; Elya; Aely; • (El, ou le dernier livre)*. Paris: Gallimard, 2008.
Jabès, Edmond. *Le Livre des ressemblances: Le Livre des ressemblances; Le Soupçon, Le Désert; L'Ineffaçable, L'inaperçu*. Paris: Gallimard, 1991.
Jabès, Edmond. *Un Regard*. Paris: Fata Morgana, 1992.
Jabès, Edmond. *Le Seuil; Le Sable; Poésies complètes 1943–1988*. Paris: Gallimard, 2009.
Weiss, Jason, 'Edmond Jabès', *Writing at Risk: Interviews in Paris with uncommon writers*, 167–206. Iowa City: University of Iowa Press, 1991.

Secondary material

Barthes, Roland. *Œuvres completes*. Edited by Éric Marty. 5 vols. Paris: Seuil, 2002.
Blanchot, Maurice. *L'Amitié*. Paris: Gallimard, 1971.
Blanchot, Maurice. *L'Espace littéraire*. Paris: Gallimard, 1955.
Brandt, Joan. *Geopoetics: The politics of mimesis in poststructuralist French poetry and theory*. Stanford, CA: Stanford University Press, 1997.
Cahen, Didier. *Edmond Jabès*. Paris: Pierre Belfond, 1991.
Caws, Mary Ann, and Richard Stamelman, eds. *Écrire le livre: autour d'Edmond Jabès: colloque de Cerisy-La-Salle*. Seyssel: Champ Vallon, 1989.

Crasson, Aurèle, and Anne Mary. 'L'Écriture hors frontières: dessins d'Edmond Jabès', *Genesis*, 37 (2013): 129–35.

Crasson, Aurèle, and Anne Mary, eds. *Edmond Jabès . ( )*. Paris: Hermann, 2012.

Deguy, Michel. *La Poésie n'est pas seule: court traité de poétique*. Paris: Seuil, 1987.

Derrida, Jacques. *De la grammatologie*. Paris: Minuit, 1967.

Derrida, Jacques. *L'Écriture et la différence*. Paris: Seuil, 1967.

elhariry, yasser. 'Demeure, Jabès', *French Forum* 39 (2014): 129–44.

Fernandez Zoïla, Adolfo. *Le Livre: Recherche autre d'Edmond Jabès*. Paris: Jean-Michel Place, 1978.

Foti, Véronique M. 'Repetition/subversion: Derrida, Jabès and the language of difference', *Soundings: An Interdisciplinary Journal* 68.3 (Fall 1985): 372–87.

Fredericksen, Brooke. 'Dwelling in words: the early poetry of Edmond Jabès', *French Forum*, 18.3 (September 1993): 335–54.

Glavey, B., and W. J. T. Mitchell, 'Image', in *Princeton Encyclopedia of Poetry and Poetics*, edited by Roland Greene, Stephen Cushman, Clare Cavanagh, Jahan Ramazani and Paul Rouzer, 660–2. Oxford: Princeton University Press, 2012.

Guglielmi, Joseph. *La Ressemblance impossible: Edmond Jabès*. Paris: Éditeurs français réunis, 1978.

Hawkins, Beth. *Reluctant Theologians: Franz Kafka, Paul Celan, Edmond Jabès*. New York: Fordham University Press, 2003.

Hlibchuk, Geoffrey. 'The poetics of exception: contemporary North American poetry and the ghosts of relation'. Doctoral thesis, State University of New York at Buffalo, 2008.

Idel, Moshe. *Language, Torah, and Hermeneutics in Abraham Abulafia*. Albany: State University of New York Press, 1989.

Jacob, Max. *Lettres à Edmond Jabès*. Pessac: Opales, 2003.

Jaron, Steven. *Edmond Jabès: The hazard of exile*. Oxford: Legenda, 2003.

Joubert, Jean-Louis. 'Edmond Jabès'. In *Dictionnaire de poésie de Baudelaire à nos jours*, edited by Michel Jarrety, 359–63. Paris: Presses Universitaires de France, 2001.

Kronick, Joseph G. 'Edmond Jabès and the poetry of the Jewish unhappy consciousness', *Modern Language Notes* 106 (1991): 967–96.

Lançon, Daniel. *Jabès, l'Égyptien*. Paris: Jean-Michel Place, 1998.

Lévy, Sydney. 'The question of absence'. In *The Sin of the Book: Edmond Jabès*, edited by Eric Gould, 147–59. Lincoln: University of Nebraska Press, 1985.

Marteau, Frédéric. 'L'Obsession grammatographique: Ponge, Perec, Jabès', *Textimage* 3 (Summer 2009). Accessed 19 January 2021. http://www.revue-textimage.com/04_a_la_lettre/marteau1.html.

Michaux, Henri, *Œuvres complètes*. Edited by Raymond Bellour. 3 vols. Paris: Gallimard, 2004.

Mole, Gary D. 'Edmond Jabès, les arts plastiques, et Bram van Velde', *Studi Francesi* 141 (2003): 589–97.

Mole, Gary D. *Lévinas, Blanchot, Jabès: Figures of estrangement*. Gainesville: University Press of Florida, 1997.

Motte, Warren F. *Questioning Edmond Jabès*. Lincoln: University of Nebraska Press, 1990.

Nancy, Jean-Luc. *Résistance de la poésie*. Bordeaux: William Blake & Co., 2004.

Pimienta, Guy. 'Édifier/Éditer ou comment taire le vide'. In *Edmond Jabès: l'exil en partage*, edited by Aurèle Crasson, 157–66. Paris: Hermann, 2013.

Reverdy, Pierre. 'L'Image', *Nord-Sud* 2.13 (March 1918): 3–7.

Richter, Gerhard. *Afterness: Figures of following in modern thought and aesthetics*. New York: Columbia University Press, 2011.

Segol, Marla. *Word and Image in Medieval Kabbalah: The texts, commentaries, and diagrams of the Sefer Yetsirah*. New York: Palgrave Macmillan, 2012.

Stamelman, Richard. *Lost Beyond Telling: Representations of death and absence in modern French poetry*. London: Cornell University Press, 1990.

Tacik, Przemysław. *The Freedom of Lights: Edmond Jabès and Jewish philosophy of modernity*. Oxford: Peter Lang, 2019.

Taïeb, Lucie. 'Lire la présence de l'histoire dans *Le Livre des questions*'. In *Les Poésies de langue française et l'histoire au XXe siècle*, edited by Laure Michel and Delphine Rumeau, 101–12. Rennes: Presses Universitaires de Rennes, 2013.

Waldrop, Rosmarie. *Lavish Absence: Recalling and rereading Edmond Jabès*. Middletown, CT: Wesleyan University Press, 2002.

Wybrands, Francis. 'L'image imprévisible'. In *Saluer Jabès: les suites du Livre*, edited by Didier Cahen, 78–85. Paris: Opales, 2000.

3 'Brûler les états / Brûler les étapes': Ghérasim Luca

Of the many slogan-like formulas by Romanian-born poet Ghérasim Luca, the above injunction, contained in the poem 'La Parole' ['Speech'], is among the most apt to characterise his body of work.[1] 'Brûler les états / brûler les étapes' ['Burn the states / burn the stages'] would seem to suggest that for Luca, the poem is the site of an antagonism, twofold in nature. Revealing the poet's enduring commitment to principles originating in the surrealist movement, the first form of antagonism relates to the signature operations of reason as they inhere in the steps of deductive reasoning: 'les étapes'. Linked to this, the second concerns the forms of centralised authority; thus, the slogan also bespeaks antagonism towards established authority (here, that of the state, but also, elsewhere in the work of Luca, that of the nation and, especially, the *patrie* [fatherland]), that figure articulating a form of Oedipal constraint. Just as Luca sets out to usurp the patrimonial functions which accrue to a given language, his work equally seeks to induce a crisis within the mechanisms of discursive rationality.

A bilingual, self-declared stateless author, Luca eventually left behind one language (Romanian) in favour of another (French). However, his own commentary on his work suggests a willed detachment from both of these: 'OUBLIE TA LANGUE MATERNELLE / SOIS ÉTRANGER À LA LANGUE D'ADOPTION ÉTRANGÈRE / SEULE / LA / NO MAN'S LANGUE' ['FORGET YOUR MOTHER TONGUE / REMAIN FOREIGN TO THE ADOPTED FOREIGN LANGUAGE / ONLY / NO MAN'S LANGUAGE'], he declares in a notebook.[2]

For Yasemin Yildiz, commenting on the work of the German Romantic philosopher Friedrich Schleiermacher, the *Muttersprache* [mother tongue] 'stands for a unique, irreplaceable, unchangeable biological origin that situates the individual automatically in a kinship network and by extension in the nation'.[3] According to Yildiz, the significance habitually attributed to the mother tongue is that it offers first language speakers a sense of organic connection to their putative shared national or ethnic origins. Promoting fictions of kinship and territoriality, this 'monolingual paradigm',[4] Yildiz argues, even today, in contexts where multilingualism is explicitly invoked, continues to dominate institutional understandings of the relationship between subjectivity, language and national community.

Luca, as will be apparent over the course of this chapter, is a writer who emerges as acutely and critically aware of the stakes of the paradigm of monolinguality. However, it is not Luca's switching of codes – his actual multilingualism or bilingualism – which is of principal interest here, nor the immediately personal stakes of his rejection or embrace of an acquired language over an inherited one. Rather, the above quotation from the poet tells primarily of a sense of estrangement from the very apparatus of linguistic expression itself, and from the intuitive understanding that treats a given language as an object available to possession or appropriation depending on one's status as native or non-native speaker ('forget *your* mother tongue').

As well as antagonising language's patrimoniality, Luca sets out to interfere in the workings of discursive rationality, that is the assumption that rationality constitutes an inherent property of discourse. Among the most explicit statements of the poet's anti-rationalism is to be found in *Un loup à travers une loupe* ['A wolf through a magnifying glass'], a text originally published in Romanian as *Un lup văzut printr-o lupă* at the height of the poet's immersion in the international surrealist movement. Taking up key surrealist motifs of eroticism, hallucination and sadistic violence, it explores the interrelation between the inner workings of the psyche and external reality:

> Il n'y a que le rationalisme qui a eu l'insolence de coller au cerveau humain les moustaches de la logique et des statistiques et de fixer la tête de l'homme sur un socle vers lequel progresse nuit et jour, en voiture ou à cheval, la paralysie, alors que les prémisses et les conclusions tournent autour d'elle telle une paire de bottes ou comme le buste de Beethoven élevé à la dignité de statue équestre, il n'y a que le rationalisme qui aimerait voir dans le signataire de ce cri un cas de misanthropie galopante, cette formule étant probablement apte à mettre un terme à sa course sénile d'une prémisse à une conclusion, et à lui donner une satisfaction entière.[5]

> [It was only rationalism that had the insolence to plaster the moustaches of logic and statistics onto the human mind and to set

> the head of man on a plinth towards which paralysis moves day and night, by car or on horseback, while premises and conclusions swirl around it like a pair of boots or like the bust of Beethoven promoted to the dignified position of an equestrian statue, it is only rationalism which would like to see in the signatory of this cry a case of galloping misanthropy, this formula probably being able to put an end to its senile race from a premise to a conclusion, and to give it complete satisfaction.]

In its form alone, this single, sweeping sentence evokes a continuous flow of thought unhindered by the obstacles of rational deliberation. For Luca, the premises, conclusions and other hallmarks of such deliberation induce a form of paralysis that is fundamentally deleterious to the life of the individual, and he underscores the need to negate rationalism's effects, not least by subverting its mode of linguistic expression. Although the text was composed in Romanian, its thesis is of course transferable to other linguistic contexts, notably to French, the poet's 'langue d'adoption étrangère' ['adopted foreign language']. French was frequently spoken in intellectual or bourgeois contexts in central Europe in the nineteenth and early twentieth centuries, and it was also the language of surrealism for Luca and his peers, and the one through which they were able to make contact with other surrealists across the globe.

Further to this, however, it is also worth acknowledging the historical assertions which have been made on behalf of the French language. Beginning with René Descartes's decision to compose his *Discours de la méthode* ['Discourse on method'] in French rather than Latin, claims have been made on behalf of the French language as the supposedly privileged vehicle of rational thought. For Jean-Jacques Rousseau, writing in his *Lettre sur la musique française* ['Letter on French music'], the French language was 'celle des philosophes et des sages' ['that of the philosophers and the wise'] and 'faite pour être l'organe de la vérité et de la raison' ['made for being the organ of truth and reason'].[6] Meanwhile, fellow eighteenth-century writer Antoine de Rivarol, author of the *Discours sur l'universalité de la langue française* ['Discourse on the universality of the French language'], in an example of acute monolingual bias, extolled the exceptional *clarté* [clarity] of the French language: 'Ce qui n'est pas clair n'est pas français ; ce qui n'est pas clair est encore anglais, italien, grec ou latin' ['What is not clear is not French; that which is not clear is still English, Italian, Greek or Latin'].[7] Overlooking the fact that some other European languages follow a largely identical grammatical structure, Rivarol claimed that the sequencing of subject, verb and object in French corresponded to fundamental operations of thought universal to all peoples: 'voilà la logique naturelle à tous les hommes; voilà ce qui constitue le sens commun' ['such is the logic natural to all men; this is what constitutes common sense'].[8] Such claims go no small way towards establishing the supposed 'exceptionality' of French in the post-Enlightenment period: while rationality emerges as a capacity of all peoples and nations, it is one that is held to find its most proper expression in the French language, thus enhancing that language's claim to universality as well as to its specificity in patrimonial terms.

Luca's decision to make French the principal idiom of his creative endeavours deserves consideration in the above contexts. As part of a creative enterprise that takes on a paradoxically quasi-metaphysical scope, he casts poetry as a revolutionary form of engagement at the limits of sense and syntax. Thus, according to Krzysztof Fijalkowski, his work constitutes an 'exploration avoisinant la philosophie et l'interprétation des modalités de la connaissance, où le jeu, l'humour noir, et plus encore une sorte de vibration du verbe d'un sens à l'autre se conjuguent' ['an enquiry bordering on philosophy and the interpenetration of modes of knowledge, and in which play, a dark humour and above all a kind of shuddering of the word from one sense to another are conjured together'].[9] For Luca, poetry constitutes a performative transgression of precisely the kinds of semantic and cognitive stability explicitly condemned in the writings of his Romanian period, which, like *Un loup à travers une loupe*, are more conventionally discursive in form. Thus, in collections ranging from *Héros-limite* ['Hero-limit'] to *La Proie s'ombre* ['Self-shadowing prey'], he sets out to subject the operations of language to a dialectical process with the aim of subverting their rationalising bent and the patrimonial attachments they invite. Throughout his work, language is pulverised into a shifting body of phonemic matter and is invested with novel combinatory possibilities that are revealed through homophony and apparently haphazard word play. In ways that allude to his condition as a writer who has foregone attachments to nation or state, Luca thus alerts the reader to the corrosive effects of the monolingual paradigm.

'Une position anti-nationale à outrance': a life fundamentally, legally, necessarily apatride

Ghérasim Luca was born Salman[10] Locker[11] in July 1913 in Bucharest, Romania, to Berl, a tailor (who died following his enlistment in the Romanian army the following year), and Sophia, a clothing factory worker. His family were Ashkenazi Jews, and in addition to his native Romanian, which would be the idiom of his early published work, he spoke Yiddish, as well as French and German. Luca's intellectual and literary aspirations were stimulated from an early age, and by his late teens, together with a group of young writers and artists including Aurel Baranga, Paul Păun and Jules Perahim, he had founded a new literary review entitled *Alge* ['Algae'], first published in 1930. Together, these young intellectuals formed a second wave of the Romanian surrealist movement, after figures such as Benjamin Fondane and Ilarie Voronca. It was Aurel Baranga who first suggested to his friend that he should adopt the pen name 'Gherasim Luca', after he came across a death notice carrying this name in a Bucharest newspaper. Intriguingly, the obituary commemorated an archimandrite of the Mount Athos Monastic State in Greece and 'emeritus linguist'.[12] The acute accent on the name appears in Luca's publications in French, and both parts of the name are technically intended as a single surname. The adoption of pen names was relatively commonplace among his peers in avant-garde circles.[13] However, Luca's casting off of his birth name and assumption of a new literary identity can be read more specifically as an expression of an aversion to the connotations of self-identicality attached to the proper name as well as to a certain patrilineal ordering of human culture, one that is consistent with his non-Oedipal credo.

Luca's heterodox literary credentials were established from a young age: in 1931, contributions by Luca, Baranga, Perahim and Paul Păun to the single edition of a journal entitled *Pulă* ['Cock'] saw each of them charged with affront to public decency and they served several days in prison. While he was supportive of the communist movement in his youth, the most significant influence on the poet and his peers in this period is that of surrealism. The period of Luca's youthful participation in the Romanian surrealist movement culminated in the publication in 1945 of the manifesto *Dialectique de la dialectique* ['Dialectic of dialectics'].[14] Coauthored with Dolfi Trost, the text is distinctive in that it is the most complete expression of Luca's adherence to the international surrealist movement. The authors endorse surrealism's disdain for nationalism, the state and institutional authority. However, their manifesto calls for a radical reorientation of the movement's revolutionary energies away from a set of techniques such as collage and automatic writing which Luca and Trost claimed were increasingly available to recuperation by forces external to the aims of surrealism; it thus also marks the moment at which Luca had already begun to part ways with some of the movement's core tenets. Although this text is accounted for at greater length in recent valuable studies by Krzysztof Fijalkowski, Iulian Toma and Yannick Torlini,[15] it is useful to dwell here briefly on its significance and the singular qualities of Luca's creative engagements with respect to the cultural movements of surrealism and Dada.

Denis Lejeune argues that the objective of surrealism is to access 'man's mental apparatus in its purest form'. Comparing surrealism with Dada, Lejeune claims that 'the former is positive, it consists in working toward a constructive goal, while the latter's intention was to attain as complete a dismantling of positives as possible'.[16] Although his project may at some level share in what Stephen Forcer calls the 'performed collapse of language, sense and reason' characteristic of Tristan Tzara and Dada,[17] and although it retains a commitment to the surrealist exploration of the unconscious, it is the supposed positive/negative orientation of these movements that sets Luca's project apart from both. Dating from *Dialectique de la dialectique*, two distinguishing features of Luca's project emerge: these are the negation of negation and non-Oedipus. In *Dialectique de la dialectique*, Luca and Trost claim that the surrealist revolution 'ne peut être maintenu et développé que par une position dialectique de permanente négation et de négation de la négation' ['can only be maintained and developed by a dialectical position of permanent negation and negation of negation'].[18] For the authors, the negation of dialectical negation was the means by which humanity could overcome the tyranny of its own intellectual and affective constructions.

While it bears the hallmarks of dialectical materialism, *Dialectique de la dialectique* also deploys a psychoanalytical vocabulary and presents the class struggle as an expression of a father–son conflict. Although Luca and Trost salute the revolutionary ambitions of various radical social movements, they argue that the rhetoric of fraternity common to such movements has done little to displace the Oedipal complex as the basis of the proletariat's struggle with the bourgeoisie.[19] 'Pour nier cet état, les dents de la révolution doivent mordre profondément la passivité inconsciente et naturelle de l'homme' ['In order to deny this state, the teeth of revolution must bite deeply into man's unconscious and natural passivity'],[20] the authors announce, declaring their intent to break the cycle of Oedipal conflict by attacking the unconscious mainsprings of those identitarian attachments of class and nation. With specific reference to the question of nationality, therefore, the work rejects what it characterises as 'un internationalisme humanitaire et révolu, qui continue de permettre aux particularités nationales de s'affirmer à l'abri d'une égalité réformiste ['an outdated humanitarian internationalism, which continues to allow specific national features to assert themselves free from any reformist egalitarianism'], while instead advocating 'une position anti-nationale à outrance, concrètement de classe et outrageusement cosmopolite, remontant dans ses aspects les plus violents jusqu'à l'homme lui-même' ['an excessively anti-national position, one which is concretely class-based and outrageously cosmopolitan, and which in its most violent aspects draws on man's own nature'].[21]

While much continues to be ascertained about Luca's contribution to Romanian surrealism, no doubt due to his relative silence on the matter, and his comparatively minimal emphasis on biographical issues more generally, the poet's experience of the period of the Shoah or Holocaust in his home country is not much documented in scholarship. However, it has as its backdrop intense, organised anti-Semitic persecution and traumatic events such as the Bucharest and Iaşi pogroms which took place in 1941. In the affectionate account of his memories of his friend Luca which he contributed to a recent special edition of the journal *Europe*, Thierry Garrel notes: 'Je me souviens que Luca ne parlait pas de la période de la guerre en Roumanie. Juste une fois, qu'il avait été prisonnier dans un camp de travail forcé' ['I remember Luca did not speak about wartime in Romania. Only once, to say that he had been prisoner in a forced labour camp'].[22] Despite Luca's apparent disinclination to speak about this harrowing period of his life, a group of documents held at the Bibliothèque littéraire Jacques Doucet in Paris sheds some additional light on his activities during World War II. Luca had projected the publication of an anthology of work by Romanian Jewish poets, and the documents held in a file on this subject show that he made an application to the American Joint Distribution Committee's 'Scholarships and Fellowships of the Department of Cultural and Educational Reconstruction of the Conference On Jewish Material Claims Against Germany' (BLJD, GHL, MS 54). Notes in Luca's handwriting for what appears to be a draft application to this scheme include the following information, under a section entitled 'PAYS DE RÉSIDENCE DEPUIS 1933':

> À Bucarest jusqu'à janvier 1939, date de l'arrivée au pouvoir du premier gouvernement anti-Sémite Goga-Cuza ; j'ai dû quitter la Roumanie en 24 heures par crainte de représailles pour mes articles anti-hitlériens. En 1940 je rentre en Roumanie. En 1947, tentative échouée de quitter clandestinement le pays que je quitte légalement en 1951 comme émigrant. A Jaffa (Israël) de 1951 à 1952 et à Paris de 1952 à 1957.[23]

[In Bucharest until January 1939, the date of the coming to power of the first anti-Semitic government, that of Goga-Cuza; I had to leave Romania in the space of 24 hours for fear of reprisals for my anti-Hitler articles. In 1940, I returned to Romania. In 1947, failed attempt to leave the country illegally; I left legally in 1951 as an emigrant. In Jaffa (Israel) from 1951 to 1952 and Paris from 1952 to 1957.]

It should be noted that there seems to be an error in the first statement here: the short-lived regime led by Octavian Goga and Alexandru Cuza, which was responsible for the introduction of a number of anti-Semitic laws (including one which reviewed criteria for citizenship of Romania by Jews), in fact ran from December 1937 to February 1938.[24] A further set of notes shows the gruesome nature of the labour which the poet was forced to undertake following the arrival of the Nazis in Romania in October 1940:

NATIONALITÉ DU DOCUMENT DE VOYAGE: Apatride ex-Roumain (Carte No.....)

[...]

DATE D'ENTRÉE DANS LE PAYS OÙ VOUS RÉSIDEZ EN CE MOMENT: 9 mars 1952.

[...]

RACONTER BRIÈVEMENT LES PREUVES DE VOTRE QUALITÉ DE VICTIME DES NAZIS:

Depuis l'entrée de l'armée hitlérienne en Roumanie et jusqu'à la fin de la guerre, j'ai fait des travaux forcés, d'abord au creusement de tranchées (au camp de concentration « Polygon Cotroceni »), puis utilisé pour balayer des rues, déblayer les ruines et ramasser les cadavres pendant les bombardements aériens, etc.[25]

[NATIONALITY OF TRAVEL DOCUMENT: Ex-Romanian stateless person (Card Number ...)

[...]

DATE OF ENTRY INTO THE COUNTRY WHERE YOU CURRENTLY RESIDE: 9 March 1952.

[...]

GIVE A BRIEF ACCOUNT OF THE EVIDENCE FOR YOUR STATUS AS A VICTIM OF THE NAZIS:

> Beginning with the arrival of Hitler's army in Romania and until the end of the war, I carried out forced labour, first digging trenches (at the 'Polygon Cotroceni' concentration camp) and I was then used to sweep streets, clear ruins and retrieve corpses during aerial bombardments, etc.]

Later poems by Luca such as 'Œdipe Sphinx' ['Oedipus Sphinx'] and 'À LA SANTÉ DU MORT ['TO THE HEALTH OF DEATH'] from *Paralipomènes*, allude explicitly to atrocities ('exécutants fusillés' ['executioners shot dead'];[26] a 'crime commis au nom de la loi' ['a crime committed in the name of the law'][27]), and take on a powerful resonance when considered in light of the experiences noted above. Preceded by his official change of name in 1946, Luca's subsequent departure for Israel (where he lived for a time in difficult circumstances in the company of Dolfi Trost) was in turn followed by his effectively permanent exile in France from 1952. The move to France was marked also by a distancing from aspects of the surrealist movement, particularly surrealism's collective manifestations. However, Luca continued to hold its leader, André Breton, in considerable esteem. Over subsequent years, Luca's poetic practice shifted noticeably towards texts developed for spoken delivery which exploited his considerable energies as a performer.[28]

Repeatedly, in documents such as those above, as well as in his notebooks and correspondence with authors, Luca self-identifies as 'apatride' ['stateless'] or 'apatride ex-Roumain' ['stateless ex-Romanian']. Typical in this respect is a draft of a letter to a journal editor contained in an undated notebook: 'Monsieur le Rédacteur, Je tiens à vous signaler la regrettable erreur qui s'est glissée dans les deux ou trois lignes que vous avez bien voulu me consacrer dans votre dernier numéro. En effet, je ne suis pas roumain – avec ou sans majuscule – mais *apatride*' ['Dear Editor, I wish to draw to your attention the regrettable mistake which slipped into the few lines which you were kind enough to devote to me in your most recent issue. I am not, in fact, Romanian – with or without a capital letter – but *stateless*'].[29] The title page of the manuscript for *Le Palais de la connaissance* has the following word-play: 'L'APPAS TRIE // L'APPÂT TRIE' ['The charm sorts // The bait sorts'],[30] while other comments are more solemn and informed by the historical experience of the Shoah: 'Fondamentalement et même légalement je suis nécessairement apatride. Ni ma langue passée ni ma langue présente ne justifient à mes yeux (après Auschwitz) l'appartenance à un patrimoine national' ['Fundamentally and even legally, I am necessarily stateless. Neither my past language nor my present one justify to my eyes (after Auschwitz) belonging to a national heritage'].[31] As he echoes here some of the opening quotations in this chapter, it is clear how Luca does not reject one national tradition in favour of another. Rather, Luca's experience of the Shoah only served to heighten his acute critical sense of languages as agents and vectors of patrimonial value.

Thierry Garrel also recalls that during the period of their friendship Luca 'faisait comme apatride la queue avec tous les immigrés devant la Préfecture de police pour renouveler son permis de séjour' ['as a stateless person used to queue with all the immigrants in front of the Prefecture of Police in order to renew his residence permit'].[32] Nonetheless, the Office français de protection des réfugiés et apatrides [French Office for the Protection of Refugees and Stateless People] does not possess any documentation relating to Luca, although it may simply have been the case that he did not seek the protection of that office. In any case, Luca's 'apatride' status does not seem to have been a definitive obstacle to travel abroad and, despite encountering considerable administrative difficulties, he was able to make foreign trips on a number of occasions to destinations including the USA, Cuba and Sweden.[33] Thierry Garrel notes that Luca eventually took French nationality and married his partner of 40 years, Micheline Catti.[34] In February 1994, the poet committed suicide by drowning in the Seine. As Thierry Garrel recalls in a note that is all the more poignant for Luca's lifelong circumvention of various forms of assignation (whether by name or nationality), his body was recovered from the river, and subject to one last formal identification:

> Je me souviens du chandail en laine que nous lui avions offert au retour d'un voyage en Écosse et que le commissaire de police de Boulogne-Billancourt m'a montré pour authentifier son corps qui venait d'être repêché dans la Seine, quai de Stalingrad, en face de l'île Saint-Germain.[35]
>
> [I remember the woollen sweater that we had given him after a trip to Scotland, the one that the Boulogne-Billancourt police commissioner showed me to authenticate his body which had just been recovered from the Seine at the quai de Stalingrad, opposite the île Saint-Germain.]

Non-Oedipus: *L'Inventeur de l'amour* (1945)

First published as a prose text in Romanian in Bucharest in 1945,[36] *Inventatorul iubirii* (*L'Inventeur de l'amour*) ['The inventor of love'] contains one of the first explicit formulations of the 'non-Oedipal' posture assumed by Luca, along with *Moartea moartă* (*La Mort morte* ['The dead death'], published in the same volume as *Inventatorul iubirii*) and the manifesto *Dialectique de la dialectique* ['Dialectic of dialectics'] written with Dolfi Trost. At the core of his attack in the book on the putative ubiquity of the Oedipus complex is his conviction that it describes a form of social and cultural normativity, amounting to a supposedly unified theory of the human condition. The excerpt quoted here is from Luca's own French translation, reworked as a text in verse:

> Depuis quelques milliers d'années
> on propage
> comme une épidémie obscurantiste
> l'homme axiomatique : Œdipe
>
> l'homme du complexe de castration
> et du traumatisme natal
> sur lequel s'appuient les amours
> les professions
> les cravates et les sacs à main
> le progrès, les arts
> les églises
>
> Je déteste cet enfant naturel d'Œdipe
> je hais et refuse sa biologie fixe
>
> Et si l'homme est ainsi parce qu'il naît
> alors il ne me reste plus qu'à refuser
> la naissance
> je refuse tout axiome
> même s'il a pour lui l'apparence
> d'une certitude[37]
>
> [For thousands of years
> like an obscurantist epidemic
> we have propagated
> axiomatic man: Oedipus

he of the castration complex
and the trauma of birth
which provide the basis for love
professions
neckties and handbags
progress, the arts
churches

I hate this natural child of Oedipus
I hate and refuse his rigid biology

And if man is such because he is born
then I just have to refuse
birth
I refuse any kind of axiom
even if it looks to be
something known for certain]

Crucial here is the consideration that the Oedipus complex is fundamentally bound up with the meanings attributed to the event of birth: 'si l'homme est ainsi parce qu'il naît' ['if man is such because he is born']. Although the formula may puzzle at first, Luca's intention is not to deny the physical reality of parturition. Rather, his posture here betokens a refusal to submit to those 'forces of circumscription – and in the first instance, the vocabulary of psychoanalytical generalisation – to which being a subject in the world, part of an objectifying arrangement, exposes the "je"', according to Michael G. Kelly.[38] Taking this perspective further, the poet's target therefore seems to be the ubiquity of nativity as the principle on which human institutions are predicated and the paralysing complexes (among them, birth trauma and castration) to which it gives rise. Luca's aims then extend to a rejection of nativity (and its associated paradigms of filiation, patrilineality, kinship and so on) as the foundational mechanism of culture. For the remainder of his writing career, he continually renewed his denunciation of what he describes as 'la condition oedipienne de l'existence dans son retour biologiquement réactionnaire vers le passé, dans les vestiges castrants, traumatiques et horribles de la naissance, dans son parasitisme sublimal sur les ruines des parents et du frère' ['the Oedipal condition of existence in its biologically reactionary return towards the past, in the horrible, traumatic, castrating residue of birth, in its subliminal parasitism on the ruins of parents and the brother'].[39]

A further objection raised by the poet is to what he sees as the axiomatic status enjoyed by the Oedipal theory, that is, to its potential to proliferate generalisations or propositions that are effectively beyond contention. It is Luca's view that axiomatic generalisations effectively induce a form of linguistic and epistemological straitjacketing of the real, and function to maintain causal explanations and explanatory paradigms. In their address to the French surrealists of 1945, *Dialectique de la dialectique*, meanwhile, Luca and Trost's eye-catching stated ambition was, by contrast, no less than to 'surmonter la froideur de la causalité universelle' ['to overcome the coldness of universal causality'], that is to overturn the universally binding causality principle.[40]

Throughout his work, Luca seems to assume that the categories of axiom and idiom present a common set of problems, and he frequently deploys and deconstructs examples of idioms. Examples of figures of speech and other received expressions featuring in the poems which follow in this chapter include: 'muet comme une carpe' ['as quiet as a carp [mouse]']; 'laisser la proie pour l'ombre' ['letting go of the prey to grasp at its shadow']; 'comme un poisson dans l'eau' ['like a fish in water'] and 'c'est l'arbre qui cache la forêt' ['You can't see the wood for the trees']. Not least because they employ organic imagery, 'les proverbes et toutes les formes moralisantes et sceptiques tirées de l'abécédaire comme des pierres funéraires' ['proverbs and all those moralising and sceptical formulas drawn from the alphabet book like tombstones'] support a domesticating function: with each reiteration they assert a form of patrimony, subtly affirming a collective inheritance of or ownership of language, one which Luca at every turn seeks to contest.[41] Indeed, as Laura Erber writes, in a suggestive account of the significance of the author's statelessness for his poetics, what Luca, as stateless author, demands 'of the language that he uses is precisely to be able to use it without having to submit to its heritage'.[42]

A letter which, the surrealist art critic and essayist Sarane Alexandrian notes, Luca addressed to him from Bucharest on 9 June 1947, captures the changing emphasis of Luca's radicality as he increasingly dissociated himself from any instituted movement of contestation. While the various 'isms' listed here may have been apt to produce a critique of aspects of the Oedipal condition, they are in Luca's view powerless to act upon it:

> Il n'y a pour moi aucun doute : la lutte mythique entre la liberté et son contraire se donne actuellement entre Œdipe et non Œdipe. L'invivable vie œdipienne, si férocement mais exactement décrite par

les systèmes (marxisme, futurisme, existentialisme, naturalisme...) doit être follement dépassée, par un bond formidable dans une sorte de vie dans la vie, d'amour dans l'amour, indescriptible, indiscernable, et irréductible au langage des systèmes. Je parle de la vie et de l'amour non-oedipiens (accessibles pour le *comportement* surréaliste poursuivi à outrance), c'est-à-dire de la négation absolue du cordon ombilical, nostalgique et régressif, source lointaine de notre ambivalence et de notre malheur.[43]

[There is no doubt in my mind: the mythical struggle between freedom and its opposite is currently taking place between Oedipus and non-Oedipus. That unbearable Oedipal life, which is so ferociously and yet scrupulously characterised by systems of thought (whether Marxism, futurism, existentialism or naturalism ...) must be frantically surpassed, by a tremendous leap into a kind of life within life, of love within love, one that cannot be described, or perceived, or reduced to the language of systems. I'm talking about non-Oedipal life and love (of a kind accessible through surreal *behaviour* pursued to excess), that is to say, the absolute negation of the nostalgic and regressive umbilical cord, that distant source of our ambivalence and our misfortune.]

Aside from his rhetorical casting off of the subject's native, 'umbilical' attachments, a noteworthy feature of this passage is Luca's intuition that non-Oedipal life eludes discursive construal; it cannot be reduced to 'the language of systems'. Although the texts dating from the Romanian-language period of Luca's *oeuvre* tend to conform to relatively conventional discursive forms such as the essay or the manifesto, broadly speaking, those dating from the beginning of Luca's exile in France adopt a more radical quality characterised by forms of verbal play that are 'improper', irreverent and sophisticated in equal measure. The following sections will address a range of different manifestations of that radicality, starting with two collections which focus on what is suppressed in the accession to language.

Le Chant de la carpe (1973) and *Paralipomènes* (1976): mutings and omissions

The title of the 1973 collection *Le Chant de la carpe* ['The song of the carp'] alludes to the proverbial mutism of the carp. The title is evocative for speakers of French in that it recalls the simile 'muet comme une carpe' ['quiet as a mouse [carp]'], although Luca's recasting of the carp's mutism as song is significant. The fish's silence here designates a retraction of speech, and, arguably, a failure or refusal to submit to the norms of discursive communication. As Jean-Christophe Bailly notes, in an essay on a later collaboration between Luca and the artist Piotr Kowalski, the collection's title 'nomme un battement muet, animal, mais qui désigne aussi le silence retiré dans la langue, que la langue contourne, n'atteint pas et laisse pourtant derrière elle comme son propre sillage' ['names a silent, animal beat, but which also designates the silence that has withdrawn into language, one that language passes by, does not reach and yet leaves behind itself as if in its own wake'].[44] In this way, Luca seeks to open our ears to the acoustic drama of that which language mutes; of that which is unsaid, if not the unsayable.

Perhaps nowhere in Luca's *oeuvre* is this quality more spectacularly displayed than in a text from the collection entitled 'Passionnément' ['Passionately'], a poem first published in the 1947 *plaquette* [booklet] entitled *Amphitrite*. In this poem, Luca dramatises an experience of linguistic dispossession, a 'not-having' of speech which is intimated via a poetics of stammering. Throughout the poem, the reader and spectator are treated to the spectacle of a 'langue étrangère qui s'égare dans ma bouche' ['foreign tongue that goes astray in my mouth'], to borrow a formula from *Un loup à travers une loupe* ['A wolf through a magnifying glass'].[45] The angst-laden sensation of foreignness at issue here is not in respect of one language over another, namely, of French, which by this stage in Luca's life has superseded Romanian as the poet's principal medium of creative engagement. Instead, the spectacle offered by this poem is that of the liquidation of the linguistic functions of affirmation and articulation themselves. Let us consider the following excerpt:

> pas pas paspaspas pas
> pasppas ppas pas paspas
> le pas pas le faux pas le pas
> paspaspas le pas le mau
> le mauve le mauvais pas
> paspas pas le pas le papa
> le mauvais papa le mauve le pas
>
> le mauvais papa le mauve le pas
> paspas passe paspaspasse
> passe passe il passe il pas pas

il passe le pas du pas du pape
du pape sur le pape du pas du passe
passepasse passi le sur le
le pas le passi passi passi pissez sur
le pape sur papa sur le sur la sur
la pipe du papa du pape pissez en masse
passe passe passi passepassi la passe
la basse passi passepassi la
passio passiobasson le bas
le pas passion le basson et
et pas le basso do pas

paspas do passe passiopassion do
ne do ne domi ne passi ne dominez pas
ne dominez pas vos passions passives ne
ne domino vos passio vos vos
ssis vos passio ne dodo vos
vos dominos d'or
c'est domdommage do dodor
do pas pas ne domi
pas paspasse passio
vos pas ne do ne do ne dominez pas
vos passes passions vos pas vos
vos pas dévo dévorants ne do
ne dominez pas vos rats
pas vos rats
ne do dévorants ne do ne dominez pas
vos rats vos rations vos rats rations ne ne
ne dominez pas vos passions rations vos
ne dominez pas vos ne vos ne do do
minez minez vos nations ni mais do
minez ne do ne mi pas pas vos rats[46]

'Non pas être bègue dans sa parole, mais être bègue du langage lui-même' ['not to stammer in one's speech, but to stammer in language itself']: Gilles Deleuze's enduring assessment of the project of writers such as Luca or Samuel Beckett is apt to account for the awkwardness and attendant cognitive unease which characterise this poem.[47] Maximising the sense of confusion and ludic possibilities issuing from a sequence of deliberate linguistic stumbles, it is the adequacy of the very system of language itself which is at issue here.

Key to 'Passionnément' is how Luca exploits the connotative properties of the signifier 'pas', both as the linguistic marker of negation in French, and more subtly as 'step' (the lapsus being understood as a 'faux pas de la langue' ['a misstep of the tongue']). In a text which, in Michael G. Kelly's terms, 'says what it dramatizes itself as trying to say', Luca makes the hierarchical order of syntax secondary to the 'lateral' play of lapsus and paronomasia.[48] This shift, present at the syntactical level, is emblematic of a broader dynamic of contestation of authority: at key moments, anti-patriarchal or anti-clerical connotations surge forth in the childishly amusing and/or provocative exhortations to 'pissez sur / le pape sur papa' ['piss on / the pope on papa'] and 'minez vos nations' / 'crachez sur vos nations' ['explode your nations' / 'spit on your nations']. Similarly, the elevation of the 'mauvais papa' ['bad dad'] invites a contrast with the legal term 'bon père de famille' ['good family father'] which featured in the French civil code from 1804 until 2014. Connoting a conduct based on prudence, reasonableness, industriousness and moral authority, the notion of the 'bonus pater familias' moreover locates a model kind of civility within both masculine authority and the function of progeniture, one to which, as we will see in the next chapter, Michelle Grangaud is also alert in her text *État civil* ['Civil status']. 'Le bon père de famille' thus 'embodies' precisely the kind of proprietorial control and patrilineality which 'Passionnément' exults in dispelling.

Throughout this piece, stammering seems to intimate the condition of a subject that is no longer proprietorially in command of its manifestation in language and is confronted with its own dissolution. And yet, the poem intimates that the production of utterance retains a quality of affirmation, even if it is no longer tied into a narrative of *self*-accomplishment or *self*-affirmation by the subject. It seems significant that it is the fragment 'pas' or 'not' that is so much to the fore here, as it is via this proliferation of negations that the final, resoundingly declarative words of the poem ring out in an embrace of the *inter*subjective through passion: 'je t'aime passio passionnément' ['I love you passio passionately'].

Like *Le Chant de la carpe*, the collection *Paralipomènes* ['Paralipomena'] of 1976 continues this fascination with the ludic (re-)introduction into language of what is suppressed in the process of its elaboration. Connoting a set of items omitted from a work and added as a supplement, the *Paralipomènes* constitute, according to Luca, a 'répertoire des oublis d'un livre' ['a repertory of the omissions of a book'].[49] Rather than designating the supplementary material appended to a body of published volumes, these 'oversights' primarily seem to have currency for Luca at a very fundamental, syntactical level, where they have potential to interfere with the processes of discursive signification. As an example, let us turn now to two poems within *Paralipomènes* which belong to the *dé-monologue* [de-monologue], a genre which, as early as 1962–3, Luca described in a notebook as a 'science de la perte du moi' ['science of the loss of the self'].[50] If the dialogue presumes an interaction between two speaking partners, the *dé-monologue* signals the very dissolution of mutually exclusive entities: 'En passant / du / dialogue / au dé-monologue // un coup de « dé » / abolit / toujours / le hasard // Hors-la-loi des contraires' ['Moving / from / dialogue / to de-monologue // a throw of the "dice" ["dé"] / always / abolishes / chance // Outwith the law of contrasts'].[51] The emphasis of this excerpt, with its brief echo of Stéphane Mallarmé's *Un Coup de Dés jamais n'abolira le Hasard* ['A throw of the dice will never abolish chance'], is on the dissolution of the finite self. However, it is also worth underscoring how the neologism additionally evokes the introduction of a singularly unruly, *demonic* impulse into language, one which is visible in a poem from the collection, 'Qui voyez-vous ?' ['Who do you see?'].

Playing on the problems of recognition, 'Qui voyez-vous ?' turns on an aporia intrinsic to the intersubjective encounter, as in the following extract:

> Nous ne voyons personne
>
> Nous voyons parfois quelqu'un
> sinon comme quelqu'un qu'on voit
> du moins comme quelqu'un
> qu'on voit parfois
> Parfois nous voyons quelqu'un
> mais en général
> nous ne voyons personne
> Quand nous voyons quelqu'un
> nous ne voyons personne
> mais personne ne voit
> qu'en ne voyant personne
> on voit toujours quelqu'un[52]
>
> ['We see no one
>
> We sometimes see someone
> if not like someone we see
> at least like someone

that we sometimes see
Sometimes we see someone
but in general
we see no one
When we see someone
we see no one
but no one sees
that in seeing no one
we still see someone']

Here, the distinctions between the terms 'quelqu'un' ['someone'] and 'personne' [no one'] are progressively elided through a series of shifts. Across the poem, successive formulations range forward and back from subjective framings ('nous ne voyons personne' ['we see no one']) to objective ones ('quelqu'un voit que nous ne voyons personne' ['someone sees that we see no one']), and from transitive forms of the verb ('nous voyons parfois quelqu'un' ['we sometimes see someone']) to reflexive ones ('nous nous voyons' ['we see ourselves']), while generalising statements contrast with time-specific ones ('parfois' ['sometimes'], 'pas toujours' ['not always']). Indeed, part of the play Luca indulges in here derives from the fact that 'voir' ['to see'], linguistically, requires the existence of an object (here, either 'personne' ['no one'] or 'quelqu'un' ['someone']), even where none is substantially present to the gaze: 'personne ne voit / qu'en ne voyant personne / on voit toujours quelqu'un' ['no one sees / that in seeing no one / we still see someone'].

The previous chapter of this book explored various texts in which Edmond Jabès effectively obstructs readerly attempts to view his poetics as governed by an intentional practice or strategy. Similarly, it is difficult to imagine how the above features of Luca's poem might reflect a rhetorical tactic (at least one which might reflect a unitary intention, to be traced through movements of the text or a set of positions assumed). To try to deduce some such unitary, sequential order beneath the various propositions contained in 'Qui voyez-vous ?' only leads the reader or listener to a state of bewilderment; this is because from one line to the next, the constituent elements of any one statement or account of the encounter between two interlocutors themselves become the object of a displacement. In these conditions, it could be argued that the response offered to the titular question is to present this encounter as a mobile one and to problematise the *voir* [the act of seeing], exposing the objectifying logic of a scopic regime that places vision and knowledge on the same plane. The text thus seems to speak against what it ostensibly endeavours to make sayable, namely the *who* implied by the poem's question, and in doing this it articulates an abiding anxiety over the nature of personhood.

Arguably the answer to the question posed in the title 'Qui voyez-vous ?' is in part also supplied by the next poem from the 'Dé-monologue' section of *Paralipomènes*, which is structurally similar and begins with the word 'personne' [no one], the last word of 'Qui voyez-vous ?'. Given that both texts were primarily destined for a public reading, the homophony of the title of this poem, 'Les cris vains' ['Vain cries'], with the term 'l'écrivain' ['the writer'] hints at a possible answer. The two poems indeed present similarities, including the shift from subjective to objective framings ('nous n'avons rien à dire' // 'comme si personne ne nous disait / même pas nous / que nous n'avons rien à dire' ['we have nothing to say'// 'as if no one said to us / not even ourselves / that we have nothing to say']) and from transitive to reflexive forms of the verb. In passing, Luca's approach here can be contrasted with Paul Éluard, in *Quelques-uns des mots qui jusqu'ici m'étaient mystérieusement interdits* ['Some of those words that until now were mysteriously forbidden to me'] of 1937. Éluard writes of his 'empire d'homme' ['human empire'] and the power of those 'Mots que j'écris ici / Contre toute évidence / Avec le grand souci / De tout dire' ['Words I write here / Contrary to all the odds / From my great anxiety / to say everything'].[53]

There is also an identical preoccupation with the indeterminacies produced by linguistic negation: 'le rien que nous ne nous disons / continuellement / nous nous le disons / comme si nous ne nous disions rien' ['the nothing that we say to ourselves / continually / we say it to ourselves / as if we were saying nothing to ourselves']. A radical challenge to transitivity is apparent here again: just as was the case with 'voir' ['to see'] in the preceding poem, this poem dwells on the paradox that 'dire' ['to say'] requires an object ('rien' ['nothing']) just as none is effectively present. Whichever formulation is adopted, 'rien' linguistically forces the speaker with each iteration to pass off the continuous and the undifferentiated as a discrete object of knowledge. The inherent vanity of writing is thus exposed:

> Personne à qui pouvoir dire
> que nous ne faisons rien
> que nous ne faisons
> que ce que nous disons
> c'est-à-dire rien[54]

[No one to whom we can say
that we are doing nothing
that we are only doing
what we are saying
that is, nothing.]

To write, for Luca, is to operate within this regime of radically attenuated creation, and to acknowledge the effective futility of one's labour within a system of rationalised production and exchange. Predicated as this notion is on the idea of a loss to the writing subject, the spirit of this example is not far from the 'création au moyen de la perte' ['creation by means of loss'] which Georges Bataille sees as characteristic of poetry.[55]

'Comment s'en sortir sans sortir': a 'langue dans la langue'

Bataille's celebrated formulation, which situates poetry at the limits of discursive economy, speaks to the bewildering infralinguistic manoeuvres characteristic of Luca. To borrow the terms of an article by Sibylle Orlandi, these manoeuvres give a sense of a transgressive 'langue dans la langue' ['language within language'] which remains stubbornly of the order of linguistic matter and not of discursive meaning and its rational, extralinguistic determinants.[56] In 'Comment s'en sortir sans sortir' ['How to get by without getting out'], a text from the 1967 collection *Apostroph'Apocalypse*, Luca plays on the homophony between the expressions 's'en sortir' (designating the act of freeing oneself from constraint or difficulty) and 'sans sortir' (meaning 'without leaving'). Yet although both formulations originate in an action of leave-taking, the term 'sortir' in this piece seems wilfully detached from any connotation of transcendence or a *dépassement de soi* [surpassing of oneself]:

On sort du sort
Allegés d'émeraudes

On s'en sort par lapsus linguæ
        par lapsus vitæ
par lapsus linguæ
par lapsus vitæ, on s'en sort

Et, sans sort,
essenc' « or » des sens a-légers

Poisson sans poids ni son
    dans l'eau sans voyelles[57]

Signalling a sudden liberation from a preordained fate ('On sort du sort' ['We come out of fate']), the text seems to promise lightening or elevation of the senses ('sans sort / essenc' « or » des sens a-légers'). Yet in a poem where repetition, by way of chiasmus and homophony, allows distinct, even contrary, meanings to emerge, the promised release does not lie outside or beyond language, but instead corresponds to an idea of a difference lurking within the same. Just as is the case at certain points in 'Le Tourbillon qui repose' ['The resting whirlwind'], the governing logic which sets parts of speech in relation to each other, on the principle that each unit is external to and functionally distinct from the last in the order of syntax, is jettisoned. At its every turn, 'Comment s'en sortir sans sortir' problematises that gesture of syntactical plotting or mapping out, where meaning is established on the basis of a teleological movement from one point to the next. Substituting the smoothness of syntactical progression for a kind of dizzying circularity, articulate thought decomposes into its constituent phonemic matter and is invested with novel combinatory possibilities.

In relation to this last point, it is worth underscoring the link between Luca's poetic practice in this text, as in many others, and aspects of Kabbalistic tradition. In a study of transnationalism within the Romanian avant-gardes, Sami Sjöberg notes that writers such as Luca and Isidore Isou identified in the Kabbalah 'a repository of original and idiosyncratic conceptions of language, meaning production, and textual techniques, which went hand in hand with the avant-gardist tendency to subvert common sense and normalized logic'.[58] '*LE MOT-ACTE ORIENTE L'ETRANJUIF ERRANT EN LANGUE SÉDENTAIRE*' ['*THE WORD-ACT GUIDES THE STRANJEW WANDERING IN SEDENTARY LANGUAGE*'], declares Luca in his notebooks,[59] placing a form of restless wandering at the core of his poetic practice: for Luca, as for Edmond Jabès, the Jewish dimension of his work is significant, even if it is difficult to establish. If 'Jewishness' is taken to imply an identity position, Luca deems it necessary to indicate the qualified nature of his own strangeness to the tradition via the neologism 'étranjuif' ['stranjew']. However, although he displays strong scepticism about any sort of instituted religious affiliation or practice, he nonetheless situates aspects of his poetic practice in relation to the Kabbalah. Another notebook entry elaborates on this 'contradictory' attitude:

> DEPUIS TOUJOURS JE SUIS TANTÔT LE CABBALISTE « JUIF » SANS TRADITION LÉGITIME DONC DÉJÀ AU CENTRE D'UNE CONTRADICTION CAR CABBALE EST SYNONYME DE TRADITION TANTÔT LE SORCIER « NOIR » D'UNE IMPOSSIBLE TRIBU EXTRÊME OCCIDENTALE CE QUI VU QUE JE NE JUIS RIEN D'AUTRE QU'UN BLANC UN SALE BLANC ME PLONGE D'AUTANT PLUS DANS L'IMPOSSIBLE.[60]
>
> [I HAVE ALWAYS BEEN AT TIMES THE 'JEWISH' KABBALIST WITHOUT LEGITIMATE TRADITION THEREFORE ALREADY AT THE CENTRE OF A CONTRADICTION BECAUSE KABBALAH IS SYNONYMOUS WITH TRADITION AND AT OTHERS THE 'BLACK' SORCERER OF AN IMPOSSIBLE EXTREME WESTERN TRIBE WHICH GIVEN THAT I AM NOTHING MORE THAN A DIRTY WHITE MAN PLUNGES ME EVEN MORE INTO IMPOSSIBILITY.]

While, in formal terms, Luca's poems invoke comparisons with practices of incantation and letter combination, individual texts allude frequently to mystic practices and to ancient or magical ceremonial rites involving the verbal and the numerical.[61] More generally, it is the Kabbalah's blend of word and action (*'LE MOT-ACTE'* [*'THE WORD-ACT'*]) which seems to have appealed to Luca. And just as Jabès's writing muses on the voids and plenums in the originary act of *Tzimtum*, texts by Luca such as 'Autres secrets du vide et du plein' ['Other secrets of the void and the full'] from the collection *Héros-limite* ['Hero-limit'] likewise explore the possibilities of an originary negativity.

Returning to 'Comment s'en sortir sans sortir', the 'muddling through' connoted by 's'en sortir' is thus precisely that: a halting motion, void of all smoothness, and detrimental to the subject's (and reader's or listener's) sense of ease. Recalling our earlier analysis of the text 'Passionnément' ['Passionately'], it is therefore noticeable that the poem extols the lapsus (understood as fault, slip or *faux pas* ['misstep']), whether in language ('lapsus linguae') or in life ('lapsus vitae'), as the privileged mechanism of individuation. Indeed, this may explain Luca's approach to that proverbial figure of ease, the fish in water. As he notes in a line from *L'Inventeur de l'amour* ['The inventor of love'] which displays his aversion to idiomatic reasoning, 'Mes mouvements / n'ont pas la grâce axiomatique / du poisson dans l'eau // du vautour et du tigre // ils paraissent désordonnés / comme tout ce qu'on voit / pour la première fois // Je suis obligé d'inventer / une façon de me déplacer / de respirer / d'exister' ['My movements / do not have the axiomatic grace / of fish in water // of the vulture and the tiger // they seem disordered / like everything we see / for the first time // I have to invent / a way to move / to breathe / to exist'].[62]

Théâtre de bouche (1987) and *La Proie s'ombre* (1991), I: 'le non-être généralisé'

In the extended citation from 'Comment s'en sortir sans sortir' ['How to get by without getting out'] above, it is noticeable that although the proverbial 'poisson dans l'eau' ['fish in water'] decomposes into the elements 'poids' ['weight'] and 'son' ['sound'], it is ultimately divested of both of these material attributes. Let us turn now to two late texts in our corpus which attest further in this way to the loosening grip on our cognitive operations of the category of being: *Théâtre de bouche* ['Mouth theatre'] and *La Proie s'ombre* ['Self-shadowing prey'].

The text *Théâtre de bouche*, dating from 1987, dramatises the agony of 'l'homme axiomatique' ['axiomatic man'] – namely, Oedipus, according to *L'Inventeur de l'amour*.[63] Adopting a format that is variously suggestive of the outline of a mathematical theorem, an administrative form, and a drama which illustrates a philosophical thesis, replete with dramatis personae, the prefatory text to the volume tracks the sexual intrigue and climax of 'l'homme axiomatique' followed by his collapse into errancy, and his eventual death:

Axiome :
l'homme

Thème :
l'homme axiomatique

Thèse :
l'extase vexée

Axe d'accès – ascèse – fixe :
X

X :
rixe à exiger et à exercer
Sexe à explorer à l'excès

Ile exilée
Dans exister

L’homme axiomatique
exanthématique
thématique
tic éthique

Le sexe l’exhale
l’exsude
l’extirpe
l’expulse

Le sexe l’exalte
l’excuse l’expose l’explose
le relaxe

L’homme créé :
à exécrer
à exaspérer
à exécuter

A expédier sur une orbite
exorbitée
Laissez-le errer errer
vers une action extrême

Excrément des éléments

L’homme :
axe d’un mot exténué
paralaxe
d’un monde exhibé
axiome à aérer
à recréer

Axe de l’homme :
le fantôme
la femme et l’homme
l’assomment
La flamme et l’ombre

l'appât et l'assaut
la partie sombre
d'une lame d'eau
et de couteau
il perd son ombre

Père excité
Expert du pire
Existe puis expire
Perplexité.[64]

[Axiom:
man

Theme:
axiomatic man

Thesis:
vexed ecstasy

Access axis – asceticism – fixed:
X

X:
necks to be wrecked and exercised
Sex to be explored to excess

exiled island
in existing

Axiomatic man
exanthematic
thematic
ethical tick

Sex exhales him
Exudes him
extirpates him
expels him

Sex exalts him
excuses him exposes him explodes him
relaxes him

Created man:
to be execrated
to be exasperated
to be executed

To be sent into orbit
out of orbit
Let him wander wander
towards extreme action

Excrement of the elements

Man:
axis of an exhausted word
parallax
of a world exhibited
axiom to be aerated
to be recreated

Axis of man:
the ghost
the woman and the man
knock him out
Flame and shadow
bait and assault
the dark part
of water's edge
and of knife edge
he loses his shadow

Excited father
Expert in the worst
Exists then expires
Perplexity.]

The 'm' phoneme at points supplies patterns of consonance within this piece, but above all it is the 'x' sound which is the shared property around which it pivots. Successive stanzas play on the possible associations of 'x', as an unknown quantity in algebra, or as an unknown or unspecified person or thing, but also as a mark of erasure. Just as many of the consonantal sequences incorporating the letter moreover feature the Latin/Greek prefix 'ex' ['out of'/'outside'/'outwards'], from 'exhale' to 'excès' ['excess'] to 'excrément' ['excrement'] to 'excité' ['excited'], the 'ex' of 'x' does not foretoken a shift into the extralinguistic, but a detaching of each semantic unit from the previous one, so that they remain external to each other. Thus, it is not just these individual signifiers that are effectively placed under the sign of 'x', but every signifier featuring in the poem, and indeed the entire system of signification to which they belong. As a manuscript note by Luca states: 'X […] INVOQUE / L'IMPLOSION D'ÊTRE / LE NON-ÊTRE GÉNÉRALISÉ' ['X […] INVOKES / THE IMPLOSION OF BEING / GENERALISED NON-BEING'].[65] In this way, 'x' arguably does not designate a value to be revealed but, rather, what the text dramatises is the collapsing of value itself, a paradigm which extends over the whole text, dissolving the distinctions between mutually exclusive entities.

While *Théâtre de bouche* attests in this way to a collapse of the operation of cognitive categories, of all Luca's collections it is arguably *La Proie s'ombre* ['Self-shadowing prey'] which most dramatically illustrates the above paradigm. *La Proie s'ombre* is a late collection by Luca whose title alludes both to the dictum 'lâcher la proie pour l'ombre' (conveying 'to give up what one has already got to go chasing after shadows') and, arguably, by extension also to a fable by La Fontaine which tells of a dog that drops its prey in order to vainly chase after its reflection in a lake.[66] Not least through its jarring linguistic form, Luca's title signals an evolution of the particular *morale* of the fable. As 'ombre' [shadow] passes over from noun to pronominal verb ('s'ombre'), a homophony effect emerges between that unusual verbal arrangement (as much a disruption as a construction) and the noun *sombre* which recalls the imaged or imagined quarry (and, at least momentarily also, the dog itself) which sinks into the river. Whereas La Fontaine's *morale* could be said to illustrate the way illusory aims distract us from the rewards already substantially within our grasp, the title of Luca's collection suggests that, in becoming its own reflection or shadow, the 'real' prey that we assume to lie within our possession is to all intents and purposes as much of an illusion as its imagined counterpart.

La Proie s'ombre takes as its point of a departure a text (La Fontaine's *Fables*) which can be characterised as a 'canonical work in the national patrimony, indeed a foundational text in the elaboration of French cultural identity',[67] as generations of French schoolchildren can attest. However, the various poems of which Luca's collection is composed can be read in part as casting suspicion on what we might term the patrimonial effects of proverbial wisdom. The fable and its associated figure of speech accomplish a function both domesticating and enracinating, attaching a particular disposition of being to a given linguistic territory and arguably stabilising linguistic usage in the process, as generations of speakers utter it in turn; they thus establish a sense of collective ownership of language. However, the first text from *La Proie s'ombre*, 'Le Tourbillon qui repose' ['The resting whirlwind'], sets out precisely to contest these functions, and to collapse the opposition of appearance and reality so integral to the moral of the fable mentioned above.

In 'Le Tourbillon qui repose', individual parts of speech or whole clauses are scattered across successive lines, thus conjuring up the rotating, vertically oriented movement of a whirlwind. From one line to the next, this whirlwind appears to be about to prompt a comparison with something else. However, as can be seen in the following excerpt, the reader's efforts to track these comparisons are continually blocked, as horizontal integration gives way to a bewildering form of vertical accumulation, clause upon clause, semblance upon semblance:

> Ce qui passe pour parfaitement immobile
> pousse ce qui semble curieusement ambulatoire
> à faire semblant d'être fixe sinon immuable
>
> Ainsi ce qui a l'air de s'arrêter malgré tout
> passe pour s'agiter follement autour
>
> Ce qui bouge ou pas dans un coin obscur
> de la pièce ou plutôt ce qui glisse
> entre les pas de ce qui bouge
> ou repose au beau milieu d'un tourbillon
> et surtout le mobile qui a l'air
> de foncer par petits bonds immobiles
> au-dessus
> font semblant d'être parfaitement
> ce qui a l'air d'être
> curieusement ambulatoire
> et avec ce qui fait semblant de passer
> pour ce qui fait semblant d'être
> fixe sinon immuable
> poussent ce qui est parfaitement immobile
> à se faire passer pour
> ce qui pousse à faire semblant
> de passer pour curieusement ambulatoire[68]
>
> [What passes for perfectly still
> pushes what seems curiously ambulatory
> to pretend to be fixed or unmoving

So what seems to stop despite everything
passes for shaking madly around

What moves or not in a dark corner
of the room or rather what slides
between the steps of what moves
or rests right in the middle of a whirlwind
and especially the mobile that seems
to dash along in little motionless leaps
above
pretend to be perfectly
what seems to be
curiously ambulatory
and with what pretends to pass
for what pretends to be
fixed or unmoving
push what is perfectly still
to pretend to pass for
what pushes it to pretend
to pass for curiously ambulatory]

From the first indefinite relative pronoun, which is echoed several times in these opening lines, with each subsequent clause, reality and appearance become entangled in ever more absurd relations ('ce qui fait semblant de passer / pour ce qui fait semblant d'être' ['what pretends to pass / for what pretends to be']). Motion offers the illusion of stasis, while stasis passes itself off as motion. The paradoxical 'petits bonds immobiles' ['little motionless leaps'] conveys that it is futile to imagine this vortex as an entity that moves from one point to another, since through pure centrifugal force, it comes to liquidate origins and throw into confusion the very markers of any supposed progression through space. The titular 'repose' here might be understood thus by way of this paradoxical non-movement, which does not equate to staying in one place, but evokes estrangement from movement and space as categories of understanding.

In this way, it is not so much that the poem signals that it is difficult to establish conceptual distinctions; distinction itself as an epistemological horizon is under threat. The 'tourbillon qui repose / au beau milieu du malgré tout' ['whirlwind that rests / right in the middle of the despite everything'][69] seems ultimately to allude to a resoundingly contrarian, self-destructive impulse that lurks within words (here, *within* the contrastive expression 'malgré tout' ['despite everything']), disturbing or displacing dominant or totalising constructions as well as the drive to particularise. The chaos solicited by the whirlwind's passage is that of a violence done to language itself, and, literally in some cases, to its constituent parts of speech, which, it is suggested, can be brandished in menacing gestures: 'ce qui agite follement le surtout / surtout le surtout-pas du mobile' ['what shakes madly the especially / the hardly of the mobile'].[70] With the exception of a few figures such as a 'mobile', a 'coin' ['corner'] and a 'puits' ['well'], barely anything retains the precision of a detail in this poem, and one of the few such nouns, 'bougie' ['candle'], evolves into an inflection of the verb 'bouger' ['to move']. It would seem that such parts of speech are thus no longer stable categories in themselves but leach into each other, introducing a creeping semantic slippage:

> mais chaque bougie en chacun
> chaque coin qui bouge en chacun
> fait semblant de nous glisser entre les pas
> de chacun
> non pas de glisser en chacun[71]
>
> [but each candle in each one
> each corner that moves in each one
> seems to slip between the steps
> of each one
> not to slip into each one]

As Dominique Carlat writes, one of the primary concerns of the poem is 'cette expérience subjective d'un rythme qui permet de dépasser les contradictions habituellement tenues pour immuables par la logique formelle' ['this subjective experience of a rhythm which surpasses those contradictions that formal logic usually takes to be perennial'],[72] and the reader is indeed struck by the recurrence of 'ce qui' and other forms of repetition ('à dépasser' … 'à dépasser' … 'de n'être' … 'de naître' ['to surpass' … 'to surpass' … 'to be' … 'to be born'])[73] and chiasmus ('chaque être qui bouge dans un coin / chaque coin qui bouge dans un être' ['every being that moves in a corner / every corner that moves in a being']).[74] Taking this point further, in a recording of this text,[75] in the line 'non pas de glisser en chacun' ['not to slip into each one'], Luca tellingly places particular stress on the pronoun 'en' ['in'/'into']. The kind of *glissement* [slippage] evoked in this excerpt is thus not that of a passage from an outside to an inside, the one remaining exclusive of the other, but one which resonates in the margins of any one subject position; it neither has the regularity of a step, nor is available to rational understanding as movement.

La Proie s'ombre (1991), II: anti-thought incarnate

Staging, as Michael G. Kelly writes, 'an obsessive circling in and around the phenomenon of thought itself',[76] another poem from *La Proie s'ombre*, 'Vers le non-mental' ['Towards the non-mental'], explores the efforts of thought as it strains to apprehend itself. And yet these very efforts are self-defeating, since, for Luca, to think upon thought is to repeatedly block, or introduce bewildering circularity into, that most fundamental of cognitive operations: comparison. In its third stanza, the text alights on the figure of the 'table tournante' ['turning table']:

> En tournant
> non pas comme une table
> ou du moins pas encore
> la pensée tourne sur elle-même
> avec une frénésie statique
>
> Comparable au ver de terre
> sous un haut talon
> et non pas au verre d'eau
> sur une table tournante[77]
>
> [While turning
> not like a table
> or at least not yet
> thought turns on itself
> with a static frenzy
>
> Comparable to the earthworm
> under a high heel
> and not to the glass of water
> on a turning table]

The 'table tournante' ['turning table'] recalls a practice associated with the spiritualist séance, in which participants seated around a table make contact with the spirit world. As the letters of the alphabet are called out, sudden tilts of the table enable those present to spell out a message from a spirit.[78] If a comparison based on a transition from spirit to matter is invoked here, only to be cast aside, it suggests that so too is a conception that sees thought as an absence brought to presence: 'La pensée n'est donc pas encore / comparable à l'ombre / qui tourne autour d'une table /

tournante' ['Thought is not yet / comparable to the shadow / which turns around a turning / table']. Shifting sylleptically away from the 'verre d'eau' ['glass of water'] which conjures up the spiritualist context, thought is instead allied once more with the figure of the 'ver de terre' ['earthworm'], now encircling a corpse on which it will presumably feast:

> Elle tourne autour
> d'un ver de terre qui tourne
> autour d'un corps
> qui retourne au ver de terre
> et à la terre qui tourne[79]
>
> [It turns around
> an earthworm that turns
> around a body
> that returns to the earth worm
> and to the earth that turns]

Though worm and body here offer a metaphor of decomposition, it seems unlikely that the metaphor is intended to figure the efforts of a thought directed towards a given object. This is because, in hallucinatory style, the poem's repeated slippages (from 'vers' ['towards'] to 'ver' ['worm'] to 'verre' ['glass']; from 'tête' ['head'] to 'tempête' ['storm']) hint at the very failure of thought to constitute in any durable sense any one 'thing' to which it is positively external. Disintegration in this poem seems operative instead to characterise what is a suspicion cast on thought's signature operations as they manifest themselves in language (most noticeably comparison), on the axiomatic modes which characterise it ('Elle nie la vérité tournante / de la terre' ['It denies the turning truth / of the earth']) and (in a key instance of 'négation de la négation' ['negation of negation']) on the binaries that sustain it. Thus, as part of this undermining of propositional logic, in the final lines, thought is compared to 'l'ombre d'un doute' ['the shadow of a doubt']:

> […] plutôt à la frénésie statique
> De l'ombre d'un doute
>
> Qui tourne encore dans sa tête
> Et qui tourne mal
> Comme tout ce qui tourne

Autour du bien et du mal
Avec un mal de tête comparable
A la frénésie statique d'une pensée
Comparable à l'incomparable[80]

[[...] rather to the static frenzy
Of the shadow of a doubt

That still turns over and over in one's mind
And that goes awry
Like everything that revolves
Around good and evil
With a headache comparable
To the static frenzy of a thought
Comparable to the incomparable]

The drama of 'Vers le non-mental', which is that of thought's failure to constitute an object from which it is positively external, is underscored by the following citation from Luca's manuscripts:

> Je crois savoir que ma poésie se situe un peu en marge de la pensée et qu'elle tend de plus en plus vers son antipode, vers cet anti-pensée incarnée qu'on appelle objet tel un objet dont la « pensée » est odeur ou rayon, ma pensée serait-elle l'émanation opaque d'un mental voué aux pires sabotages.[81]
>
> [I understand that my poetry is slightly on the fringes of thought and that it tends more and more towards its exact opposite, towards that anti-thought incarnate that is known as an object, such as an object whose 'thought' is the odour or light ray, my thought would thus be the opaque emanation of a mind devoted to the worst kind of sabotage.]

Insisting on poetry's position within a domain poles apart from that of rationality, Luca underscores the deleterious effects of the former on the latter and elevates the particulate, non-objectified motifs of the odour or the light ray as its privileged images.

Just as 'Vers le non-mental' bespeaks the difficulties of rational thought in apprehending its object, 'La Forêt' ['The forest'], a later text from *La Proie s'ombre*, also takes up this theme. Much as the title of the collection involves a play on the figurative expression 'lâcher la proie pour l'ombre', this poem seems to decompose the constituent parts of the expression 'c'est l'arbre qui cache la forêt' (equivalent to the English saying 'you can't see the wood for the trees'), which alludes to a failure to achieve objectivity. While the poem's setting is that of the forest, its primary concern is with language genesis. Throughout this text, successive strophes offer a phonological decomposition of the component parts of the expression ('forêt' ('orée') / 'arbre' ('br') ['forest' ('edge') / 'tree']) and other terms from the same lexical field of organic nature ('branche', 'terre' ['branch', 'earth']):

> La forêt pendue à l'arbre
> cache l'arbre au pendu
> et le pendu dans l'arbre
>
> […]
>
> Au cœur du mot ARBRE
> la tête du mot BRANCHE
> tranchée[82]
>
> [The forest hanging from the tree
> hides the tree from the hanged man
> and the hanged man in the tree
>
> […]
>
> At the heart of the word TREE
> the head of the word BRANCH
> severed]

Now, it is worth recalling that organic metaphors of trees, branches and stems figure often in the stories told about the origin of language. They feature in the field of historical linguistics, as, for instance, in the arboreal models of the relation between language systems and their common origin in Proto-Indo-European developed by the German comparative linguist August Schleicher (1821–68). Explanatory schemas of this type which draw on such organic motifs can serve a legitimising ideological function based on nationalist or ethnolinguistic concerns, as Thomas Bonfiglio argues in his study *Mother Tongues and Nations: The invention of the native speaker*. Discussing the work of the Swiss Romantic-era linguist Adolphe Pictet (1799–1875), Bonfiglio notes that such natural or botanic motifs offered 'a framework for understanding and enracinating humans and their language'.[83] In 'La Forêt', Luca, that herald of the 'no-man's langue', whose adopted name pays homage to an 'emeritus linguist',[84] seems in many ways alert to the particular valence of the arboreal metaphor in his poem's account of the origins of language:

> Pendue à la plus haute branche
> la forêt originelle
> tire sa langue originale
> de ses *C*RIMES sans initiale[85]
>
> [Hanging from the highest branch
> the primeval forest
> bases its original language
> on its *C*RHYMES without initials]

In this excerpt, it is noticeable that the line '*C*RIMES sans initiale' ['*C*RHYMES without initials'] foreshadows a final poem in *La Proie s'ombre* which enumerates a long list of ideologies and doctrines all identifiable by the fact that they share the same 'isme' ['ism'] suffix.[86] In the context of the approach to language's genesis in 'La Forêt', it would appear that the suggestion is that it is from this collected pool of doctrines and ideologies that the 'langue originale' ['original language'] notionally draws its source. However, in a gesture at odds with a positivistic vision of language as arboreal entity, Luca inverts the customary paradigm of enracination and the implied organic continuity of tree to branch. A recurrent pattern across the piece is thus that of hanging or decapitation: the linguistic events at issue here are captured in instances of phonemic truncation, rather than in those images of organic descent usually associated with such arboreal motifs:

> Loin de tomber au pied du mot AR*B*RE
> la tête du mot *B*RANCHE monte
>
> La tête du mot *B*RANCHE
> monte à la tête du mot AR*B*RE
> et le BARRE[87]
>
> [Far from falling at the foot of the word TREE
> the head of the word BRANCH rises

The head of the word BRANCH
rises to the head of the word TREE
and strikes it out]

Here, the gesture of blocking signals an assault on the forms of genealogical continuity and the biological metaphors which support them. Indeed, a culminating image later in the text is an anti-hereditarian and anti-authoritarian one: that of a regicide ('le mot *PROIE* sans queue ni tête / tue le mot ROI dans son âme et son corps' ['headless and tailless, the word PREY / kills the word KING in body and soul']).[88]

'La Forêt' has much in common with Luca's notebooks which are held at the Bibliothèque littéraire Jacques Doucet. These often follow the same pattern of composition and display a similarly pulsating intensity. One of the most striking features of the poem is the repetition of strophes: these accumulate in a pulsating, constantly building, forward-moving surge of verbal matter that comes to cram successive pages and brings to mind the incantatory quality of the poet's spoken performances. As those performances reveal, Luca's compositions are characterised by the elaboration of a seemingly unbroken phonetic sequence whose internal displacements bring about a transformation of an entire semantic field. The closing section of this chapter will now consider the significance of this motif for Luca's project.

Conclusion: becoming postmonolingual

Through the readings proposed over the preceding pages, a series of elements of Luca's poetics as they are manifest in different collections have become apparent. To encounter a poem by Luca is to bear witness to a condition of weakening which advances across the whole edifice of language. This weakening is progressive and fundamentally deleterious. Its targets include the habitual order of syntax, the mutual exclusivity of parts of speech and the entities they designate, and forms of reasoning based on idioms or other figures of speech. Underlying it is a critique of the inherently identitarian or patrimonial function which such linguistic features support, but more broadly, through it, Luca casts suspicion on language's instituted forms, and notably their authority to authenticate that which *is*. The nature of this weakening is such that its progression cannot so much be traced, in a linear fashion, from one point to the next. Rather, it is triggered at multiple, discrete sites, invoking something that happens *to* language, and to its minute constituent matter: in such and such a phoneme, here, or suffix or other semantic particle, there.

In a 1958 letter to the Argentinian poet Tilo Wenner, who had requested to translate some of his work, Luca describes 'le déroulement physique du langage' as a central preoccupation of his poetry:

> Comme le déroulement physique du langage occupe dans mes poèmes une place centrale, je vous demanderai d'accompagner votre traduction de sa version originale. Ce n'est pas une préoccupation d'ordre « esthétique » qui me dicte cette exigéance [*sic*] (vous pensez bien que la littérature constitue le dernier de mes soucis), l'écriture n'étant pour moi que le « support » – dans le sens alchimique du terme – d'une démarche analogue à la kabbale (une kabbale anarchique et athée, bien sûr, mais non moins rigoureuse que celle des mystiques du moyen-âge), chaque incursion dans la structure intime du mot devant marquer la transgression concrète d'un obstacle intérieur et l'ouverture d'une porte dans mon esprit.[89]
>
> [As the physical progression of language occupies a central place in my poems, I would ask you to include the original text with your translation. It is not an 'aesthetic' concern that dictates this requirement (you can imagine that literature is the last of my concerns), writing being for me only the 'base' – in the alchemical sense of the term – for a process analogous to Kabbalah (an anarchic and atheistic Kabbalah, of course, but no less rigorous than that of the mystics of the Middle Ages), each foray into the intimate structure of the word marking the concrete transgression of an inner obstacle and the opening of a door in my mind.]

Luca, it should be noted, explains that his requirement that Wenner include the source text in his proposed translation is not motivated by a desire to preserve the work's aesthetic value; as this chapter has shown at multiple junctures, the poet's approach consists in a radical subversion of value itself (aesthetic or otherwise) and the stabilising function which it accomplishes across a text. Thus, the formula 'le déroulement physique du langage' ['the physical progression/uncoiling of language'] adopted by the poet is a useful one in this context, since it invokes a kind of displacement at work multiply and simultaneously, one that liquidates the markers of its own progression, rather like a ripple moving across water. If we emphasise this motif here, it is precisely because Luca himself does so. For if Luca's compositions subvert the operation of motifs such as that of the tree which imply genealogical continuity, it is all the more noticeable that the poet embraces the vibratory, non-organic, non-terrestrial paradigm of the wave.[90] Non-static and ephemeral, the wave poses a challenge to cognitive appropriation, as the poem 'La Question' ['The question'] intimates: 'Les ondes vides / quêtent pénètrent et sondent / l'être du vide / que le vide même féconde' ['The empty waves / seek out penetrate and probe / the being of the void / that the void itself enriches'].[91]

In the opening pages of this chapter, we considered the poet's intended *glissement* [slippage] from the English expression 'no man's land' to 'no man's langue'. The shift from 'land' to 'language', and thus away from the grounding and enracinating connotations of 'land', also helps to illuminate Luca's subsequent embrace of the subatomic, particulate motif of the light or sound wave, a figure materially transformed by its own action and inseparable from that action. Through the motif of the wave, the voice exceeds itself, speaking always from somewhere other than where it last spoke. An excerpt from a manuscript entitled 'Commentaires de Ghérasim Luca sur *Autres secrets du vide et du plein*' ['Commentaries by Ghérasim Luca on *Other secrets of the void and the full*'] affirms the wave's cardinal significance for Luca: 'Je parcours aujourd'hui une étendue où le vacarme et le silence s'entrechoquent, où le poème prend la forme de l'onde qui l'a mis en marche' ['Today I walk through an expanse where commotion and silence collide, where the poem takes the form of the wave that set it in motion'].[92]

Such a formula invites the reader to consider the peculiar status of poetry for Luca. At some level, it speaks to his embrace of the vibratory energies of oral performance, and thus to poetry's departure from the textual support of the book. In this respect, Luca's approach is in significant ways distinct from a conception of poetic activity beginning with Mallarmé – and continuing through the work of Jabès – which allies the poetic with its *aboutissement dans le livre* [culmination in the book]. Such a shift in Luca's work designates not just a move beyond the printed, bound volume. Leaving behind the conventionality of text for the contingency of spoken performance and the 'improper' accidents of orality, it also bespeaks a distancing from the values of the written and a liberation of that which the instituted forms of language suppress in their progression towards lexical/semantic stability and discursive rationality.

A case in point is the short humorous text 'Au procès des assonances' ['At the trial of the assonances']:[93] this poem relates the appearance before a tribunal of 'dix-neuf jeunes assonances' ['nineteen young assonances'].[94] The indicted 'redoutables pourfendeurs d'Empire' ['fearsome scourges of the Empire'][95] are 'accusées de complot contre le langage' ['accused of conspiracy against language'].[96] The prosecution is composed of philologists, etymologists, and a linguist who demands the heads of the accused 'afin que le Glossaire / le Dictionnaire et le Nomenclature / soient sauvegardés' ['in order that the Glossary / the Dictionary and the Nomenclature / be safeguarded'].[97] The various branches of the formal study of language, with their declension of functions and technical nomenclature, engage in a kind of quasi-judicial 'gatekeeping' of the uses of the word. In a telling instance of one of the key dialectical oppositions that motivate Luca's work, here, assonance, that feature of poetic language based on chance resemblance of sound, is cast as a dangerous affront to the values of the written as embodied by the institution of linguistics. Ultimately more comfortable to qualify his practice not as poetry, but as what he terms *ontophonie*,[98] in Luca's work originary *logos* is pulverised in a radically disseminatory phonesis, a making of sounds at the limits of sense and language, one exempted from the demands and responsibilities attached to the mother tongue.

Luca's work is, as Jean-Christophe Bailly writes, an attempt to 'atteindre à la conscience de soi de la langue, soit la poésie définie comme cette conscience' ['reach language's own awareness of itself, or poetry defined as that self-awareness'].[99] Taking this perspective further, his work offers us the spectacle of a language at the moment of its 'becoming postmonolingual', to return to a concept introduced by Yasemin Yildiz. This is not in the sense that his poetry or *ontophonie* signals its porosity to other established idioms, but rather that it exposes language's own internal porosities, its capacity to produce reflexively contrasting meanings and the kind of intended complications peculiar to *La Proie s'ombre* and other collections that disturb monolingual serenity. Via an inimitable pursuit of a 'langue dans la langue' ['language within language'], Luca's texts set out to subvert the authority that accrues to a language's privileged utterances and to shatter convictions in the exclusive authority or self-sufficiency of the *langue propre*. By unsettling the particular totalising force that any instituted language assumes in respect of those who use it (whether by birth or adoption), it is our contention that the stateless poet offers a way for thinking postmonolingually.

Notes

1 Ghérasim Luca, *Héros-limite suivi de Le Chant de la carpe et de Paralipomènes*, pref. by André Velter (Paris: Gallimard, 2001), 217.

2 This excerpt from a preparatory notebook for the work *Apostroph'Apocalypse* is quoted in: Dominique Carlat, *Gherasim Luca l'intempestif* (Paris: José Corti, 1998), 253.

3 Yasemin Yildiz, *Beyond the Mother Tongue: The postmonolingual condition* (New York: Fordham University Press, 2012), 9.
4 Yildiz, *Beyond the Mother Tongue*, 251.
5 Ghérasim Luca, *Un loup à travers une loupe* (Paris: José Corti, 1998), 70. The text was first published in Romanian: Gherasim Luca, *Un lup văzut printr-o lupă* (Bucharest: Negatia Negatiei, 1945).
6 Jean-Jacques Rousseau, *Œuvres complètes*, ed. by Louis Barré (Paris: J. Bry aîné, 1856–7), 9: 247.
7 Antoine de Rivarol, *Œuvres choisies,* pref. by M. de Lescure (Paris: Librairie des Bibliophiles / E. Flammarion, successeur, 1880), 1: 44.
8 Rivarol, *Œuvres choisies*, 43.
9 Krzysztof Fijalkowski, 'Ghérasim Luca : « le désir désiré »'. In *« Infra-noir », un et multiple : un groupe surréaliste entre Bucarest et Paris, 1945–1947*, ed. by Monique Yaari (Oxford: Peter Lang, 2014), 48.
10 Or 'Solman', or indeed 'Zolman' according to various spellings of this first name. The poet was also known by those familiar to him as 'Zola'.
11 Or 'Loker', according to a text relating the decision of the Romanian department of justice concerning his change of name. That document, as well as the poet's correspondence, manuscripts and other papers are held at the Bibliothèque littéraire Jacques Doucet, Paris (henceforth 'BLJD') in the Fonds Ghérasim Luca ('GHL'). See BLJD, GHL, PP 1. Further references to Luca's manuscripts will take the following form: BLJD, GHL, PP 1.
12 See: Carlat, *Gherasim Luca l'intempestif*, 41. In a notebook from 1962, Luca recalls that: 'MON NOM VIENT DU MONT ATHOS, L'ARCHIMANDRITE D'UN CLOÎTRE PHONÉTIQUE LE PORTAIT AVANT MOI ET C'EST BARANGA CE JUIF-GOÏ QUI, VERS L'ÂGE DE 16 ANS, ME L'AVAIT SUBITEMENT PROPOSÉ' ['MY NAME COMES FROM MOUNT ATHOS, THE ARCHIMANDRITE OF A PHONETIC CLOISTER CARRIED IT BEFORE ME AND IT WAS BARANGA THAT JEW-GOY WHO SUDDENLY SUGGESTED IT TO ME AT THE AGE OF 16']. BLJD, GHL, MS 188.
13 For some commentary on the adoption of pseudonyms by Luca's contemporaries, see: Petre Raileanu, *Gherasim Luca* (Paris: Oxus, 2004), 17.
14 Ghérasim Luca and Dolfi Trost, *Dialectique de la dialectique: message adressé au mouvement surréaliste international* (Bucharest: Slova, 1945).
15 See: Krzysztof Fijalkowski, 'Ghérasim Luca : « le désir désiré »', in *« Infra-noir », un et multiple : un groupe surréaliste entre Bucarest et Paris, 1945–1947*, ed. by Monique Yaari (Oxford: Peter Lang, 2014), 47–100; Iulian Toma, *Gherasim Luca ou l'intransigeante passion d'être*, pref. by Jacqueline Chénieux-Gendron (Paris: Honoré Champion, 2012); Yannick Torlini, *Ghérasim Luca, le poète de la voix: ontologie et érotisme* (Paris: L'Harmattan, 2011).
16 Denis Lejeune, *The Radical Use of Chance in 20th Century Art* (Amsterdam and New York: Rodopi, 2012), 114.
17 Stephen Forcer, *Dada as Text, Thought and Theory* (Oxford: Legenda, 2015), 48.
18 Luca and Trost, *Dialectique de la dialectique*, 13–14.
19 'La position du frère-père, maintenue dans l'inconscient du prolétariat, retient celui-ci dans un esclavage envers lui-même et lui fait conserver les déformations provenant de la nature et de l'économie capitaliste' ['The position of the brother-father, which the proletariat retains in its subconscious, keeps it enslaved to itself and maintains it in a deformed state as dictated by nature and the capitalist economy']. Luca and Trost, *Dialectique de la dialectique*, 22.
20 Luca and Trost, *Dialectique de la dialectique*, 23.
21 Luca and Trost, *Dialectique de la dialectique*, 23.
22 Thierry Garrel, 'Je me souviens de Ghérasim Luca', *Europe* 1045 (May 2016): 36.
23 BLJD, GHL, MS 54.
24 I have not discovered any references to Luca's anti-Hitlerian articles, although for a discussion of the poet's journalism in this period, see: Marta Petreu, 'Les idées politiques de Gherasim Luca dans sa période roumaine', *Synergies Roumanie* 2 (2007): 57–64.
25 BLJD, GHL, MS 54.
26 Luca, *Héros-limite*, 261.
27 Luca, *Héros-limite*, 206.
28 For a record of such performances, see in particular the following documentary: *Comment s'en sortir sans sortir*, dir. by Raoul Sangla, Éditions Corti, 2008, DVD, ISBN 336-3-310000-02-1.
29 BLJD, GHL, MS 188.

30 BLJD, GHL, MS 103.
31 Quoted in: Carlat, *Gherasim Luca l'intempestif*, 251.
32 Garrel, 'Je me souviens de Ghérasim Luca', 32.
33 Michel Deguy describes losing his bearings late at night in New York with Luca during a trip to the city: 'Tout *Polyphonix* échoua down town ...'. Michel Deguy, *Brevets* (Seyssel: Champ Vallon, 1986), 13.
34 Garrel, 'Je me souviens de Ghérasim Luca', 40.
35 Garrel, 'Je me souviens de Ghérasim Luca', 31.
36 Gherasim Luca, *Inventatorul iubirii: urmat de Parcurg imposibilul și de Moartea moartă* (Bucharest: Editura Negația Negației, 1945), 13.
37 Ghérasim Luca, *L'Inventeur de l'amour* suivi de *La Mort morte* (Paris: José Corti, 1994).
38 Michael G. Kelly, 'Poetic utterance and the cosmopolitan indisposition: on Ghérasim Luca'. In *The Cause of Cosmopolitanism: Dispositions, models, transformations*, ed. by Patrick O'Donovan and Laura Rascaroli (Bern: Peter Lang, 2011), 282.
39 Ghérasim Luca, 'Cubomanies et objets', *Supérieur inconnu* 5 (October–November 1996), 97.
40 'Utilisant des procédés pathologiques (échographie, stéréotypie), et mettant à la portée du fonctionnement réel de la pensée des appareils mécaniques, tels le pantographe et la machine à couper le papier (la pantographie, la cubomanie), nous essayons de surmonter la froideur de la causalité universelle' ['Using pathological procedures (such as ultrasound and stereotypy), and making mechanical devices, such as pantographs and paper cutting machines (pantography, cubomania), accessible to the true functioning of thought, we try to overcome the coldness of universal causality']. Luca and Trost, *Dialectique de la dialectique,* 28. While the various *procédés* listed here are offered as means to thwart the functioning of causal reasoning, in his later work, the form of Luca's frontal assault on the principle of causality is primarily linguistic: 'L'effet est fête / faute hâte / écho et cause' ['The effect is feast / fault haste / echo fault and cause']. See: 'La Paupière philosophale', Luca, *Héros-limite*, 102.
41 Ghérasim Luca, *Le Vampire passif, avec une introduction sur l'objet objectivement offert, un portrait trouvé et dix-sept illustrations* (Bucharest: Éditions de l'Oubli, 1945; repr. Paris: José Corti, 2001), 67.
42 Laura Erber, 'No man's langue: rethinking language with Ghérasim Luca'. In *Socioaesthetics: Ambience – imaginary*, ed. by Anders Michelsen and Frederik Tygstrup (Boston: Brill, 2015), 103. As Carlat similarly argues, 'La langue de l'apatride tente d'échapper aux structures linguistiques instituées – les langues nationales comme institutions et critères d'appartenance à une *patrie*' ['The language of the stateless person tries to escape established linguistic structures – national languages as institutions and criteria for belonging to a *fatherland*']. Carlat, *Gherasim Luca l'intempestif*, 252.
43 Sarane Alexandrian, 'Le Poète sans repartir: jamais plus ici, toujours là', *Supérieur inconnu* 5 (October–November 1996), 74.
44 Jean-Christophe Bailly, *Piotr Kowalski* (Paris: Fernand Hazan, 1988), 71.
45 'Nous franchissons un corridor, traversons un pont, inventons une forêt : la langue étrangère qui s'égare dans ma bouche, alors que sous une averse de feuilles et de larmes nous courons enlacés à la rencontre du premier abîme venu, a le goût indéchiffrable de l'air que seul le vide des gouffres émane' ['We cross a corridor, cross a bridge, invent a forest: the foreign language which goes astray in my mouth, while we run arm in arm under a shower of leaves and tears to meet the first abyss, has the indecipherable taste of the air that emanates only from the voids of the abyss']. Luca, *Un loup à travers une loupe*, 31.
46 Luca, *Héros-limite*, 169–71.
47 Gilles Deleuze and Claire Parnet, *Dialogues* (Paris: Flammarion, 1977), 10.
48 Michael G. Kelly, 'Poetic utterance and the cosmopolitan indisposition', 291.
49 Luca, *Héros-limite*, 264.
50 BLJD, GHL, MS 188.
51 Luca, *Héros-limite*, 203–4.
52 Luca, *Héros-limite*, 211.
53 Paul Éluard, *Œuvres complètes*, I (Paris: Gallimard, 1968), 713–14.
54 Luca, *Héros-limite*, 213.
55 'Le terme de poésie, qui s'applique aux formes les moins dégradées, les moins intellectualisées de l'expression d'un état de perte, peut être considérée comme synonyme de dépense : il signifie, en effet, de la façon la plus précise, création au moyen de la perte' ['The term poetry, which applies to the least degraded, the least intellectualised forms of the expression of a state

of loss, can be considered as synonymous with expenditure: it means, in fact, in the most precise way, creation through loss']. Georges Bataille, *Œuvres complètes*, 10 vols. (Paris: Gallimard, 1970), I: 307.

56 Sibylle Orlandi, 'Gherasim Luca, Paul Celan: un au-delà de la langue dans la langue ?', *TRANS-* 17 (2014), accessed 22 January 2021, https://doi.org/10.4000/trans.890.

57 Luca, *Héros-limite*, 263.

58 Sami Sjöberg, 'An other transnationalism: Romanian Jewish emigrants in Francophone avant-garde literature', *French Studies*, 73.1 (January 2019), 37. See also: Tom Sandqvist, *Dada East: The Romanians of Cabaret Voltaire* (London: MIT Press, 2006).

59 BLJD, GHL, MS 188.

60 BLJD, GHL, MS 187.

61 See the 'antique / rite de vérité' of *Théâtre de bouche*: Ghérasim Luca, *Théâtre de bouche* (Paris: José Corti, 1987), 46.

62 Luca, *L'Inventeur de l'amour*, 9.

63 Luca, *L'Inventeur de l'amour*, 13.

64 Luca, *Théâtre de bouche*, 7–10.

65 BLJD, GHL, MS 184.

66 'Chacun se trompe ici-bas. / On voit courir après l'ombre / Tant de fous, qu'on n'en sait pas / La plupart du temps le nombre. / Au Chien dont parle Esope il faut les renvoyer. / Ce Chien, voyant sa proie en l'eau représentée, / La quitta pour l'image, et pensa se noyer ; / La rivière devint tout d'un coup agitée. / À toute peine il regagna les bords, / Et n'eut ni l'ombre ni le corps' ['We deceive ourselves in this world; / We see so many fools chasing after shadows / So many are there that often, / We can rarely count the number. / Refer them back to the dog of which Aesop speaks. / This dog, seeing the reflection of his prey in the water, / Let go of it for its image and nearly drowned himself. / The river became astir / And the dog barely made it back to the bank, / Having lost both the shadow and the prey']. La Fontaine, *Œuvres complètes*, 2 vols. (Paris: Gallimard, 1954), I: 145.

67 Ralph Albanese Jr., 'La Fontaine and the teaching of Frenchness'. In *The Shape of Change: Essays in early modern literature and La Fontaine in honor of David Lee Rubin* (Amsterdam: Rodopi/Brill, 2002), 315.

68 Ghérasim Luca, *La Proie s'ombre* (Paris: José Corti, 1991), 16–17.

69 Luca, *La Proie s'ombre*, 21.

70 Luca, *La Proie s'ombre*, 23.

71 Luca, *La Proie s'ombre*, 19–20.

72 Carlat, *Gherasim Luca l'intempestif*, 241.

73 Luca, *La Proie s'ombre*, 18.

74 Luca, *La Proie s'ombre*, 19.

75 Ghérasim Luca, *Ghérasim Luca par Ghérasim Luca*, double audio CD, ed. by Nadèjda and Thierry Garrel, José Corti, 2002.

76 Michael G. Kelly, 'A voice from the shadows', *Berlin Review of Books*, May 2013, accessed 22 January 2021, http://berlinbooks.org/brb/2013/05/a-voice-from-the-shadows/.

77 Luca, *La Proie s'ombre*, 33.

78 In this connection, handwritten notes at the Bibliothèque littéraire Jacques Doucet (BLJD, GHL, MS 185) show Luca to have been a close reader of esoteric and alchemical sources such as the following: Oswald Wirth, *Le Symbolisme hermétique dans ses rapports avec l'alchimie et la franc-maçonnerie* (Paris: Librairie initiatique, 1909); René Alleau, *Aspects de l'alchimie traditionnelle* (Paris: Éditions de Minuit, 1953); Serge Hutin, *Les Sociétés secrètes* (Paris: Presses universitaires de France, 1954). The poet's interest in such sources is elsewhere reflected in the volume *La Paupière philosophale* (Paris: Corti, 2016).

79 Luca, *La Proie s'ombre*, 34.

80 Luca, *La Proie s'ombre*, 37.

81 BLJD, GHL, MS 218.

82 Luca, *La Proie s'ombre*, 61.

83 Thomas Paul Bonfiglio, *Mother Tongues and Nations: The invention of the native speaker* (New York: Walter de Gruyter, 2010), 159.

84 As Carlat asks, 'Quelle science linguistique évoque-t-on lorsque, dans les années trente, l'on qualifie une personnalité de « linguiste émerite » ? Sont essentiellement retenus le savoir positif, la connaissance de l'histoire des langues, de leur filiation, de leur contexte géographique et national' ['What kind of linguistics is one talking about when, in the thirties, one labels a

significant person as an "emeritus linguist"? This essentially refers to positive knowledge, knowledge of the history of languages, their lines of descent and their geographic and national context']. Carlat, *Gherasim Luca l'intempestif*, 42.

85 Luca, *La Proie s'ombre*, 65.

86 For instance: 'Animisme / atomisme / conformisme / dynamisme / euphémisme / islamisme'. Luca, *La Proie s'ombre*, 95.

87 Luca, *La Proie s'ombre*, 65.

88 Luca, *La Proie s'ombre*, 71.

89 Letter to Tilo Wenner, 13 June 1958, BLJD, GHL, Correspondence.

90 In a further letter to the Argentinian author Julio Llinás on 29 March 1960, Luca elaborates on the significance of the sound wave for his poetic practice, underscoring its supposed dermatological and neurological effects on the reader: 'L'onde sonore qui traverse le langage porte dans la structure de son frissonnement une idéation capable de fracasser les pires résistances au « message » : en agissant directement sur la peau du lecteur et le système nerveux qui l'habille, l'échange « mental » englobe une grande partie de sa participation corporelle' ['The sound wave that traverses language contains within its rippling structure a way of forming ideas that is capable of shattering the worst varieties of resistance to the "message": by acting directly on the reader's skin and the surrounding nervous system, "mental" exchange accounts for a large part of his physical participation']. Letter to Julio Llinás, 29 March 1960, BLJD, GHL, Correspondence.

91 Luca, *Héros-limite*, 227.

92 BLJD, GHL, MS 42.

93 Ghérasim Luca, 'Au Procès des assonances', *Cahiers de la bibliothèque littéraire Jacques Doucet*, 2 (1998), 97–104.

94 Luca, 'Au Procès des assonances', 99.

95 Luca, 'Au Procès des assonances', 102.

96 Luca, 'Au Procès des assonances', 99.

97 Luca, 'Au Procès des assonances', 102.

98 The poet notes that 'le terme même de poésie me semble confus, je préfère peut-être celui d'ontophonie. Celui qui ouvre le mot ouvre la matière, et le mot n'est que le support matériel d'une quête qui a la transmutation du réel pour fin' ['The very term poetry seems confused to me, I prefer that of ontophony. The one who opens up the word opens up matter, and the word is simply the material basis for a quest aimed at the transmutation of the real']. Gherasim Luca, 'Interview' (by Serge Bricianer), *Oiseau-tempête*, 4 (Winter 1998), 32.

99 Jean-Christophe Bailly, *Piotr Kowalski* (Paris: Fernand Hazan, 1988), 63.

Bibliography

Primary material

Luca, Ghérasim. Fonds Ghérasim Luca, Bibliothèque littéraire Jacques Doucet, Paris.

Luca, Ghérasim. *Amphitrite: mouvements sur-thaumaturgiques et non-oedipiens*. Bucharest: Socec, 1947.

Luca, Ghérasim. 'Au Procès des assonances', *Cahiers de la bibliothèque littéraire Jacques Doucet* 2 (1998): 97–104.

Luca, Ghérasim. *Comment s'en sortir sans sortir*. Directed by Raoul Sangla. Paris, José Corti, 2008. DVD.

Luca, Ghérasim. 'Cubomanies et objets', *Supérieur inconnu* 5 (October–November 1996): 97–99.

Luca, Ghérasim, *Ghérasim Luca par Ghérasim Luca*. Edited by Nadèjda and Thierry Garrel, José Corti, 2002. CD.

Luca, Ghérasim. *Héros-limite* suivi de *Le Chant de la carpe* et de *Paralipomènes*, preface by André Velter. Paris: Gallimard, 2001.

Luca, Ghérasim, 'Interview' (by Serge Bricianer), *Oiseau-tempête*, 4 (Winter 1998): 32–3.

Luca, Gherasim. *Inventatorul iubirii: urmat de Parcurg imposibilul și de Moartea moartă*. Bucharest: Editura Negația Negației, 1945.

Luca, Ghérasim. *L'Inventeur de l'amour* suivi de *La Mort morte*. Paris: José Corti, 1994.
Luca, Ghérasim. *Un loup à travers une loupe*. Paris: José Corti, 1998.
Luca, Gherasim, *Un lup văzut printr-o lupă*. Bucharest: Negatia Negatiei, 1945.
Luca, Ghérasim. *La Paupière philosophale*. Paris: Corti, 2016.
Luca, Ghérasim. *La Proie s'ombre*. Paris: José Corti, 1991.
Luca, Ghérasim, *Théâtre de bouche*. Paris: José Corti, 1987.
Luca, Ghérasim. *Le Vampire passif, avec une introduction sur l'objet objectivement offert, un portrait trouvé et dix-sept illustrations*. Bucharest: Éditions de l'Oubli, 1945; repr. Paris: José Corti, 2001.
Luca, Ghérasim, and Dolfi Trost, *Dialectique de la dialectique: message adressé au mouvement surréaliste international*. Bucharest: Slova, 1945.

Secondary material

Albanese, Ralph Jr. 'La Fontaine and the teaching of Frenchness'. In *The Shape of Change: Essays in early modern literature and La Fontaine in honor of David Lee Rubin*, 315–35. Amsterdam: Rodopi/Brill, 2002.
Alexandrian, Sarane. 'Le Poète sans repartir: jamais plus ici, toujours là', *Supérieur inconnu* 5 (October–November 1996): 71–8.
Alleau, René. *Aspects de l'alchimie traditionnelle*. Paris: Éditions de Minuit, 1953.
Bailly, Jean-Christophe. *Piotr Kowalski*. Paris: Fernand Hazan, 1988.
Bataille, Georges. *Œuvres complètes*, 10 vols. Paris: Gallimard, 1970.
Beledian, Krikor. 'L'Écriture comme réécriture chez Chahan Chahnour/Armen Lubin', *Modern Languages Open* 1 (2019). Accessed 22 January 2021. http://doi.org/10.3828/mlo.v0i0.222.
Bonfiglio, Thomas Paul. *Mother Tongues and Nations: The invention of the native speaker*. New York: Walter de Gruyter, 2010.
Carlat, Dominique. *Gherasim Luca l'intempestif*. Paris: José Corti, 1998.
Deguy, Michel. *Brevets*. Seyssel: Champ Vallon, 1986.
Deleuze, Gilles and Claire Parnet, *Dialogues*. Paris: Flammarion, 1977.
de Rivarol, Antoine. *Œuvres choisies*. Preface by M. de Lescure. 2 vols. Paris: Librairie des Bibliophiles / E. Flammarion, successeur, 1880.
Éluard, Paul. *Œuvres complètes*, 2 vols. Paris: Gallimard, 1968.
Erber, Laura. 'No man's langue: rethinking language with Ghérasim Luca'. In *Socioaesthetics: Ambience – imaginary*, edited by Anders Michelsen and Frederik Tygstrup, 98–116. Boston: Brill, 2015.
Fijalkowski, Krzysztof. 'Ghérasim Luca: « le désir désiré »'. In *« Infra-noir », un et multiple : un groupe surréaliste entre Bucarest et Paris, 1945–1947*, edited by Monique Yaari, 47–100. Oxford: Peter Lang, 2014.
Forcer, Stephen. *Dada as Text, Thought and Theory*. Oxford: Legenda, 2015.
Garrel, Thierry. 'Je me souviens de Ghérasim Luca', *Europe* 1045 (May 2016): 31–44.
Hutin, Serge. *Les Sociétés secrètes*. Paris: Presses universitaires de France, 1954.
Kelly, Michael G. 'Poetic utterance and the cosmopolitan indisposition: on Ghérasim Luca'. In *The Cause of Cosmopolitanism: Dispositions, models, transformations*, edited by Patrick O'Donovan and Laura Rascaroli, 271–92. Bern: Peter Lang, 2011.
Kelly, Michael G. 'A voice from the shadows', *Berlin Review of Books*, May 2013. Accessed 22 January 2021. http://berlinbooks.org/brb/2013/05/a-voice-from-the-shadows.
La Fontaine, *Œuvres complètes*, 2 vols. Paris: Gallimard, 1954.
Lejeune, Denis. *The Radical Use of Chance in 20th Century Art*. Amsterdam and New York: Rodopi, 2012.
Orlandi, Sibylle. 'Gherasim Luca, Paul Celan: un au-delà de la langue dans la langue ?', *TRANS-* 17 (2014). Accessed 22 January 2021. https://doi.org/10.4000/trans.890.
Petreu, Marta. 'Les idées politiques de Gherasim Luca dans sa période roumaine', *Synergies Roumanie* 2 (2007): 57–64.
Raileanu, Petre. *Gherasim Luca*. Paris: Oxus, 2004.
Rousseau, Jean-Jacques. *Œuvres complètes*. Edited by Louis Barré. 12 vols. Paris: J. Bry aîné, 1856–7.
Sandqvist, Tom. *Dada East: The Romanians of Cabaret Voltaire*. London: MIT Press, 2006.

Sjöberg, Sami. 'An other transnationalism: Romanian Jewish emigrants in Francophone avant-garde literature', *French Studies*, 73.1 (January 2019): 33–49.
Toma, Iulian. *Gherasim Luca ou l'intransigeante passion d'être*. Preface by Jacqueline Chénieux-Gendron. Paris: Honoré Champion, 2012.
Torlini, Yannick. *Ghérasim Luca, le poète de la voix: ontologie et érotisme*. Paris: L'Harmattan, 2011.
Wirth, Oswald. *Le Symbolisme hermétique dans ses rapports avec l'alchimie et la franc-maçonnerie*. Paris: Librairie initiatique, 1909.
Yildiz, Yasemin. *Beyond the Mother Tongue: The postmonolingual condition*. New York: Fordham University Press, 2012.

4

Taking leave of one's self: Michelle Grangaud between *propre* and *commun*

The *oeuvres* of Lubin, Jabès and Luca are marked by pervasive anxieties with regard to the proper name, identity and the figuration of the 'je'. In each, poetry is coincident with or constituted by a condition of exile or non-belonging, and variously characterised by, for instance, effects of provisionality, the interruptive spacing of textual matter or the performative suppression of language's patrimonial attachments. In our consideration of these poets, personal trajectories have been a determining factor, and each poet considered has belonged to the categories of 'migrant', 'exiled' or 'stateless' writer. Even if these are distinguishing qualities of the profiles of the writers in question, it would be limiting for this study to suggest that such qualities are the exclusive preserve of writers occupying these categories. Among the problems of restricting discussions of mobility, displacement and marginalisation to literature by migrants is the risk of a persistent othering of writers in this category. By contrast, in the context of Québécois literature, for instance, Catherine Khordoc has called for a transnational perspective that considers both migrant and non-migrant writing together.[1] Without adopting a transnational approach, the present chapter will consider the question of non-belonging for a writer who does not herself belong to the category of migrant.

For the poet and Oulipo member Michelle Grangaud, non-belonging does not appear to be linked to a personal experience of migration, even if her early life was one marked by the traumas of postcolonial transition and she was more or less compelled by historical circumstance to leave then French Algeria, where she was born. While she is perhaps most noted for her inventive approach to the anagram in the collections

Mémento-fragments (1987) and *Stations* (1990), Grangaud is also the author of a range of works variously organised around other textual constraints such as the inventory, lipograms and anadiplosis. One of the first women members of Oulipo, she rejects the idea of creative inspiration and originality issuing historically from romanticism and shares in Oulipo's interest in the production of texts according to strict constraints.

Founded in 1960 by Raymond Queneau and François Le Lionnais, Oulipo, or the Ouvroir de littérature potentielle, is a collective focused on the production of writing through the application of mathematical procedures and textual constraints. Rejecting the emphasis on psychic automatism and the impulses of the unconscious present in the then-dominant surrealist movement, members of Oulipo seek to underscore the methodical and systematic character of their experiment and dedicate themselves to the discovery of constraints and the generation of new text types. In the most general terms, while surrealism is interested primarily in exploring possibilities of thought, Oulipo seeks to interrogate those of language. Jacques Roubaud, for instance, criticises what he sees as the debilitating generalisation of automatic writing by the surrealists, emphasising instead the importance of perpetuating a variety of fixed poetic forms.[2] The primary interest of literary work for the members of Oulipo lies in the discovery, application and description of new constraints rather than the particular semantic, psychoanalytical or even political charge they might carry. In keeping with its attempts to demystify the author function, Oulipo eschews emphasis on personal expression and the values of lyric, and promotes instead a conception of the text primarily as an artefact or construct. As the American writer and member of Oulipo Harry Mathews noted, '[Oulipo] is first and last a laboratory where, through experiment and erudition, possibilities of writing under arbitrary and severe restrictions are investigated'.[3]

Although Oulipo has gained a reputation for the pursuit of arcane literary games, its activity often has a profoundly ontological reach. As Alison James argues in a study of Georges Perec, Oulipo reveals 'an anxiety at the heart of the exploration of forms and … a profound concern with what is at stake – psychologically, aesthetically, and epistemologically – in literary creation'.[4] The works of Michelle Grangaud speak directly to this anxiety of creation and, moreover, to that concerning identity and linguistic non-belonging which is common to the other poets who are the focus of this study. Throughout the work of Grangaud, beyond the concern with the technical elaboration of text, there is a recurrent thematic preoccupation with the institutions (such as libraries, asylums or the transport system) that characterise life in an administered society, and their socialising effects at a level beyond that of the anecdotal 'I'. As Grangaud declares in comments to Serge Gavronsky, her writing endeavours to '[hold on] to the anagrammatic lesson of a nonintentional discourse and, this goes without saying, without an identity'.[5] For Grangaud, as for other Oulipians, the methodical application of constraints can be liberating. This is because it leads to the production of a kind of writing unhindered by the conventions of the 'free' expression of the self, one where the technical elaboration of the work surpasses aesthetic concerns. Grangaud's publications in this way disclose a fascination with the liberating possibilities of the anagram, anadiplosis and myriad other constraints whose application permits an actualisation of possibilities.

Biography: oneself at a certain distance from oneself

> It is not easy to speak about oneself, at least correctly. It is not easy for me to speak about my writing. When I think about it, it all appears commonplace, anecdotal, futile. Others know how to speak correctly about writing and about their own writing. When I say 'correctly,' I mean placing oneself at a certain distance from oneself, neither too close nor too far away. In my case it is with a degree of awkwardness that I situate myself.[6]

Born on 11 October 1941 in Algiers, Michelle Grangaud grew up in the neighbourhood of Hydra in a devout French Protestant family which had been present in Algeria for two generations. The poet's early life was to be marked by the events of the Algerian War of Independence. 'J'ai bien vu l'Histoire de l'Algérie; j'espère que je l'ai bien fait sentir dans *Calendrier des fêtes nationales* ["Calendar of national festivals"]', she tells John C. Stout in an interview, referring to her 2003 work of that name.[7] As a teenager, she was witness to bombings which she recalls in detail in the same interview and in the prose text *Jours le jour* ['Days the day'].[8] Some additional insight into the social and political turmoil experienced by Grangaud during the years preceding independence in Algeria is offered in an autobiographical text by her brother Jean-Paul, a leading paediatrician based in Algiers. Unlike other members of the Grangaud family, Jean-Paul Grangaud remained in Algeria after independence and took the unusual step of adopting Algerian nationality. In his account of his formative years, he offers a vivid picture of the milieu into which his sister was born. Grangaud notably recalls how his sister Michelle was involved in the hiding of a member of the dissident paramilitary group

Organisation Armée Secrète on the family property in 1962 while the man in question was being actively sought by gendarmes in the vicinity.[9] Leaving Algeria later that year, Michelle Grangaud went on to work as a classics teacher in the Montpellier area for a number of years, and from the late 1970s has lived in Paris, where she left behind teaching (a career she considered too repetitive) for a job as an administrator in the Paris educational authority.[10]

Michelle Grangaud's first published work, *Mémento-fragments*, appeared in the P.O.L imprint in 1987.[11] Composed of anagrams of titles of books, paintings, pieces of music and other sources, the book was to establish Grangaud as a leading literary practitioner of the anagram. In 1995, she became only the second female member of the Ouvroir de littérature potentielle (Oulipo), after Michèle Métail. Among the constrained writing techniques which she has pioneered as a member of Oulipo are the *sexagrammatine*, a hybrid form which blends the anagram and the sestina, and the *avion*, an 'abréviation de «abréviation»' ['abbreviation of "abbreviation"'].[12] At the time of writing, she is the author of over 15 published works, in prose and verse.

With regard to *Mémento-fragments*, one possible partial anagram of the title of the book itself – 'Nom émet fragments' ['Noun emits fragments'] – elicits a central preoccupation of Grangaud's poetics, namely her desire to disrupt the epistemological valence of the proper noun. In a commentary on the P.O.L website, she notes that:

> … il fallait bien lui donner un nom, pour le distinguer de tous les livres déjà écrits, par d'autres, sans compter ceux que j'avais l'intention d'écrire. Ceci dit, je ne tenais pas autrement à lui donner un nom. Je ne suis pas fanatique des noms qu'on appelle propres. Je leur préfère, de beaucoup, les noms communs. Une des choses que j'apprécie, avec les noms communs, c'est qu'ils permettent de fabriquer des poèmes anagrammatiques, et c'est ce que j'avais fait avec *Mémento-fragments* …[13]
>
> [… it was really necessary to give it a name, to set it apart from all the books already written, by others, not to mention those I intended to go on to write. That said, in other respects, I had no particular desire to give it a name. I'm not terribly enthusiastic about those nouns called proper. I much prefer common nouns instead. One of the things that I appreciate with common nouns is that they enable me to produce anagrammatic poems, and that is what I did with *Mémento-fragments* …]

Grangaud's statements here betray an attitude of anxiety or circumspection with regard to the giving of a name, that most proprietary of attributes. This is a facet of her poetics that is common to Armen Lubin and Ghérasim Luca. As much as for Lubin and Luca, in the case of Grangaud, this anxiety extends in particular to the giving of one's *own* name: in one comment, she openly regrets not having thought of taking for a name her social security number.[14] Grangaud's intent is ultimately to subvert the connotations of univocity, indivisibility and self-identicality that attach to the proper noun, that is, to names and identities of all kinds. Issuing from this in turn is her imaginative investment in the anagram and the common noun. While the anagram opens up the possibility of fragmenting or dissolving those attributes that are proper to the proper noun, the common noun achieves a comparable effect, since it denotes all those entities of a similar kind or class, as opposed to the particulars of any singular individual.

It is in her persistent circling around the question of the common and the proper, and the ambiguities produced by the opposition of these linguistic categories, that the poet's contribution to the various reflections on statelessness and non-belonging contained in this study is most pressing. Although the author was more or less compelled by circumstance to leave the territory of her birth, and despite the fact that the question of nationality was clearly at issue for members of her family, Grangaud's sense of non-belonging is not so intensely bound up with a personal experience of migration in the way it is for Jabès, Lubin or Luca. It is not so much that her work addresses the specificities of the migrant condition, but that it exposes in critical fashion the purchase of the categories of having and belonging over our ordinary semantics. Grangaud sees non-belonging as coincident with our contemporary social condition: ultimately, her writing builds on this conviction to elicit the sense that there is something fundamentally *inappropriable* in language's mediation of human relations, in other words, that they are not reducible to the properties of a 'subject'. In a body of work that speaks both eloquently and playfully to the concerns of post-foundationalist philosophy and to aspects of our contemporary social condition, Grangaud offers us a paradoxically invigorating account of the limits of an ontology dominated by what the philosopher Roberto Esposito terms a 'semantics of proprium',[15] that is, one which can be apprehended only via the proprietary attributes of a subject, and a lexical field of having or belonging. Subtly indicating the limits of the categories by which we are politically, socially and linguistically constituted, Grangaud seems to view a form of radical non-belonging not as the loss of community, but as its very condition.

Improper nouns, I: anagrams and the otherness within. *Mémento-fragments* (1987) and *Stations* (1990)

Grangaud's earliest published collections, *Mémento-fragments* of 1987 and *Stations* of 1990, are both composed of anagrammatic poems, and they quickly established her as a leading practitioner of this form of constrained writing in which each line is an anagram of all other lines in the poem. *Mémento-fragments* consists of a series of anagrammatised titles of books, paintings, literary citations, street names and so on. Often asyntactical in character and featuring sudden contrasts and arbitrary juxtapositions, these poems are marked by a sense of playfulness. The title of *Mémento-fragments* alludes to motifs of possession (the memento as 'thing kept') and dispersion. It thus highlights a fundamental quality of the poems featured within this study, since readerly interest at least in part derives from how the poem gestures towards or deviates radically from the signification ascribed to the particular set of linguistic units presented by the title. In the set of comments by Grangaud featured on the P.O.L website concerning *Mémento-fragments*, Grangaud herself identifies the anagram as a 'mode de multiplication du langage par lui-même' ['a method of multiplication of language by itself'], a controlled production of an excess of signification.[16] Likewise, in her interview with John C. Stout, she comments that: '[ce] qui me fascinait vraiment, c'était ce pouvoir d'engendrement du langage par lui-même et le maniement du langage par les lettres, alors que les lettres n'ont aucun sens' ['what fascinated me really was this power of procreation of language by itself and the manipulation of language by letters, when in fact letters have no meaning'].[17]

Dating from at least the classical period, the anagram found popularity in the twentieth century with authors including Georges Perec and the German writer Unica Zürn, in whose work Grangaud first encountered the anagrammatic poem. Meanwhile, scholarly interest in the anagram was spurred by growing awareness of research on the topic undertaken by Ferdinand de Saussure. As Jean Starobinski writes, Saussure's research on anagrams in classical Greek and Roman sources reveals the problem of writerly intentionality and has the potential to reinvigorate understanding of the nature of poetic language:

> La question étant : qu'y a-t-il immédiatement derrière le vers ? la réponse n'est pas : le *sujet* créateur, mais : le *mot* inducteur. … La poésie n'étant pas seulement ce qui se réalise *dans* les mots, mais ce qui prend naissance à *partir* des mots, elle échappe donc à

l'arbitraire de la conscience pour ne plus dépendre que d'une sorte de légalité linguistique.[18]

> [The question being: what lies directly behind the line of verse? The answer is not: a *subject* who creates, but: the *word* which induces. … Poetry being not only what is accomplished *in* words, but what *starts out* from words, it thus eludes the arbitrariness of consciousness and is contingent only on a kind of linguistic legality.]

In this perspective, a text's poetic quality is not realised within words as a property which has been bestowed on them by an authorial consciousness, but rather is something that is engendered through a necessary linguistic relation.

In a more radical, anti-structural mode, Jean Baudrillard identifies in Saussure's research on anagrams the lineaments of a theory of poetic language which goes beyond the semiological theory developed by Saussure in his *Cours de linguistique général* ['Course in general linguistics']. Baudrillard argues that in rearranging the letters of a word or phrase to produce another word or phrase, the anagram subverts the linearity and unity of the linguistic sign (as composed of signifier and signified), thereby disrupting the Saussurean linguistic theory of value. The anagram thus constitutes 'quelque chose comme le noyau d'une antiéconomie politique, lieu d'extermination de la valeur et de la loi' ['something like the kernel of a political anti-economy, a place where value and the law come to be exterminated'];[19] according to this view, which is in turn central to Baudrillard's understanding of 'le poétique' in *L'Échange symbolique et la mort* ['Symbolic exchange and death'], 'le poétique' holds the potential to break with capitalist values of production and exchange operative within discursive formations.[20]

Although the anagram may traditionally have been viewed as a source of distraction or light entertainment, Grangaud herself, unsurprisingly, sees it in more ambitious terms. In her responses to a questionnaire completed for Serge Gavronsky, she states:

> Rather than a constraint, I have always felt [the anagram] to be a technique. Once acquired, it becomes a working tool. Question of meaning: constraint fixes attention on phonemes and, as a result, masks meaning, reality. Out of my anagrammatic practice emerges, nevertheless, fragments of reality, often the most violent, that surface independently of all desire to speak. This involuntary return of reality transforms, so it seems to me, the anagram into

something other than a pure exercise in virtuosity. One can say as much about all forms of poetic writing. There is a division, the intentionality of discourse (and of personal affectivity) that find themselves short-circuited, and as of that, the anecdotal falls to the side.[21]

It is worth emphasising here the Oulipian dimension of Grangaud's position in that it supports a view of writing as a form of intellectual technology rather than as an aesthetically motivated activity. In Oulipian fashion also, Grangaud rejects notions of authorial intentionality or originality. Typically, this serves to direct attention away from the work's semantic aspects and instead towards formal and procedural aspects of ordered textual production. In the context of the anagrammatic poem, the technical elaboration of the line of verse thus takes precedence over lyrical encoding or semantic continuity. The resulting effects of syntactic displacement and truncation are often so abrupt that they lead to a disquieting sense of estrangement for a reader who soon becomes accustomed to eruptions of the 'violence' alluded to by Grangaud above. Additionally, although Grangaud acknowledges the activity of the unconscious, she understands this to come about as a *consequence* (understood here as a 'return' of elements of reality) of writing by constraint rather than as dictated by arbitrary impulses of the psyche, such as might be found in the literature of surrealism.

A poem such as 'la rue Notre-Dame-des-Victoires' from *Mémento-fragments* is indicative of the 'involuntary return of reality' evoked above. Throughout the piece, anagrams of the titular street produce effects of irony and irreverence. The title's triumphalist connotations and maternal associations with the biblical Mary are displaced, ushering in a series of images of urban disarray and defiled or sickly bodies.

Vérone-Madrid et l'issue atroce
de victoires malades retourne
à l'envers moite torsade durcie
Verdun-Oslo cities à derme taré
rose virulent sort à ce diadème
décorum vies ratées à l'endroit
Anvers-Moscou et te dire dire la
Riviera-Londres tout de camées
rue des Volontaires cité-drame
escalade un remords titré voie
et il rêve coudre trois amandes

le dessin dévorait ma route cré-
nom a tout écrasé, vider le désir
de cités-lavoirs, une morte-rade.[22]

Perhaps the most striking anagrammatic decomposition in this poem, not least because it is so syntactically and semantically complete, is the forceful assertion that 'nom a tout écrasé, vider le désir' ['noun has crushed all, evacuate desire'], a sentiment which takes up the poet's critique of the proper noun and underscores an inherent violence of the act of naming. That violence is also in evidence in 'Histoire de la folie à l'âge classique', a piece in which the poet anagrammatises the title of Michel Foucault's 1961 study of practices of internment of the mentally ill (translated as *Madness and Civilization: A History of Insanity in the Age of Reason*):

l'idiote – *l'asile* – à chaque fois sa règle
isolée saquée – *dehors* il fait glacial –
haie de croquis – *gifle à l'œil* – la tasse
à qui est-ce – dehors *il a failli* – sa geôle
sage – la chose *la droite* – il se qualifie
loquet adhésif – *isolées là* – glaciaire –
haïe – *le cloaque* sédatif – sois l'argile
idéal *horticole* – sa glaise – *fêlés* – à qui[23]

As in the case of other poems in the volume, to anagrammatise here is to subvert the conventional hierarchical relation between title and textual content, that is, between the name of the text and that which it identifies. Nonetheless, Grangaud offers an oblique commentary on Foucault's study. While the book's title suggests an attitude of critical detachment from its topic, Grangaud's poem by contrast precipitates the reader into the life-world of establishments for the mentally ill. In a fortuitous connection to Foucault's discussion of *le grand renfermement* [the great confinement] of the poor and the marginal, poetic form mobilises its own forms of division, containment and submission to constraint: the anagrammatic poem is arranged across successive lines without syntactical connection between them, while internal forms of segmentation are present via syntactical clusters separated by dashes. Together, these maximise contrasts and produce sudden changes of tone, point of view and emphasis, at times evoking snatches of overheard conversation ('*dehors* il fait glacial' ['*outside*, it is icy']), brusque interrogations ('à qui est-ce' ['whose is this']) or abruptly interrupted trains of thought. The readerly experience is one of moments of syntactical fluidity which alternate with sudden, puzzling obstructions to sense or syntactical order, those obstructions usually coinciding with clusterings of nouns or nominal constructions ('haie de croquis – *gifle à l'œil* – la tasse' ['hedge of outline – *slap in the eye* – the cup']).

Such forms of readerly confusion heighten our sense of the modalities of lived experience in the establishments accounted for by Foucault, and successive lines produce combinations of images which resonate with one another to produce a critique of the precipitate cruelty and alienating effects of these establishments. Thus, there are allusions to physical obstacles (a hedge) and unhygienic conditions (*'le cloaque'* [*'the cesspit'*]); mental ill health, and the prejudicial labels which connote it ('l'idiote' ['the idiot'], *'fêlés'* ['crackpots']); internment and submission to rules (references to a door latch, asylum and isolation); and upsurges of affect (cold or physical violence). These do not map onto any one stable perspective, that of a distinct protagonist within the titular 'histoire', but rather evoke a generalised condition of claustrophobic unease, abuse and confusion.

While the material anagrammatised in the poems of *Mémento-fragments* ranges widely across book titles, place names and citations from literature, that contained in the later collection *Stations* is drawn from a single repertory of names, those of stations on the Paris metro network.[24] Moreover, by contrast with *Mémento-fragments*, each of the poems in *Stations* is identified only by its incipit, which gives the name of the station or stations in question. If a conventional function attributed to the title of a text is that of identification, this strategy arguably betokens a text's resistance to stabilising in the manner dictated by the name – the title – under whose sign it is presented. Indeed, in its undermining of the noun's unitary character and conventionality as an element of discourse, the anagram, as Jean-Claude Milner writes, 'met la langue en excès' ['places language in excess'].[25]

In a comment appearing on the website of P.O.L, Grangaud elaborates on why the placenames of *Stations* appealed to her: 'J'ai pu opérer sur ces noms propres-là, parce qu'ils ne désignaient plus telle ou telle personne mais un lieu traversé par des foules de gens et par l'histoire' ['I was able to go to work on those proper nouns because they no longer designate this person or that but a place traversed by crowds of people and history'].[26] For Grangaud, the common noun and public space are analogous and partake of the same dynamic; both are available to, and indeed solicit, various kinds of decomposition, reappropriation and redefinition. In some cases in *Stations*, an anagram is formed on the basis of the names of two stations, such as in the following example which features the Quai de la Rapée and Nationale:

> Quai-de-la-Rapée Nationale
> on naît de l'épique râââââle[27]

The two noun constructions featuring in the incipit are rearranged as a complete syntactical construction in which it is only the integrity of the noun for 'groan' which is lost, given its comic elongation into 'râââââle'. While a prominent element of the incipit is the adjectival noun 'Nationale' (a word potentially connoting a kind of nativist or ethnocentric purchase over the space in question), the subsequent line elaborates another, less exclusionary, less tangible, but no less foundational form of belonging, that of an imprecise 'on' originating in a primal-sounding groan that is strongly evocative of the pain of childbirth.

The poem 'Nation-Place-des-Antilles' in more elaborate fashion dwells on a similar question of nationality, through a revealing play upon the status of one of the most privileged sites of political congregation in French Republicanism, the place de la Nation:

> Nation-Place-des-Antilles la cité
> danse son lit plane talpe l'anodin
> il es cantse dans ce pli né
> lit tal'osane penti'delas lentos
> lacina del passe lel'incantation
> nelcap atlantide il nosse dans ce
> né lit palsionatel natinales
> solace plendit na cedillan tonelita spes[28]

Perhaps seeking to echo the snatches of foreign language conversation overheard in the large metro interchange beneath the place de la Nation, this piece seems to perform a Deleuzian 'devenir-autre de la langue' ['becoming-other of language'],[29] deflecting back radically on the naturalised usages of French. Through a combination of a dispersed spatial structure, evocative quasi-Romance sonorities that suggest glossolalia ('penti'delas lentos'; 'del passe lel'incantation'; 'na cedillan tonelita spes'), and allusions to rebirth and the lost continent of Atlantis, the text seems intended to puncture a monolingual conception of national identity and the territorial claim which that identity lays to certain privileged spaces.

Just as in the above piece, in other poems featuring in *Stations*, Grangaud experiments with the text's graphic inscription and the organisation of letters on the page:

> Boucicaut Pré-Saint-Gervais Galliéni   va la
> glace s'épie un bistouri grinçait   il saignait
> coupable un cri agité vers   le lit gris gracias
> un bain coupe ta vie   cuire un visa bistre il
> cognait la page   ici rebite la cage où il a pris
> vingt ans   oubli crispé langage écrivait sa nuit[30]

Grangaud's earlier anagrammatic poems, such as those of *Mémento-fragments*, had been predominantly arranged around the horizontal and vertical axes of the stanza and verse line. This piece, however, is organised around a diagonal cut that subverts those axes: just as in 'Nation-Place-des-Antilles', the unitary character of both stanza and verse line is undermined, since in each case anagrammatised matter spills over into the subsequent line, with the exception of the final one. Grangaud's experiments with the anagram in this way offer a quite literal illustration of Jean-Luc Nancy's statement that 'la poésie rendrait compte dans le langage de ce qui, en tant qu'art et que différence des arts, fait bord et coupe du langage' ['poetry could be said to give in language an account of what, as an art and as the difference between the arts, acts as the margin and cut of language'].[31] As that which cuts through the substance of language, and its linearity/conventionality, the anagram places the *coupe* and the margin at the core of Grangaud's understanding of poetry, rather than the matter of signification.

Improper nouns, II: the (un)folding of memory in *Souvenirs de ma vie collective* (2000)

The anagrammatic poem is, however, not the only kind of text by Grangaud in which the unitary character of the noun is subverted. A case in point is her 2000 prose text, *Souvenirs de ma vie collective* ['Memories of my collective life'], which seems to be in part inspired by fellow Oulipo member Georges Perec's *Je me souviens* ['I remember'] of 1978. In the latter text, Perec presents the reader with multiple recollections of moments in his life between the ages of 10 and 25. What is distinctive about this litany of recollections is the fact that they are not exclusive to the life of the author himself, but draw on numerous experiences of, for instance, consumerism or spectatorship, which are shared by members of his generation. These shared remembrances range from quotidian banalities to recollections of the media portrayal of historical events:

> Je me souviens quand on revenait de vacances, le Ier septembre, et qu'il y avait encore un mois entier sans école.[32]
> Je me souviens des trous dans les tickets de métro.[33]
> Je me souviens que pendant son procès, Eichmann était enfermé dans une cage de verre.[34]
> Je me souviens d'un fromage qui s'appelait « la Vache sérieuse » (« la Vache qui rit » lui a fait un procès et l'a gagné).[35]
>
> [I remember when we came back from holidays, on the 1st of September, and there was still a whole month without school.
> I remember the holes in metro tickets.
> I remember during his trial, Eichmann was locked up in a glass cage.
> I remember a cheese which was called 'The Serious Cow' ('The Laughing Cow' took them to court and won).]

Though seemingly inspired by her fellow Oulipian, Grangaud's *Souvenirs de ma vie collective* deviates significantly from Perec's model. While in Grangaud's text the object of recollection is ultimately something that is common to a collective, in Perec's the recollection originates, voluntarily or otherwise, in individual memory, the presence of which is repeatedly affirmed in the litany 'Je me souviens'. *Souvenirs de ma vie collective*, moreover, seems to suggest a different paradigm, in so far as any trace of a recollecting *je* is conspicuously absent from the work, other than in the 'ma' of its title. The stimulus for recollection is thus transferred away from the self to the homophonous properties of successive words, as the final word or words of a given sentence share similar properties of sound to the first word or words of the next sentence. The constraint deployed here can be understood as an instance of the rhetorical figure of *anadiplosis*, a term which, etymologically, designates a 'doubling' or '*fold*ing up'. It also shows similarity to a related term within versification, *rime enchaînée*, even if Grangaud's text is not composed in rhymed verse. In versification, *rime enchaînée* designates a form of rhyme that consists of the repetition of the closing syllable or syllables of a line of verse at the beginning of the following line, usually in poetry where an end-of-line rhyme pattern is also present. Unlike *rime enchaînée*, in which sense typically carries over from one line to the next, the anadiplosis in

Souvenirs de ma vie collective is marked by a splitting of sound and sense; as continuity of sense is jettisoned, sound is retained:

> Éther qui, par ses qualités naturelles paraît situé entre la vie et la mort.
> Morve produite par le rhume et les larmes.
> Art mélodique engendrant la rythmique du vers.
> U vert selon Rimbaud.
> Beau temps qui ne présage rien de bon dans l'attente du cyclone.[36]
>
> [Ether which, by its natural qualities, seems to be situated between life and death.
> Mucus produced by colds and tears.
> Melodic art creating the rhythmics of verse.
> U green according to Rimbaud.
> Fine weather which does not bode well ahead of the cyclone.]

In classical rhetoric, the purpose of anadiplosis is often that of supplying additional emphasis to the noun in question; it also has a mnemonic function. By contrast, it would seem that the constraint deployed in Grangaud's text does not function additively in this way. What it performs is a 'pli' or fold in the text, as each noun marking the end of a line separates into its constituent phonemes, thus unsettling the construction of sense and subverting referential value, a feature which is supplemented by Grangaud's recourse to the technique of textual montage. Now, the fascination with the figure of the fold in modern French poetry can be traced back at least to the poetry of Stéphane Mallarmé. As Marian Zwerling Sugano writes, elaborating on the significance of the 'pli' in Mallarmé, the 'pli' 'is a corrupt container: it contains without fully enclosing, allowing the inside to be discernible from the outside but nevertheless a part of it. … the "pli" re-poses the question of whether language can in some way *contain* an extralinguistic reality and vice versa'.[37] Grangaud's text likewise subverts a certain notion of language as 'container'. Indeed, the subtitle of *Souvenirs de ma vie collective* is *Sujets de tableaux sans tableaux* ['Subjects of paintings without paintings'], arguably connoting a subversion of the 'containment' function through the eschewal of context and frame. In this connection, Grangaud's short 1996 text *On verra bien* ['We shall see'] also meditates on the connotations of the 'pli' in the French language, playing on the term's meanings as 'pleat', 'fold' and 'habit':

> En suivant du doigt le côté du pli, on peut aller soit en avant, soit en arrière. Et bien qu'on ne sache jamais si l'avant n'est pas plutôt

l'arrière et inversement, on sait qu'on va dans une direction donnée, ce qui n'est quand même pas rien. Trouver dans le rien quelque chose qui n'est pas rien, c'est déjà quelque chose.[38]

> [By following the side of the pleat with one's finger, one can go either forward or backward. And even if we never know if the front is actually not rather the back and vice versa, we know that we are moving in a given direction, which is no small matter. To be able to find in the nothing something that is not nothing is already something.]

The 'pli', then, for Grangaud, is a figure (that of an absence generative of a presence) that disrupts the teleology of action and text. This elusive ontology of the 'pli' has a bearing also on the constraint featuring in *Souvenirs de ma vie collective*: by virtue of its variant on conventional anadiplosis, according to which the very same *word* is carried over from one line to the next, the reader is thus presented with an inventory of successive statements which seem to bear no trace of discursive or narrative consistency, although they do in the main draw on collective knowledge or social reality. The figure is a source of constant variation, continually detaching the experience of reading from any single, unified perspective, and producing contrasts of the monumental and the intimately banal. At the diegetic level of individual statements, this sense of disorientation is mirrored through examples which evoke physical obstacles and unarticulated space:

> Sardanapale assiégé dans Ninive par Arbakès.
> Caisses en carton, empilées contre le mur du parking du supermarché, voisinant avec les caddies.
> Difficulté à trouver la porte adéquate, à la Maison de la radio.[39]

> [Sardanapalus besieged in Nineveh by Arbakes.
> Cardboard boxes, piled against the walls of the supermarket car park, adjacent to the shopping trolleys.
> Difficulty finding the appropriate door, at the Radio headquarters.]

In a manner that is comparable to Grangaud's work on the anagram, the constraint here effectively undermines the line's pre-ordainedness as a discrete unit of sense structured around the kernel of the proper noun. Various self-referential examples throughout the text intimate the reach of the constraint, such as in the telling *mise-en-abyme* of 'sens' and 'absence' in the following lines:

> Thématique mallarméenne de l'absence.
> Sens qui n'est fait que de glissements successifs dont on ne voit jamais le bout.[40]
>
> [Mallarmean thematic of absence.
> Sense which is made solely of successive slippages with no end in sight.]

Similarly, as the first and second lines of the following example indicate, a certain attenuation of subjectivity is implied by the text's repeated and disorienting 'redistributions détonantes' of meaning, its persistent *brisure* [fragmentation] of words and lines.

> Bris de mots ou de vers pouvant donner lieu à des redistributions détonantes.
> Antonyme d'humain qui n'est pas forcément inhumain.
> Mendès-France instituant un dispositif social faisant une large place à la consommation du lait.[41]
>
> [Fragment of word or of verse capable of giving rise to explosive redistributions.
> Antonym of human which is not necessarily inhuman.
> Mendès-France founding a social system largely structured around the consumption of milk.]

And yet the rhetorical evacuation of the *je*, of perspectival consistency and of other accessories of subjecthood does not of necessity equate to an 'inhumain' suppression of sensation or affect, which are abundantly present in numerous evocations of aural, visual and other impressions, like the mucus, tears and melodies of one of the citations above. Memory thus seems to possess a dual association for Grangaud, and a further pairing would seem to suggest its obliterative and productive possibilities:

> Cendre impersonnelle répandue dans l'air du temps et formée par l'ensemble de tous les renoncements.
> Semences de souvenirs semées par chaque instant, mais dont la plupart ne pourront jamais éclore.[42]

[Impersonal ash spread through the spirit of the times and formed by all the renunciations.
Seeds of memories sown by every instant, most of which will not bloom.]

In another significant pairing of absence and presence, the anadiplosis 'lacune/universalité' seems to turn on the paradoxically universalising drive of the text's devaluation of individualised identity:

Fondement de la Vérité basés sur une lacune.
Universalité, dans les sociétés humaines, du rire, du langage et du tabou.[43]

[Foundation of Truth based on a gap.
Universality in human societies, of laughter, of language and taboo.]

Above all, Grangaud seems to identify a peremptory and unruly agency of language over subjective intention or recollection. Attesting to language's continual unfolding, which is actualised with each passing word, *Souvenirs de ma vie collective* intimates that to be a linguistic being is to become exposed to a continual and disorienting short-circuiting of intentionality. What this in turn discloses is an abiding sense of the inherent virtuality of all human situation in respect of language, rather than the content of some mythic shared recollection. Like the Capronian *res amissa* evoked in the Introduction to this book (see p. 7), poetry here comes about by dint of a care in language for that which is forever lost to language.

In addition to its musings on the linguistically generative possibilities of the 'pli', *On verra bien* also elaborates on the specificities of the term 'côté' ['side']:

C'est bien ce qu'il y a de bizarre, et si j'osais je dirais de tordu, avec le côté, c'est que justement on ne peut pas y aller de côté. J'ai essayé plus d'une fois. J'ai toujours échoué. C'est que le côté n'a pas de côté. Il se contente d'en être un. Il est tout en être, et il n'a pas d'avoir.[44]

[That's certainly what's bizarre, and if I dared, I would say twisted, about the side, it is precisely that you cannot go aside of it. I've tried more than once. I've always failed. It's because the side has no side. It is happy enough to be one. It is all being, it has no having.]

As the text's gentle play on the term implies, the *côté*, as border or edge, exhibits a similarly elusive ontology to that of the *pli*. Possessing no substantive essence of its own, the *côté* interferes with the principle of self-identicality and, thereby, the semantics of proprium: being 'tout en être', and having no 'avoir', it thus goes to the core of Grangaud's understanding of the anagram and anadiplosis. Grangaud's experiments with these constraints thus open onto a kind of *impropriety*, not just in the sense that they often thematise violence or feature abrupt contrasts. Like the border and the fold, both the anagram and anadiplosis are improprietous in that they underscore a general condition of language, which is that of language's inability to contain itself: to contain itself, that is, to the sphere of the proper and the purview of an individual subject.

État civil (1998): the limits of identification

In texts dating from the latter part of her writing career, Grangaud's interests broadly shift away from particular constraints and poetic forms (such as the haiku, which is adopted in her 1991 collection *Geste* ['Gesture']) and embrace instead a variety of text *types* that frequently draw on or allude to the use of archival materials (such as records of civil status or historical dictionaries) and lists or registers (in the form of calendars of events or notable persons). Thus, in her mature career, there has been a shift towards a kind of writing motivated by the classificatory operations integral to those types of texts.

État civil ['Civil status'], of 1998, is one such text. In many respects, *État civil* can be said to belong to a category of literature designated as the 'factographie' ['factography'] by Marie-Jeanne Zenetti in a recent study of works by Annie Ernaux, Charles Reznikoff and Georges Perec. Characterised by patterns of montage as well as various techniques of information capture such as notation and transcription, such works are characteristic of a trend marked by the desertion of traditional narrative modes dominated by the novel. Often based on sources such as official documents or archives, 'factographic' texts perform a sophisticated interrogation of modes of referentiality and the nature of the real.[45]

Grangaud's own contribution to this phenomenon adopts the clinical inventorial tone of the State's official record of births, marriages and deaths in the life of the individual. According to Alain Rey's *Dictionnaire historique de la langue française* ['Historical dictionary of the French language'], a text which Grangaud later draws on liberally in the context of her work *Les Temps traversés* ['Times traversed'], the term 'état civil' designates 'ce qui distingue l'individu dans la sociéte et la famille' ['what sets apart the individual in society and family'] as well as 'le service public qui dresse les actes constatant ces faits' ['the public service that draws up the certificates attesting to these events'].[46] The term refers both to the social position of the individual as established through a certain number of life events, and to the particular document which, in the legal or administrative sense, takes cognisance of those events. In certain usages, it can simply connote an individual's name.[47]

Reading the prose of the civil register, one is struck by the peculiar stylistic and epistemological charge conferred on it by legislative authority. One of the cardinal characteristics of this kind of prose is its exclusive concentration on empirical detail, a feature that Grangaud strives to emulate in *État civil*, and which she additionally claims to have modelled on the French civil code.[48] Bringing to an extreme the rationalising drive to document and particularise human activity that motivates the State's administrative records, from one disconnected utterance to the next Grangaud's text multiplies and juxtaposes – to often whimsical effect – factual commentaries, banalities and candid statements about intellectual and emotional life. As Charles Dobzynski notes in an apt formulation, 'Le poète s'y fait l'huissier farfelu d'une saisie marxienne (au sens Groucho) de nos biens terrestres et de nos comportements animaux' ['The poet casts herself as a giddy court official compiling a register of our earthly belongings and animal behaviours in the style of Marx (Groucho, that is)'].[49] The following passage is indicative of Grangaud's prose in *État civil*:

> Dans la cuisine, l'éponge ocre jaune glisse sur le bois laqué blanc où est tombée une goutte de café puis est replacée dans le petit bac, au bord de l'évier, la surface blanche à nouveau immaculée.
> État d'un système, grandeurs physiques et observables.
> Pour le corps, chacun ne peut percevoir que la face antérieure du sien propre, l'articulation du cou n'autorisant pas une rotation complète.[50]
>
> [In the kitchen, the ochre sponge sweeps over the white lacquered wood surface where a drop of coffee has fallen, then it is returned to the little tub, next to the sink, the white surface immaculate once more.
> State of a system, physical and observable magnitude.
> Regarding the body, each person is incapable of perceiving his own from the rear, the articulation of the neck not enabling a complete rotation.]

The spare, methodical detailing of excerpts such as this one could conceivably point to the influence of the prose of the Alain Robbe-Grillet of *Instantanés* ['Snapshots']. However, Grangaud's avowed debt is to American objectivist poets such as Charles Reznikoff.[51]

As Jacques Derrida notes, as much as the term 'consignation' alludes to an act of deposition or assignation, it equally denotes a gathering together of signs.[52] In keeping with this sense of the term, Grangaud's *État civil* is an encyclopaedic project which inventories a vast, synchronic cross-section of discourses, with sources drawn from radio reports, dictionary-style definitions and excerpts of dialogue at a global scale. In her work on the anagram, it is one constraint which predominates, whereas in *État civil*, a wide variety are deployed, including stammering, lipograms and holophrasis, and, above all, montage. The text is organised into three sections – 'N', 'M' and 'D', denoting 'Naissances' ['Births'], 'Mariages' ['Marriages'] and 'Décès' ['Deaths'] – but at first appears to maintain only an oblique concern with each of these themes. In its opening lines, for instance, the text dwells on images of darkness, then light; slowly, elements of a narrative emerge, suggesting a plane's approach to an airport, followed by a landing and a passage through immigration controls. Gradually, it appears that 'Naissances' seems preoccupied with moments of coming to knowledge and the formation of various 'plis' or recurrent patterns, such as the flashing red light on a dark background which is the text's inaugural image. The section on 'mariages' explores themes of sexuality (often indirectly through the linguistic motif of 'conjugaison' ['conjugation']) and pregnancy, while 'Décès' deals in death and other forms of ending.

'Ces registres sont de trois sortes, N pour naissances, M pour mariages et D pour décès. J'avais d'abord remarqué que ce sont, dans l'ordre, les consonnes du mot « nomade »' ['These registers are of three kinds, N for births, M for marriages and D for deaths. I first noticed that these are, in that order, the consonants of the word 'nomad'], Grangaud notes.[53] Essentially territorialising in its function, the *état civil* is predicated on an understanding of citizenship as a sedentary phenomenon, and official documents such as birth certificates frequently designate a place of residence. Grangaud's discernment of a latent 'nomad' figure lurking within the bureaucratic categories peculiar to the *état civil* points to a fascination with what haunts the category of the individuated, sedentary subject designated by its proper name. As she notes in one interview, the project of *État civil*, 'au départ, était de dire tout ce que moi, en tant qu'individu quelconque, je pouvais avoir en commun avec n'importe quel autre moi, le plus différent possible de moi. C'était de définir ce que chacun peut avoir en commun avec tous quand on est un être humain' ['at the outset, was to say everything that I, as an ordinary individual, could have in common with any other I, as different as could be from me. It was to define what each person can have in common with everyone when one is a human being'].[54]

The project thus deviates from the outset from the civil register's protocol of identification; as a survey of any of the pages of *État civil* shows, it is impracticable to attempt to assign any consistently unitary identity to the source of the assertions, factual statements or snatches of dialogue which feature within the text's montage. The application of a set of arbitrary constraints across the text (such as montage, stammering and declension) offers a means of 'working out', and even transgressing, a social grammar, one that, as the following citation demonstrates, is fundamentally patriarchal in character:

> L'autorité est un caractère spécifiquement humain.
> La nuit, la silhouette élancée des gratte-ciel fait penser à des minarets.
> L'autorité est l'attribut du père.
> Les toits rougeâtres des petits pavillons banlieusards sont dominés par les tours énormes et vitrées où sont installés des bureaux.
> Le père est prince est prince le père est principalement interdicteur.
> L'ancien hôtel, qui a l'aspect d'une gigantesque pâtisserie, est coiffé par une grande enseigne publicitaire rouge et blanche.
> Zone Urbaine Prioritaire.
> En principe, le père est censé se soumettre comme tout un chacun aux interdictions qu'il impose aux autres.
> Je cherche un mot, c'est diphtérie qui me vient à l'esprit, mais je sais que ce n'est pas le mot que je cherche, je cherche un mot.
> Toute règle souffre d'exception.
> Je crois que c'est la diff, la diffamation, non, la diffraction, non, la diff, la diff, la difformité, la difficulté, non la différence, voilà, la différence.
> Le père incarne la loi et dispose du pouvoir d'exception.[55]
>
> [Authority is a specifically human characteristic.
> At night, the slender figure of the skyscrapers brings to mind minarets.
> Authority is the attribute of the father.
> The reddish roofs of the little suburban houses are overlooked by the enormous glazed towers in which offices are located.

The father is a prince is a prince the father is principally prohibitor.
The old hotel, which looks like an enormous pastry, is topped by a large red and white advertising sign.
Priority Urban Zone.
In principle, the father is supposed to himself submit like everyone else to the same prohibition which he imposes on others.
I look for a word, it is diphtheria that comes to mind, but I know that it is not the word I am looking for, I look for a word.
Every rule suffers from exception.
I think that it's diff, defamation, no, diffraction, no, diff, def, deformity, difficulty, no difference, there, difference.
The father incarnates the law and possesses the power of exception.]

Commenting on the line 'Toute règle souffre d'exception' ['Every rule suffers from exception'], Jean-François Puff notes of *État civil*: 'C'est dire que le projet initial, qui consiste à inventorier tout ce qui est commun à tous les humains, implique *du même coup* une exposition de cela qui est propre au sujet écrivant, les règles qui sont exprimées étant autant d'occasions de subjectivation ou de manifestations d'exception' ['In other words, the initial project, which consists of inventorying everything that is common to all humans, *by the same token* implies the exposure of that which is proper to the writing subject, the rules which are expressed being just so many chances for subjectivation or manifestations of exception'].[56] By way of illustration of Puff's argument, in the passage above, strongly axiomatic statements alternate with stammerings that implicitly point to an undermining of language's capacity to articulate axiomatic value.

In *État civil*, even the most proprietary attributes which one might think of as securing an individual voice – the linguistic 'je' ['I'] and the 'moi' ['me'] – are in constant circulation, as the text underlines their appropriation and reappropriation by alternate actors in the context of successive statements. And whereas the convention which places the prefix 'pro-' before the word 'noun' would suggest that nouns and pronouns relate to each other by means of straightforward substitution, for Grangaud the pronoun has an altogether more collectivising function, although not in the sense that it connotes a plural grouping of individuals. One particular section of the work muses *inter alia* on the linguistic categories of nouns and pronouns, through the following montage of utterances:

Jetant jetant je t'entends, tu mens, tu m'entends ?
Les noms désignent une identité séparée.
Métastase, oui, je vois, c'est un cancérologue célèbre, non ?

C'est un cas un cas c'est un camarade.
Les noms désignent une entité séparée.
Les pronoms désignent une entité collective.
Regroupées avant l'ouverture, les employées du grand magasin écoutent le chef de rayon expliquer qu'il faut nettoyer les présentoirs.
Tout le monde dit 'je'. 'Je' est tout le monde.
Le Panama fabrique des cigarettes.
Il dit que tout le monde se ressemble, et bien sûr, il a raison, mais moi je trouve que tout le monde est quelqu'un d'autre et j'ai raison aussi.
Une personne est à la fois quelqu'un, personne et tout le monde.
La foire aux livres d'occasion est éclairée par des lanternes de papier couvertes d'idéogrammes.
Je peux me sentir pas pas me sentir pareil aux voix aux voisins mais je ne me sens sans sans je ne me sens pas, sans pas, je ne me sens pas être la même chose qu'eux.[57]

[Throwing, throwing, I hear you, you lie, do you hear me?
Nouns refer to a separate identity.
Metastasis, yes, I see, she's a famous oncologist, isn't she?
It's a case a case it's a comrade.
Nouns refer to a separate entity.
Pronouns designate a collective entity.
Gathered together before opening time, the female employees of the department store listen to the department manager explaining that the displays must be cleaned.
Everyone says 'I'. 'I' is everyone.
Panama produces cigarettes.
He says that everyone looks like everyone else, and of course he's right, but I think everyone is someone else and I'm right too.
A person is at the same time someone, nobody and everyone.
The second-hand book fair is lit by paper lanterns covered with ideograms.
I can feel not not feel the same as the voices as the neighbours but I do not feel without without I do not feel, without not, I do not feel that I am the same thing as them.]

Here, mechanical third-person iterations of various linguistic categories are brought into contrast with a range of first-person utterances which, in self-reflexive ways, offer an account of a subject's difficult accession to language. This effect is heightened by montage's characteristic piecing together of heterogeneous discourses, in such a way as to create effects of ambiguity or ironic distancing. As Raluca Manea comments in a persuasive analysis of *État civil*, 'In combining the language of various organizations of data …, the inventory mines the authority of each discourse it borrows from'.[58] Against the bland statements of grammatical conventions, instances of stammering and naïve or perplexed assertions bespeak the efforts of subjects at grips with their own linguistic self-differentiation. Émile Benveniste notes in *Problèmes de linguistique générale* ['Problems in general linguistics'] that, given its substitutive value, 'la définition ordinaire des pronoms personnels comme contenant les trois termes *je, tu, il* y abolit justement la notion de « personne »' ['the standard definition of personal pronouns as containing the three terms *I, you, he* does away with the notion of "person"'].[59] It is in this sense that the pronoun is paradoxically both particularising and anonymising, having a resonance that is both individual and, as the passage above suggests, collective. Here, Grangaud offers a subtle commentary on the nature of personhood and the linguistic categories that conventionally accommodate it.

Some features of the passage can be elucidated by recourse to the Oulipian notion of clinamen, which is notably characterised by Georges Perec as 'la variation que l'on fait subir à une contrainte' ['the variation to which one subjects a constraint'].[60] Originating in the name which the Roman author Lucretius ascribed to the unpredictable deflection of atoms falling through space, 'clinamen' is understood to refer to the apparent accidents or arbitrary play produced in the application of a textual constraint. Clinamen is not so much evidence of a surrealist discovery of the illogical within systems but from an Oulipian perspective points to a kind of naturally existing unpredictability or variation, one which allows for a corresponding variation in the application of constraint, the emphasis being less on the psychological experience of the illogical and more on the observation and manipulation of the generative effects of a 'jolt' in the system. In relation to Grangaud here, it is useful to note the etymological link of 'clinamen' to 'déclinaison' ['declension']. In the long citation above, as a subject appears to grapple with the indefinite pronouns, the text elicits a structural indeterminacy intrinsic to the constraint imposed by the declension of subject pronouns: 'Tout le monde dit "je". "Je" est tout le monde.' / 'Il dit que tout le monde se ressemble, et bien sûr, il a raison, mais moi je trouve que tout le monde est quelqu'un d'autre et j'ai raison aussi. / Une personne est à la fois quelqu'un, personne et tout le monde' ['Everyone says "I". "I" is everyone.' / 'He says that everyone looks like everyone else, and of course he's right, but I think everyone is someone else and I'm right too. / A person is at the same time someone, nobody and everyone.'] Brought to these extremes, the process of declension seems to involve a turning away from its own ostensible purpose, namely that of marking out a set of subject positions within the system of language.

The passage above instead seems to return the reader momentarily to an undifferentiated, *quelconque* [nondescript] state somewhere on the outside of those positions, or to heighten awareness of what they cannot accommodate. On this point, amid its 'factographic' drive to register a vast array of empirical detail, the passage alludes to structural gender inequalities (the female employees receiving cleaning instructions from a male manager) in the world of work. Taken alongside the previous citation's assertion of the paternal character of authority, the passage captures a sense of a social and linguistic world organised primarily around the enfranchised masculine subject. Elsewhere, in the 'Mariages' section of the text, the poet offers multiple, often ironically detached observations on women's experience of pregnancy and childbirth. There, in one passage she dwells on how the inheritance of her paternal surname was inseparable from her birth: 'Quand je suis née, mon père a pris un brevet sur ma personne, son nom comme un estampillage, ses droits d'auteur. … L'esprit de famille se confound avec celui de propriété' ['When I was born, my father took out a patent on me, his name as a stamp, his copyright … The sense of family is bound up with that of property'].[61]

In her questionnaire for Serge Gavronsky, Grangaud states that her gender plays a role in her work but that she is unable to explain precisely what that role is.[62] The fact that she does not more affirmatively state the female-gendered qualities of her writing may be due to her suspicion of the category of identity more generally. Nonetheless, in examples like that just cited, her work reflects a persistent critical alertness to oppressive gender dynamics (whether they manifest through patriarchal structures in the social world or through the ubiquity of the patronym in the giving of personal names), a fact which is worth considering in the context of her membership of the highly male-dominated Oulipo group.[63]

The suspicion of identity is reflected also in the curious passage entitled 'Portrait du zèbre' which completes the 'Naissances' section:

> Ce qui caractérise le zèbre, c'est sa peau.
> L'égalité est une civilisation qui date de l'antiquité.
> La peau est une surface sensible qui fait communiquer l'intérieur avec l'extérieur. Mais c'est aussi ce qui enferme le zèbre, qui en fait un individu séparé de tout le reste.

> L'antiquité s'oppose à la religion.
> Le mot individu, mot valise composé d'indivis et indu, paraît en effet le mot le plus apte à me désigner, moi le zèbre.
> La religion fabrique des livres.
> C'est par sa peau que le zèbre est identifié.
> Un zèbre doit porter, sa vie durant, les rayures qui le signalent en tant que zèbre.
> Les livres sont plats et pleins d'herbe.
> J'éprouve un sentiment désagréable, chaque fois que je vois écrit sur ma carte d'identité : signes particuliers néant. Je ne sais pas pourquoi.[64]
>
> [What characterises the zebra is its skin.
> Equality is a civilisation dating from antiquity.
> Skin is a sensitive surface that connects the interior with the exterior. But it is also what encloses the zebra, what makes it an individual separate from all else.
> Antiquity is opposed to religion.
> The word individual, a portmanteau word made up of 'indivis' and 'indu', seems indeed the word most apt to designate me, me the zebra.
> Religion produces books.
> The zebra is identified by its skin.
> A zebra must wear, throughout its life, the stripes that mark it out as a zebra.
> Books are flat and full of grass.
> I have an unpleasant feeling, every time I see the words written on my identity card: distinguishing marks none. I do not know why.]

Grangaud appears to disclose an affinity with a creature whose difference is perhaps the most marked in the animal kingdom – at least to human eyes – and yet whose markings have traditionally been understood to serve a purpose of camouflage, making it indistinguishable from its environment. This paradox is extended in the playful assertion that that most empirical of designations 'individu' ['individual'] is a portmanteau of 'indivis' ['jointly held'] and 'indu' ['unwarranted']. As the *Trésor de la langue française* dictionary informs us, from the point of view of the law 'indivis' refers to a property which 'n'est pas partagé matériellement, qui appartient en commun à plusieurs personnes, lesquelles exercent leur droit conjointement' ['is not shared physically, which belongs jointly to several people, who exercise their right to it conjointly']; 'indu', on the other hand, designates that which 'n'est pas dû; qui n'est pas conforme à la loi; qui n'est pas justifié, fondé)' ['is not owed; which is not in accordance with the law; which is not justified or legitimate'].[65]

In this way, just as elsewhere in *État civil*, Grangaud's subtle critique of the putative indivisibility of the individual resonates with some concerns of post-foundationalist political thought, particularly in the work of Jean-Luc Nancy, for whom the singularity of finite beings, as he notes in *La Communauté désœuvrée* ['The inoperative community'], 'a lieu dans le plan du *clinamen*, inidentifiable' ['takes place at the level of the *clinamen*, which is unidentifiable'].[66] Querying the manner in which language becomes tied by convention to the articulation of a self-identity, *État civil* therefore opens onto a fraught commonality of being, one based, paradoxically, on the shared perception of an apparent dissolution of the unitary self.

Calendrier des fêtes nationales (2003) and *Les Temps traversés* (2010): spatialising histories

While *État civil* exhibits a concern with classificatory processes, the final texts considered in this chapter explore the possibilities of two text *types*: the calendar and dictionary. The *Calendrier des fêtes nationales* ['Calendar of national festivals'] of 2003 is inspired by the national calendar. Here, individual entries corresponding to each day of the calendar feature long inventories of historical incidents, with no apparent common denominator other than that they occurred on identical calendar dates. Although each entry is marked by a movement from a distant past to a more recent present, in the main, the sequential and the *événementiel* in historical description yield to a synchronic if somewhat chaotic series of snapshots. This example is from the entry for 30 June:

> 30. Royaume de France, Louis Le Pieux, attaqué par ses fils & abandonné par ses guerriers, est déposé, ayant rendu les armes. – Russie, Catherine prend pouvoir avec acclamations du peuple & se fait sacrer cathédrale Notre-Dame de Kazan. – France, loi ordonne, dans chaque département, édification hôpital exclusivement réservé aux aliénés ; campagne recommandée « pour la quiétude de la résidence ». – Bitlis, Arméniens répartis 2 groupes, hommes conduits hors de ville, fusillés après avoir creusé leur propre fosse, femmes & enfants distribués à la foule. – Luxembourg, autorités allemandes font fermer dernière école juive encore tolérée par

grand-duché. – Léopoldville, Palais de la Nation, roi Baudouin déclare : « L'indépendance du Congo constitue l'aboutissement de l'œuvre conçue par le génie du roi Léopold II » ; en réponse, Patrice Lumumba : « Nous avons connu les ironies, les insultes, les coups que nous devons subir, matin, midi & soir, parce que nous étions des nègres. » – *La vita è sogno*, opéra de Gian Francesco Malipiero d'après Caldéron, exécuté à Breslau, en Pologne.[67]

[30. Kingdom of France, Louis the Pious, attacked by his sons & abandoned by his warriors, is deposed, having surrendered. – Russia, Catherine takes power to the cheers of the people & is crowned Cathedral of Our Lady of Kazan. – France, law orders, in each department, construction of hospital exclusively reserved for the insane; countryside recommended 'for the tranquillity of the residence'. – Bitlis, Armenians divided into 2 groups, men led out of town, shot after digging their own grave, women & children distributed to the crowd. – Luxembourg, German authorities close the last Jewish school still tolerated by the Grand Duchy. – Léopoldville, Palais de la Nation, King Baudouin declares: 'The independence of the Congo constitutes the culmination of the work conceived by the genius of King Léopold II'; in response, Patrice Lumumba: 'We experienced the ironies, the insults, the blows that we have to undergo, morning, noon & night, because we were negroes.' – *La vita è sogno*, opera by Gian Francesco Malipiero adapted from Caldéron, performed in Breslau, Poland.]

Among the constraints noticeable in this passage are the consistent replacement of 'et' by the ampersand diacritic, and the elimination of pronouns and definite articles. Together these confer an artificial or telegrammatic quality on the prose which functions to interrupt the linear smoothness of reading. Through these different forms of negation of diachronic progression, the text privileges a more transnational and pluralised frame of reference whose attributes are those of space, and which enables the reader to detect commonalities of form (if not of content) within a variety of historical experiences. From the 1838 French law providing for the establishment of hospitals set apart for the mentally ill, to genocidal or colonial injustices more or less notorious, the events listed here are consistently marked by the modalities of containment, displacement, elimination or exclusion.

This concern with the move from diachronic progression to synchronic structure is a feature of 2010's *Les Temps traversés*. Drawing exclusively on Alain Rey's *Dictionnaire historique de la langue française* ['Historical dictionary of the French language'], first published in 1992, Grangaud composes poems featuring only words or expressions which entered recorded dictionary usage in a given year. Each poem in the collection takes the form of a *morale élémentaire* [elementary morality], a poetic form initially developed by Raymond Queneau in his 1975 work of that name. Each of these *morales* is characterised primarily by the recourse to *bimots* [biwords], that is, in Oulipian terms, combinations of noun plus adjective. The *morale* consists of three sets of three plus one such *bimots*, followed by a seven-line interlude of between one and five syllables featuring verbs and indicators of time or space, then a final set of three plus one *bimots*. The particular linguistic moment selected by Grangaud in the following example is that of 1839–40:

1839–40

Ciel ouaté	Horizon politique Révolution industrielle	Rire rabelaisien
Roman picaresque	Scrutin proportionnel Frères siamois	Républicain communiste
Langue verte	Lactaire délicieux Musée historique	Idées italiennes

Dans la maison
de tolérance
l'anarchie
cauchemarde
nom de nom
je ne mange pas
de ce pain-là

Parti communiste	Race jaune Symphonie funèbre[68]	Maladie bleue

[1839–40

Cotton wool sky	Political horizon Industrial revolution	Rabelaisian laughter
Picaresque novel	Proportional ballot Siamese twins	Communist republican

Slang	Saffron milk cap Historical museum	Italian ideas
	In the maison de tolérance anarchy has nightmares good grief I'll have nothing to do with it	
Communist party	Yellow race Funeral symphony]	Blue disease

This technique of abstracting words from their habitual usage and exploring their possible combination with others from the same period offers the reader a synchronic image of the French language at a given point in its development which it is tempting to see in terms of Ferdinand de Saussure's notion of an *état de langue* ['language state']. In the continual historical development of a language, Saussure posits the existence of stages of relative equilibrium. Citing examples such as 'le français du XIXe siècle' ['the French of the nineteenth century'] and 'le latin du siècle d'Auguste' ['the Latin of the century of Augustus'],[69] Saussure explains that language states 'sont perpétuellement la transition entre l'état de la veille et celui du lendemain' ['are perpetually transiting between a previous state and the following one'].[70] Seemingly by analogy, Grangaud hypothesises a particular linguistic moment, wherein the linguistic subject is notionally configured at the meeting point of ideological formations such as those of race or class, and bodies of botanic, linguistic, literary or medical knowledge.

Yet even if the poem presents a project that seems at great structural remove from the lived horizon of the subject, casting the subject as the product of a series of structural determinations, it simultaneously presents the possibility of reading across these formations and bodies of knowledge in a manner more capricious or contrarian, that is, in a way which colours or even disrupts them. The truncated quality imposed by the form of the *morale élémentaire* allows the various *bimots* to reverberate semantically with each other by means of affinities or juxtapositions. This can be seen in the sense of foreboding elicited in the example here in the parallel between 'ciel ouaté' ['cotton wool sky'] and 'horizon politique' ['political horizon'] or the ironising effect of the combination of 'frères siamois' ['Siamese twins'] and 'Républicain communiste' ['Communist republican']. Similarly, patterns of affect can be detected, as taste ('délicieux' ['delicious']) and colour ('bleu', 'jaune' and 'vert' ['blue', 'yellow', 'green']) come to inflect medicine, science and racial ideology. This kind of reading acquires a particular disjunctive force within the interlude, which marks a sudden turn to historicity and the diachronic, human situation and action. In this way, the agitations of affect are signalled most strongly, as an inchoate, anarchistically minded 'je' ['I'] affirms its visceral *in*tolerance of a State-condoned prostitution of which it wants no part. The interlude is thus a scene of subjectivation, not in the sense that it marks out a distinct position to which a subject might be assigned, but rather in that it discloses a 'gap' in the emerging symbolic order, the space of a difference as yet unaccounted for.

Conclusion: towards the inappropriable

In the later phase of Grangaud's work, the poet challenges the epistemological underpinnings of the various text types she takes up. *État civil*, for instance, subtly infers the difficulty of establishing stable empirical distinctions between individual and collective in language, and *Calendrier des fêtes nationales* draws attention to the inherent chaos of historical experience which is retrospectively masked by national commemorations. Yet, in an optimistic perspective, such texts for Grangaud also present the possibility of a project, poetic and even political. In this way, in *Les Temps traversés*, the technique of abstracting words from habitual usage and exploring their possible combination with others of the same 'vintage' allows her to hypothesise an optimal *état de langue* and to glimpse 'un parallélisme entre la montée d'un idéal démocratique et le développement de la langue' ['a parallelism between the rise of a democratic ideal and the development of the language'], as she declares in a foreword to the volume.[71]

If we are to follow this parallel elicited in *Les Temps traversés* between the institutionalisation of French and the rise of democracy, it would seem that for Grangaud we are in a sense equal before the language system that allows us to say what we say as we are equal before the law. This is not insofar as language endows subjects with an equal set of competencies but because we are all equally exposed to the proclivity of a particular linguistic dynamic to cut across the subject positions we are given to occupy. Inscribing a form of non-belonging at its core, her work enacts a departure or a displacement from the received terms by which the very categories of personhood and those of social relations are conventionally designated. It thus discloses the structural determinations that constitute the subjects of a system, but also shows how these are generative of affects or intensities that point to the residual energy of a difference not yet marked. In this way, the application of constraints opens a space for the actualisation of possibilities: as the poet comments to Serge Gavronsky, 'It seems to me that it is always the greatest absence of identity that produces the most powerful singularity in the case of a writer or a poet.'[72]

In an essay that dwells on the creative possibilities of the noun, Jean-Christophe Bailly writes of his aspiration to '[considérer] les noms, non comme une appropriation de ce qui est, mais comme un mouvement humain vers l'inappropriable' ['[consider] nouns not as an appropriation of what is, but as a human movement towards the inappropriable'].[73] It is a comparable desire which animates the project of Grangaud, given the poet's determination to subvert those gestures of discursive appropriation of which the noun forms the semantic currency. Seeking to expose the proper noun's purchase over our cognitive operations and ordinary semantics, Grangaud's writing instead intimates a conviction that there is something in the nature of the human relation that does not lend itself to the gesture of appropriation.

As Astrid Poeir-Bernhard notes, with their multiple pronominal shifts and subtle but persistent attenuation of the category of personhood, Grangaud's texts disclose for the reader 'l'expérience d'une totalité qui n'a rien d'extérieur, mais qui au contraire abolit les frontières entre le dedans et le dehors, de sorte que l'on se perçoit comme une partie d'un tout' ['the experience of a totality to which nothing is external, but which, on the contrary, abolishes the boundaries between the inside and outside, in such a way that one sees oneself as part of a whole'].[74] Seeming to elude actualisation, this totality might perhaps further be thought of as a space of articulate exposure, of the kind intimated in one of the various stammerings (evocative of Ghérasim Luca) that are encountered throughout the pages of *État civil*: 'Il faut semer il faut semer il faut se méfier' ['We must sow we must sow we must be wary'].[75]

What is disclosed here is not an originating presence, that of a subject proprietorially in command of its manifestation in language, but rather the self as echo-chamber, perhaps closer to what the Jean-Luc Nancy of *La Communauté désœuvrée* ['The inoperative community'] might term its 'être en commun' ['being in common'].[76] Nancy's conception of the inoperable community, which eludes substantive categorisations of individuality or the unitary subject, and which favours instead a dynamic of differentiation and exposure, might well help to illuminate aspects of Grangaud's project, and her attachment to the category of the 'commun' ['common'] over that of the 'propre' ['proper'].[77] What Grangaud offers us, then, is a paradoxically invigorating shared sense that although language dispossesses us, this dispossession is the very condition of our being-in-common: 'Je suppose que j'ai la parole, mais c'est peut-être la parole qui m'a, moi-même, avec beaucoup d'autres' ['I suppose that I have speech, but maybe it is speech which has me, myself, with many others'].[78]

Notes

1 Khordoc proposes to show 'how writing about movement, mobility, traversing borders, origins, belonging, which appear to be recurring themes in contemporary Québécois literature, is not the exclusive domain of immigrant writers, and is present in a great many contemporary Québécois writers, regardless of their origins'. Catherine Khordoc, 'From migrant to transnational: contemporary Québécois writing (1999–2010)', *Québec Studies*, 63 (2017): 80.
2 See: Jacques Roubaud, *La Vieillesse d'Alexandre* (Paris: Maspero, 1978).
3 Quoted in: Matias Viegener and Christine Wertheim (eds.), *The noulipian Analects* (Los Angeles: Les Figues Press, 2007), 169.
4 Alison James, *Constraining Chance: Georges Perec and the Oulipo* (Illinois: Northwestern University Press, 2009), 15.
5 Serge Gavronsky, *Six Contemporary French Women Poets: Theory, practice and pleasures* (Carbondale: Southern Illinois University Press, 1997), 23.
6 Interview with Grangaud in: Gavronsky, *Six Contemporary French Women Poets*, 21.
7 John C. Stout, *L'Énigme-poésie: entretiens avec 21 poètes françaises* (Amsterdam: Rodopi, 2010), 236.
8 Michelle Grangaud, *Jours le jour* (Paris: P.O.L, 1994), 112–13.
9 Abderrahmane Djelfaoui, *Maqamat Jean-Paul Grangaud: Un itinéraire d'Alger à El-Djazaïr* (Algiers: Casbah, 2000), 41–2.
10 Jean-Baptiste Harang, 'Engrangement de Grangaud coucou des lettres', *Libération*, 19 June 1997.
11 Michelle Grangaud, *Mémento-fragments* (Paris: P.O.L, 1987).
12 Oulipo. 'Avion', accessed 25 January 2021, http://oulipo.net/fr/contraintes/avion.
13 P.O.L, '*Mémento fragment*' [sic], accessed 25 January 2021, http://www.pol-editeur.com/index.php?spec=livre&ISBN=2-86744-090-4.
14 Gavronsky, *Six Contemporary French Women Poets*, xxiii.
15 Roberto Esposito, *Communitas: The origin and destiny of community*, trans. by Timothy Campbell (Stanford, CA: Stanford University Press, 2010), 2.
16 P.O.L, '*Mémento fragment*'.
17 Stout, *L'Énigme-poésie*, 220.
18 Jean Starobinski, *Les Mots sous les mots: les anagrammes de Ferdinand de Saussure* (Paris: Gallimard, 1971), 152–3.
19 Jean Baudrillard, *L'Échange symbolique et la mort* (Paris: Gallimard, 1976), 307.
20 'Le poétique, c'est l'insurrection du langage contre ses propres lois' ['The poetic is the insurrection of language against its own laws']. Baudrillard, *L'Échange symbolique et la mort*, 312.
21 Gavronsky, *Six Contemporary French Women Poets*, 21.
22 Grangaud, *Mémento-fragments*, 53.
23 Grangaud, *Mémento-fragments*, 92.
24 Michelle Grangaud, *Stations* (Paris: P.O.L, 1990). The appeal of the Parisian metro to writers of Oulipo is reflected also in Jacques Jouet's *Poèmes de métro*, a collection composed of poems written during the course of journeys on the rail system: Jacques Jouet, *Poèmes de métro* (Paris: P.O.L, 2000). In Jouet's case, there is an experiential constraint, as opposed to the linguistic constraint imposed by the names of the stations.
25 'Ainsi l'anagramme représente, inclus dans le réseau d'impossible de la langue, un « en plus » qui s'en distingue. D'une part, il est tout entier formulable en termes de phonèmes, et suppose une analyse fondée, quant à elle, sur le principe qui fait contingente l'homophonie – en sorte

que celle-ci ne reçoit de statut que par un système qui la dévalue – ; d'autre part, il dénomme un réel qui excède toute phonologie possible : par là, par l'incontournable de son réel, il met la langue en excès, qu'on la prenne en elle-même ou dans sa représentation calculable : cette fonction d'excès, nous l'appelons lalangue' ['Thus, brought into language's network of the impossible, the anagram represents an "added value" which causes it to stand out. On the one hand, it can be formulated entirely in terms of phonemes, and presupposes an analysis based, for its part, on the principle which makes homophony into a contingent value – in such a way that homophony receives its status only through a system which devalues it –; on the other hand, the anagram names a real which exceeds all possible phonology; thereby, given the fact that its real cannot be ignored, it places language in excess, whether we consider it in itself or in its calculable representation: we call this function of excess *lalangue*']. Jean-Claude Milner, *L'Amour de la langue* (Paris: Verdier, 2009), 85.

26 P.O.L, '*Stations*', accessed 25 January 2021, http://www.pol-editeur.com/index.php?spec=livre&ISBN=2-86744-173-0.

27 Grangaud, *Stations*, 56.

28 Grangaud, *Stations*, 42.

29 'Ce que fait la littérature dans la langue apparaît mieux : comme dit Proust, elle y trace précisément une sorte de langue étrangère, qui n'est pas une autre langue, ni un patois retrouvé, mais un devenir-autre de la langue, une minoration de cette langue majeure, un délire qui l'emporte, une ligne de sorcière qui s'échappe du système dominant' ['What literature does in language appears more clearly: as Proust says, it traces precisely a sort of foreign language within language, which is not another language, nor a rediscovered patois, but a becoming-other of this major language, a minorisation of this major language, a delirium that carries it away, a witch's line that escapes the dominant system']. Gilles Deleuze, *Critique et clinique* (Paris: Minuit, 1993), 15.

30 Grangaud, *Stations*, 72.

31 Jean-Luc Nancy, *Résistance de la poésie* (Bordeaux: William Blake & Co., 2004), 29.

32 Georges Perec, *Je me souviens* (Paris: Hachette, 1978), 42.

33 Perec, *Je me souviens*, 52.

34 Perec, *Je me souviens*, 70.

35 Perec, *Je me souviens*, 58.

36 Michelle Grangaud, *Souvenirs de ma vie collective* (Paris: P.O.L, 2000), 33.

37 Marian Zwerling Sugano, *The Poetics of the Occasion: Mallarmé and the poetry of circumstance* (Stanford, CA: Stanford University Press, 1992), 34–5.

38 Michelle Grangaud, *On verra bien* (Paris: Plurielle, 1996), 5.

39 Grangaud, *Souvenirs de ma vie collective*, 24.

40 Grangaud, *Souvenirs de ma vie collective*, 56.

41 Grangaud, *Souvenirs de ma vie collective*, 145.

42 Grangaud, *Souvenirs de ma vie collective*, 161.

43 Grangaud, *Souvenirs de ma vie collective*, 168.

44 Grangaud, *On verra bien*, 5.

45 '[Le mode de fabrication des factographies] repose sur la référence à des techniques de capitation, dont on peut distinguer deux modalités essentielles : la *notation*, qui concerne la formulation et la mise par écrit de faits observables (petites scènes, brèves descriptions) et la *transcription*, fondée sur le prélèvement d'énoncés préalablement entendus ou lus avant d'être recopiés' ['[The method for producing factographies] draws on references to recording techniques, of which two essential types can be distinguished: notation, which concerns the formulation and writing down of observable facts (small scenes, brief descriptions), and transcription, which is based on a sampling of statements previously heard or read, then copied down']. Marie-Jeanne Zenetti, *Factographies: l'enregistrement littéraire à l'époque contemporaine* (Paris: Garnier, 2014), 35. Zenetti discusses a set of works by Annie Ernaux, Charles Reznikoff and Georges Perec. For more on this theme and the related phenomenon of creative 'republication' of texts in the public arena in the context of recent poetry in French, see Jeff Barda, 'Forensic poetics: legal documents transformed into strange poems', *L'Esprit créateur* 58.3 (2018): 86–102.

46 Alain Rey, ed., *Dictionnaire historique de la langue française* (Paris: Robert, 1998), 1:1322.

47 'Dans l'écriture romanesque, les personnages surgissent du néant, à ma guise. Ils me réclament aussitôt un état civil, une apparence, une histoire, une psychologie' ['In the writing of novels, the characters surge forth out of nothingness, however I wish. They immediately demand of

me a name, an appearance, a story, a psychology']. François Garde, *Marcher à Kerguelen* (Paris: Gallimard, 2018), 44.

48 As she remarks in a documentary by Pascale Bouhénic: 'La phrase dans État civil, en fait je l'ai construite en fonction du style du Code civil : quelque chose de très dense, c'est-à-dire avec le minimum de mots tirer le maximum de choses, injecter le maximum de sens, et d'un sens qui doit être très précis' ['I actually constructed the sentences in *État civil* in the style of the Civil Code: something very dense, in other words, with the minimum of words to draw out a maximum of things, a maximum of meaning, and a meaning which has to be very precise']. *L'Atelier d'écriture de Michelle Grangaud*, directed by Pascale Bouhénic (Paris: Avidia/Centre Pompidou/Bibliothèque publique d'information, 1998), VHS.

49 Charles Dobzynski, 'Poétiquement incorrects', *Europe* 837–8 (Jan–Feb 1999): 272.

50 Michelle Grangaud, *État civil* (Paris: P.O.L, 1998), 51.

51 See John C. Stout's interview with Grangaud in which she discusses Reznikoff: Stout, *L'Énigme-poésie*, 224.

52 The act of archiving, Derrida argues, is an instance of what he terms archontic power, the power to consign: 'Il faut que le pouvoir archontique, qui rassemble aussi les fonctions d'unification, d'identification, de classification, aille de pair avec ce que nous appelerons le pouvoir de *consignation*. Par consignation, n'entendons pas seulement, dans le sens courant de ce mot, le fait d'assigner une résidence ou de confier pour mettre en réserve, en un lieu et sur un support, mais ici l'acte de *con*signer en *rassemblant les signes*. Ce n'est pas seulement la *consignatio* traditionnelle, à savoir la preuve écrite, mais ce que toute *consignatio* commence par supposer. La *consignation* tend à coordonner un seul corpus, en un système ou une synchronie dans laquelle tous les éléments articulent l'unité d'une configuration idéale' ['It is necessary to combine the archontic power, which additionally brings together the functions of unification, identification and classification with what we will call the power of *consignation*. By consignation, we do not only mean, in the ordinary sense of the word, the fact of assigning residence or of entrusting with the aim of holding something in reserve, in a place and on a device of some kind, but here the act of *con*signing by *gathering together signs*. It is not only the traditional *consignatio*, that is, written proof, but everything that *consignation* presupposes from the outset. *Consignation* aims to coordinate a single corpus, in a system or a synchrony in which all the elements articulate the unity of an ideal configuration']. Jacques Derrida, *Le Mal d'archive: une impression freudienne* (Paris: Galilée, 1995), 14. In her discussion of *l'enregistrement littéraire* [literary recording], Zenetti identifies consignation as a cardinal motif of the latter. 'L'enregistrement', she writes, is 'd'abord une consignation, c'est-à-dire la transcription par écrit d'un message préexistant à des fins d'officialisation, de mémorisation ou de publication' ['Recording is above all a consignation, in other words a written transcription of a pre-existing message for the purposes of officialisation, memorisation or publication']. Zenetti, *Factographies*, 58.

53 P.O.L, '*État civil*', accessed 25 January 2021, http://www.pol-editeur.com/index.php?spec=livre&ISBN=2-86744-599-X.

54 Stout, *L'Énigme-poésie*, 226.

55 Grangaud, *État civil*, 140–1.

56 Jean-François Puff, 'Michelle Grangaud, le commun et le propre', *Figures de l'art* 30 (2015): 247.

57 Grangaud, *État civil*, 102–3.

58 Raluca Manea, '*État civil*: Michelle Grangaud on language unrest', *Contemporary French and Francophone Studies* 23 (2020): 294.

59 Émile Benveniste, *Problèmes de linguistique générale* (Paris: Gallimard, 1966), 251.

60 'Nous avons un mot pour la liberté qui s'appelle le clinamen, qui est la variation que l'on fait subir à une contrainte…c'est-à-dire la liberté que l'on prend par rapport a une contrainte, qui peut être très grande ou très petite. […] Le fait de tricher par rapport à un règle ? Là, je vais être tout à fait prétentieux : il y a une phrase de Klee que j'aime énormément et qui est : « Le génie, c'est l'erreur dans le système »' ['We have a word for freedom which is called clinamen, which is the variation to which one subjects a constraint … in other words the freedom that one takes in relation to a constraint, which can be very great or very slight. […] The fact of cheating in relation to a rule? I'm going to be completely pretentious: there is a phrase by Klee which I really like and which is "Genius is the error in the system"']. Georges Perec, '« Création et contraintes dans la production littéraire », conférence prononcée à l'université de Copenhague le 29 octobre 1981', in *Entretiens et conférences*, ed. by Dominique Bertelli and Mireille Ribière (Paris[?]: Joseph K., 2003), II: 316–17.

61 Grangaud, *État civil*, 136.

62 'Does the fact of being a woman play a role in my thinking? Without a doubt, without a doubt it plays a part, but what part I would not be able to say. It truly conceals its role. In fact, I have a tendency of suspecting it, this being-woman; it appears to me to be a bit like a false brother. The dictionary tells us that the term poetess quickly acquired a pejorative connotation. That is a societal truth, probably more so in a Mediterranean society, a fact that, unfortunately, does not affect only poetesses! In painting, music, sculpture, architecture – the feminine quote simply does not exist. No need to discuss it. And yet we have in the government a minister for women to defend us; we – we are also battered wives, daughters raped by their fathers and secretaries by their bosses in that sweet land of France with its legendary gallantry. There is much bread on the table for our minister for women, but it seems we are not eating our share of it'. Gavronsky, *Six Contemporary French Women Poets*, 23.

63 On this topic, see Dennis Duncan, *The Oulipo and Modern Thought* (Oxford: Oxford University Press, 2019), 150.

64 Grangaud, *État civil*, 91–2.

65 'Indivis'/ 'indu', accessed 23 March 2020. *Trésor de la langue française informatisé*, http://atilf.atilf.fr/.

66 'La singularité n'a jamais ni la nature, ni la structure de l'individualité. La singularité n'a pas lieu dans l'ordre des atomes, identités identifiables sinon identiques, mais elle a lieu dans le plan du *clinamen*, inidentifiable' ['Singularity never has the nature or the structure of individuality. Singularity does not take place in the order of atoms, which are identifiable if not identical identities; rather, it takes place at the level of the *clinamen*, which is unidentifiable']. Jean-Luc Nancy, *La Communauté désœuvrée* (Paris: Christian Bourgois, 1986), 23–4.

67 Michelle Grangaud, *Calendrier des fêtes nationales*: *Année folle II* (Paris: P.O.L, 2003), 107.

68 Michelle Grangaud, *Les Temps traversés* (Paris: P.O.L, 2010), 83.

69 Ferdinand de Saussure, *Cours de linguistique générale*, ed. by Rudolf Engler (Wiesbaden: Otto Harrassowitz, 1990), II: 6.

70 Ferdinand de Saussure, *Cours de linguistique générale*, II, 11.

71 Grangaud, *Les Temps traversés*, 7.

72 Gavronsky, *Six Contemporary French Women Poets*, xxiii.

73 Jean-Christophe Bailly, *Le Propre du langage: voyages au pays des noms communs* (Paris: Seuil, 1997), 58.

74 Astrid Poeir-Bernard, 'Michelle Grangaud – Anagrammes, tercets et autres textes insolites', in *OULIPO-POETIQUES*: *Actes du Colloque de Salzburg, 23–25 avril 1997*, ed. by Peter Kuon (Tübingen: Gunter Narr, 1999), 128.

75 Grangaud, *État civil*, 15.

76 'L'être *en* commun signifie que les êtres singuliers ne sont, ne se présentent, ne paraissent que dans la mesure où ils com-paraissent, où ils sont exposés, présentés ou offerts les uns aux autres. Cette comparution ne s'ajoute pas à leur être, mais leur être y vient à l'être' ['Being *in* common means that singular beings are, present themselves, appear only to the extent that they com-pear, that they are exposed, presented or offered to one another. This com-appearance is not an addition to their being, but their being comes into being through it']. Jean-Luc Nancy, *La Communauté désœuvrée* (Paris: Christian Bourgois, 1986), 146.

77 The following reflections by Roberto Esposito on the notion of community are also suggestive in the context of Grangaud's understanding of non-belonging as the paradoxical condition of community: 'The *munus* that the *communitas* shares isn't a property or a possession [*appartenenza*]. It isn't having, but on the contrary, is a debt, a pledge, a gift that is to be given, and that therefore will establish a lack.' Esposito, *Communitas*, 6.

78 Grangaud, *État civil*, 89.

Bibliography

Primary material

Grangaud, Michelle. *Calendrier des fêtes nationales*: *Année folle II*. Paris: P.O.L, 2003.
Grangaud, Michelle. *État civil*. Paris: P.O.L, 1998.

Grangaud, Michelle. *Jours le jour*. Paris: P.O.L, 1994.
Grangaud, Michelle. *Mémento-fragments*. Paris: P.O.L, 1987.
Grangaud, Michelle. *On verra bien*. Paris: Plurielle, 1996.
Grangaud, Michelle. *Souvenirs de ma vie collective*. Paris: P.O.L, 2000.
Grangaud, Michelle. *Stations*. Paris: P.O.L, 1990.
Grangaud, Michelle. *Les Temps traversés*. Paris: P.O.L, 2010.

Secondary material

Bailly, Jean-Christophe. *Le Propre du langage: voyages au pays des noms communs*. Paris: Seuil, 1997.
Barda, Jeff. 'Forensic poetics: legal documents transformed into strange poems', *L'Esprit créateur* 58.3 (2018): 86–102.
Baudrillard, Jean. *L'Échange symbolique et la mort*. Paris: Gallimard, 1976.
Benveniste, Émile. *Problèmes de linguistique générale*. Paris: Gallimard, 1966.
Bouhénic, Pascale, dir. *L'Atelier d'écriture de Michelle Grangaud*. Paris: Avidia/Centre Pompidou/ Bibliothèque publique d'information, 1998. VHS.
Deleuze, Gilles. *Critique et clinique*. Paris: Minuit, 1993.
Derrida, Jacques. *Le Mal d'archive: une impression freudienne*. Paris: Galilée, 1995.
de Saussure, Ferdinand. *Cours de linguistique générale*, edited by Rudolf Engler. 2 vols., Wiesbaden: Otto Harrassowitz, 1990.
Djelfaoui, Abderrahmane. *Maqamat Jean-Paul Grangaud: un itinéraire d'Alger à El-Djazaïr*. Algiers: Casbah, 2000.
Dobzynski, Charles. 'Poétiquement incorrects', *Europe* 837–8 (Jan–Feb 1999): 270–7.
Duncan, Dennis. *The Oulipo and Modern Thought*. Oxford: Oxford University Press, 2019.
Esposito, Roberto. *Communitas: The origin and destiny of community*, translated by Timothy Campbell. Stanford, CA: Stanford University Press, 2010.
Garde, François. *Marcher à Kerguelen*. Paris: Gallimard, 2018.
Gavronsky, Serge, *Six Contemporary French Women Poets: Theory, practice and pleasures*. Carbondale: Southern Illinois University Press, 1997.
Harang, Jean-Baptiste. 'Engrangement de Grangaud coucou des lettres', *Libération*, 19 June 1997.
James, Alison. *Constraining Chance: Georges Perec and the Oulipo*. Illinois: Northwestern University Press, 2009.
Jouet, Jacques. *Poèmes de métro*. Paris: P.O.L, 2000.
Khordoc, Catherine. 'From migrant to transnational: contemporary Québécois writing (1999–2010)', *Québec Studies* 63 (2017): 79–98.
Manea, Raluca. '*État civil*: Michelle Grangaud on language unrest', *Contemporary French and Francophone Studies* 23 (2020): 290–7.
Milner, Jean-Claude. *L'Amour de la langue*. Paris: Verdier, 2009.
Nancy, Jean-Luc. *La Communauté désœuvrée*. Paris: Christian Bourgois, 1986.
Nancy, Jean-Luc. *Résistance de la poésie*. Bordeaux: William Blake & Co., 2004.
Oulipo. 'Avion'. Accessed 25 January 2021. http://oulipo.net/fr/contraintes/avion.
Perec, Georges. '« Création et contraintes dans la production littéraire », conférence prononcée à l'université de Copenhague le 29 octobre 1981'. In *Entretiens et conférences*, edited by Dominique Bertelli and Mireille Ribière, 2 vols., II: 307–23. Paris[?]: Joseph K., 2003.
Perec, Georges. *Je me souviens*. Paris: Hachette, 1978.
Poeir-Bernard, Astrid. 'Michelle Grangaud – Anagrammes, tercets et autres textes insolites'. In *OULIPO-POETIQUES*: *Actes du Colloque de Salzburg, 23–25 avril 1997*, edited by Peter Kuon, 119–40. Tübingen: Gunter Narr, 1999.
P.O.L, '*État civil*', Accessed 25 January 2021. http://www.pol-editeur.com/index.php?spec=livre&ISBN=2-86744-599-X.
P.O.L, '*Mémento fragment*' [sic]. Accessed 25 January 2021. http://www.pol-editeur.com/index.php?spec=livre&ISBN=2-86744-090-4.
P.O.L, '*Stations*'. Accessed 25 January 2021. http://www.pol-editeur.com/index.php?spec=livre&ISBN=2-86744-173-0.
Puff, Jean-François. 'Michelle Grangaud, le commun et le propre', *Figures de l'art* 30 (2015): 239–51.
Rey, Alain, ed. *Dictionnaire historique de la langue française*, 3 vols. Paris: Robert, 1998.

Roubaud, Jacques. *La Vieillesse d'Alexandre*. Paris: Maspero, 1978.

Starobinski, Jean. *Les Mots sous les mots: les anagrammes de Ferdinand de Saussure*. Paris: Gallimard, 1971.

Stout, John C. *L'Énigme-poésie: entretiens avec 21 poètes françaises*. Amsterdam: Rodopi, 2010.

Trésor de la langue française informatisé. Accessed 25 January 2021. http://atilf.atilf.fr/.

Viegener, Matias, and Christine Wertheim (eds.), *The noulipian Analects*. Los Angeles: Les Figues Press, 2007.

Zenetti, Marie-Jeanne. *Factographies: l'enregistrement littéraire à l'époque contemporaine*. Paris: Garnier, 2014.

Zwerling Sugano, Marian. *The Poetics of the Occasion: Mallarmé and the poetry of circumstance*. Stanford, CA: Stanford University Press, 1992.

Conclusion

A brief survey of some work in contemporary French poetics can help to summarise some of the themes of earlier chapters in this book. In an essay from the volume *Actes* ['Acts'], 'Réponse à un journaliste' ['Answer to a journalist'], in which he comments on the *oeuvre* of Dante, Michel Deguy rejects the suggestion that poetry should be taken as the expression of a particular political commitment. Deguy moreover argues that it is misleading to attempt to categorise poetry as a field of knowledge analogous to those of politics or philosophy or history, since poetry is not ultimately amenable to articulation in terms of discursive or logical properties, such as causality or dialectics. In turn, since he or she has relinquished any particular stake within the broader discursive economy common to these different fields, the poet can be considered as 'sans état' (emphasising a specific meaning of 'état' which equates to 'occupation' or 'status'): 'nous pourrions dire que par état le poète est *sans état* ; celui qui suspend tout engagement pour révéler l'assise poétique de tout état' ['we could say that in terms of occupation or trade, the poet is occupation-less or trade-less; the one who suspends all commitment in order to reveal the poetic foundation of any occupation or status'].[1] Poetry is thus marked by a relinquishment or retraction of the very properties that would enable the poem to be constituted as an object of knowledge, or that would allow poetry to be counted as an occupation among others.

Meanwhile, through a survey of the period corresponding to the poetic *extrême contemporain*, Jean-Claude Pinson asks precisely how one can account for the specificity of poetry given the progressive erosion of those factors which traditionally conferred on it its cultural authority. Pinson acknowledges that poetry has had to relinquish claims that it could give access to a transcendental realm; it has foregone its privileged role in the preservation of collective tradition; it has broken with the myth of inspiration, and is no longer identifiable on the basis of formal criteria. Pinson argues that 'c'est dans l'instant où il desserre le lien communautaire et troue le réseau des représentations symboliques communes, que le poème peut le mieux suggérer, « en deçà ou au-delà de l'univers du *nommé* », quelque chose de cette « altérité non logique » qu'est le « réel »' ['it is in the moment when it loosens the community bond and pierces the network of shared symbolic representations that the poem can best suggest, "within or beyond the universe of the *named*", something of that "non-logical otherness" that is the "real"'].[2] According to Pinson, the specificity of poetry today lies in its intrinsic practices, which problematise the assignation of names. Indeed, as we have seen throughout this book, it is poetry's adoption of elliptical or equivocating or negative forms of utterance that enable it to bring language to a place where its power to name or articulate is suspended or disrupted. For Pinson, the poem effects a breach in the settled order of language; it leads to a puncturing of symbolic representations and of relations of belonging.

Like Pinson, Jacques Rancière, in his *Politique des poètes*, locates poetry precisely in such instances of (dis-)identification with a dominant social order and its associated symbolic practices. Focusing on the question of the poet's own relation to the *polis*, Rancière declares that the poet belongs to political thought via a paradoxical mode of 'unbelonging belonging': 'C'est dire ... qu'il y appartient sur un mode singulier qui est de spécifier une inappartenance. Le poète appartient à la politique comme celui qui n'y appartient pas, qui en ignore les usages et en disperse les mots' ['That is to say ... that the poet belongs to it in a singular mode, which is to specify a non-belonging. The poet belongs to politics as much as the person who does not belong to it, who turns a blind eye to its customs and scatters its words'].[3] For Rancière, the poet is the 'porte-parole des anonymes parce qu'il est celui qui bouleverse tout ordre des noms et des nominations dont se soutient l'état de la domination' ['spokesperson of the anonymous because they are the one who upsets any order of names and namings that provide the basis for the state of domination'].[4]

While the emphasis may be different in each case, it is noticeable that a common characteristic of the three foregoing commentaries is that they infer a withdrawal of the poet or of poetry from a broader domain of signification or political thought in which they would be presumed to have some part. They each emphasise that poetry has a less secure ontological value by comparison with those other domains (those which Deguy mentions are politics, philosophy and history) but that it also inherently problematises the notions of part-taking, property and possession that form their semantic currency. The poetic practice of the poets whose work has been the focus of this book discloses a similar intuition. As the foregoing chapters have argued, through their poetry, Grangaud, Jabès, Lubin and Luca perform an unbinding of the categories of having and belonging and evolve distinct forms of self-conscious attention towards language in ways that achieve critical remove from those paradigms of possession or appropriation that continually circulate through discourse. They offer a counterpoint to a pastoral view of poetry as the privileged expression of a community's inalienable, ancestral values, the expression of its *langue propre* [own language]. Yet their poetry is not marked by a simple flight into an idiosyncratic or rarefied impropriety, one where non-belonging would constitute an impasse. 'La parole poétique', Jacques Sojcher writes, 'est, dans son essence même, un risque, celui de l'apatridité' ['Poetic speech is, in its very essence, a risk, that of statelessness'].[5]

Nonetheless, poetry's risk is its singular resource: what Grangaud, Jabès, Lubin and Luca reveal is the extent to which a poetic practice inflected by exile, statelessness or non-belonging is capable precisely of turning a condition of marginality or loss into one that interrogates centralised conceptions of meaning, authority and power as they are articulated through literary work. They are in different ways attuned to the possibilities inherent in poetry as a practice of language reflexively aware both of its own suffusion by loss and of the poem's potential to momentarily produce and preserve an expression of that loss. They thus bring us close to the viewpoint of Jean-Luc Nancy, who emphasises that 'ce qui résiste avec la poésie …, c'est ce qui, dans la langue ou de la langue, annonce ou retient plus que la langue' ['what resists with poetry … is what, in language or of language, announces or keeps more than language'].[6] It is the keeping of or care for this 'more than language', this unsayable excess, that is constitutive of poetry, poetry being 'par essence plus et autre chose que la poésie même' ['in essence more than and something other than poetry itself'].[7]

Recalling Agamben's discussion of style and manner described in the introduction to this volume, it is his argument that the mature *oeuvre* of the poet Giorgio Caproni can be understood in terms of the literary pursuit of a quality that is distinctly, intimately, Capronian, one which is, however, no longer identifiable in terms of what has erstwhile come to define it. This study has argued that what applies to Caproni here applies more broadly to a certain quality of poetry that can be elicited from the study of four poets. Thus, what Agamben sees in terms of the maturation of an individual poet in the interaction of 'appropriating expropriation' and 'expropriating appropriation' is analogous with a quality of the poetic field at a particular stage in its maturation, a field itself no longer identifiable in terms of what has erstwhile come to define it in the shared conception.

Regarding the field of twentieth-century poetry in French, Michael G. Kelly argues that the 'migration of the *poetic* from an identifiable form to a quality whose recognition is a matter of constant questioning' mirrors a comparable evolution in utopian thought in the same period.[8] Although the approach of the present study is not from the perspective of utopian thought, the poetry studied here shows the possibilities of a creative engagement abstracted from the categories of selfhood, citizenship and nation, one in which new conceptions of humanity, community and being-together are at times foreshadowed. In a recent consideration of some artistic responses to the condition of statelessness, Marianne Hirsch comments that if we 'allow ourselves to be vulnerable to the provocation of these works', then they stand to illuminate 'a space beyond present political reality and beyond our own horizons of possibility'.[9] Some of the works of poetry considered in this book offer one such provocation. From the texts of Lubin which disclose an underlying irreducibility of human utterance to the accounts which are made of it and the forms which represent it; to Jabès, who in his writing seeks to get rid of the cumbersome qualities of the 'I' in favour of an almost anonymous 'We';[10] to Luca's rejection of Oedipus and his '*négation absolue du cordon ombilical*' ['absolute negation of the umbilical cord'];[11] to Grangaud, for whom language dispossesses us as the condition of our being-in-common – they each underscore the possibilities of a mode of creative engagement beyond the horizon of the proper. They may even gesture towards that which, in the terms of Roberto Esposito, 'begins where what is proper ends': the common, a term which refers neither to a symbolic representation of the community nor to a form of communitarianism, and in fact is the negation of both of these. For Esposito, the common designates a condition of being in the world that can be said to belong to everyone and no one, and which thus undermines the purchase of the categories of identity and belonging over thought.[12]

As the current century moves towards an increasingly global frame of reference for the understanding of human culture, one in which the structures of the nation state become less tenable, or less adapted to the character of human mobility across the planet, the abiding value of studying the array of poetic practices on display in this book should be apparent. This is especially the case in the context of perceptions of the loss of poetry's cultural authority or its fading capacity to articulate collective memory. This poetry brings home to us the need to interrogate certain legacies of the proper, and most notably the exemplary status that continues to be conferred by our institutions on place-bound, sedentary models of subjectivity, or models that privilege the monolingually serene and the politically enfranchised at the expense of those who are neither of these. With uncommon insight, it shows the potential to extend beyond the proper towards a different regime of engagement, that of our common non-belonging, and thus to challenge long-held assumptions about the relation between subjects, the language they use and the place from which they speak.

Notes

1 Michel Deguy, *Actes* (Paris: Gallimard, 1966), 43.
2 Jean-Claude Pinson, *Poéthique: une autothéorie* (Seyssel: Champ Vallon, 2013), 67.
3 Jacques Rancière, 'Préface', *La Politique des poètes. Pourquoi des poètes en temps de détresse*, ed. by Jacques Rancière (Paris: Albin Michel, 1992), 9.
4 Rancière, *La Politique des poètes*, 9–10.
5 'La parole poétique est, dans son essence même, un risque, celui de l'apatridité. Habiter la parole – il s'agit d'une limite inatteignable –, c'est avoir quitté l'espace et le temps usuels pour un chemin qui ne mène nulle part (car quitter un lieu pour un autre, aujourd'hui pour demain, c'est toujours se mouvoir à l'intérieur d'un espace et d'une diachronie homogènes)' ['Poetic speech is, in its very essence, a risk, that of statelessness. Inhabiting the word – it is an unattainable limit – is to have left everyday space and time for a path that leads nowhere (because leaving one place for another, today for tomorrow, is always moving within a homogeneous space and diachrony)']. Jacques Sojcher, *La Démarche poétique* (Paris: Union générale d'Éditions, 1976), 96.
6 Jean-Luc Nancy, *Résistance de la poésie* (Bordeaux: William Blake & Co., 2004), 22.
7 Nancy, *Résistance de la poésie*, 22.
8 Michael G. Kelly, *Strands of Utopia: Spaces of poetic work in twentieth-century France* (London: Legenda, 2008), 14.
9 Marianne Hirsch, 'Stateless memory', *Critical Times* 2 (2019): 432, accessed 25 January 2021, https://doi.org/10.1215/26410478-7862541.
10 Edmond Jabès, *Le Livre des marges* (Paris: Fata Morgana, 1984), 130.
11 Quoted in: Sarane Alexandrian, 'Le Poète sans repartir: jamais plus ici, toujours là', *Supérieur inconnu*, 5 (October–November 1996), 74.
12 'The first meaning of the noun *communitas* and of its corresponding adjective, *communis*, is what becomes meaningful from the opposition to what is proper. In all neo-Latin languages (though not only), "common" (*commun, comun, kommuri*) is what is *not* proper [*proprio*], that begins where what is proper ends: *Quod commune cum alio est desinit esse proprium*.' Roberto Esposito, *Communitas: The origin and destiny of community*, trans. by Timothy Campbell (Stanford, CA: Stanford University Press, 2010), 3.

Bibliography

Alexandrian, Sarane. 'Le Poète sans repartir: jamais plus ici, toujours là', *Supérieur inconnu* 5 (October–November 1996): 71–8.
Deguy, Michel. *Actes*. Paris: Gallimard, 1966.
Esposito, Roberto. *Communitas: The origin and destiny of community*, translated by Timothy Campbell. Stanford, CA: Stanford University Press, 2010.
Hirsch, Marianne. 'Stateless memory', *Critical Times* 2 (2019): 416–34. Accessed 25 January 2021. https://doi.org/10.1215/26410478-7862541.
Jabès, Edmond. *Le Livre des marges*. Paris: Fata Morgana, 1984.
Kelly, Michael G. *Strands of Utopia: Spaces of poetic work in twentieth-century France*. London: Legenda, 2008.

Nancy, Jean-Luc. *Résistance de la poésie*. Bordeaux: William Blake & Co., 2004.
Pinson, Jean-Claude. *Poéthique: une autothéorie*. Seyssel: Champ Vallon, 2013.
Rancière, Jacques. Preface to *La Politique des poètes. Pourquoi des poètes en temps de détresse*, edited by Jacques Rancière, 9–18. Paris: Albin Michel, 1992.
Sojcher, Jacques. *La Démarche poétique*. Paris: Union générale d'Éditions, 1976.

Index

CPSIA information can be obtained
at www.ICGtesting.com
Printed in the USA
BVHW040045250322
632421BV00015B/107

9 781787 356740